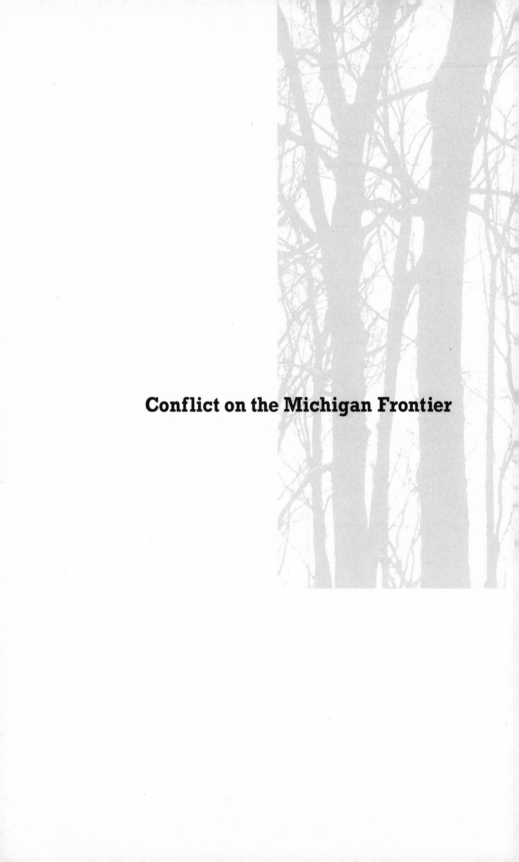

Conflict on the Michigan Frontier

Conflict on the Michigan Frontier

Yankee and Borderland Cultures, 1815–1840

James Z. Schwartz

 Northern
Illinois
University
Press
DeKalb

© 2009 by Northern Illinois University Press

Published by the Northern Illinois University Press, DeKalb, Illinois   60115

Manufactured in the United States using postconsumer-recycled, acid-free paper.

All Rights Reserved

Design by Julia Fauci

Library of Congress Cataloging-in-Publication Data

Schwartz, James Z.

Conflict on the Michigan frontier : Yankee and borderland cultures, 1815–1840 / James Schwartz.

   p.   cm.

Includes bibliographical references and index.

ISBN 978-0-87580-400-2 (clothbound : alk. paper)

1. Michigan—History—To 1837. 2. Frontier and pioneer life— Michigan. 3. Community life—Michigan—History—19th century. 4. Pioneers—Michigan—History. 5. New Englanders—Michigan—History—19th century. I. Title.

F566.S39 2009

977.4'03—dc22

2009007503

Contents

Acknowledgments

Many friends, editors, mentors, archivists, and colleagues have helped to produce this book. The staffs at the Bentley Historical Library at the University of Michigan in Ann Arbor, the Burton Historical Collection at the Detroit Public Library, the Library of Michigan in Lansing, and the Library of Congress in Washington, D.C., were enormously helpful.

Special thanks go to several scholars and editors: this book began as a paper presented at the 2000 annual conference of the Society of Historians of the Early Republic in Buffalo, New York. Toby Ditz, who served as commentator on my panel, offered encouragement and valuable criticism. I also owe a special debt to Amy S. Greenberg and Martin J. Hershock, who read early versions of this manuscript. They not only corrected errors but also offered insightful comments that helped to make it better in innumerable ways. Melody Herr, my first editor at Northern Illinois University Press, and Sara Hoerdeman, her successor, also offered valuable assistance. Additionally, I owe a debt to Jacqueline Wehrle, Michael Swinford, and Marilyn McLaughlin for their help with editing, proof reading, indexing, and fact checking.

Several reviewers and editors have offered generous help and valuable insights. These include Mark Nicholas, Michael Morrison, Roderick A. McDonald, David Macleod, Nora Faires, and Mary C. Graham.

I also would like to thank colleagues at several institutions. At the University of Michigan–Dearborn, Martin J. Hershock, Mark Kay Carter, Pam Pennock, Elaine Clark, Enoch Baker, Cameron Amin, and Georgina Hickey created a stimulating environment in which to teach. While working on this book, I survived a very cold winter in Michigan's Upper Peninsula with the aid of Robbie Goodrich, Alan Willis, Chet DeFonso, and Keith Kendall. At Eastern Illinois University, I have benefited from the criticism, friendship, and moral support of Anita Shelton, Lynn Curry, Martin Hardeman, Terry Barnhart, Debra Reid, Nora Pat Small, Amy Schneidhorst, Ralph Ashby, Michael Shirley, Jonathan Coit, Sace Elder, Jose Deustua Newton Key, Josh Birk, Charlie Titus, Bailey Young, Charles Foy, Mark Voss

Hubbard, Jonelle DePetro, Gary Aylesworth, Donna Nichols, Teresa Britton, Roger B. Beck, Edmund Wehrle, David K. Smith, Joy Kammerling, and Jeff and Lesley Ashley.

Family and friends, both two- and four-legged, also have contributed to this project: these include Martha Seijas, Marvin Sharon, Marge Sharon, David Stanislaw, Aaron Goldstein, Karen Newman, Fran Schwartz, Michael Weinstein, and Zach and Lev Weinstein, as well as Beanie and Sheba Schwartz. Special thanks go to my daughter, Eleanor C. Schwartz, and my parents, Robert and Judith Schwartz, who offered a rich intellectual environment in which to grow up.

Finally, my mentors at Wayne State University provided an invaluable model of scholarship and integrity. Marc Kruman, Alan Raucher, Ross Pudloff, Sam Scott, and Christopher Johnson helped by offering friendship and incisive criticism. But I owe my greatest debt to Sandra VanBurkleo, who proved that there really is such a thing as a free lunch. As I worked on this manuscript, she treated me to many meals, during which we batted around ideas and discussed my progress or lack thereof. I benefited greatly from her superb editing, keen mind, and wonderful sense of humor.

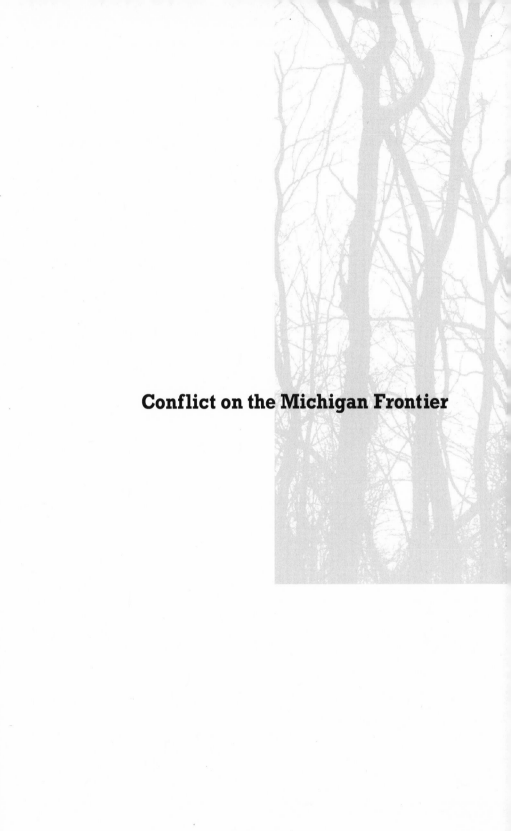

Conflict on the Michigan Frontier

Introduction

In 1832, the editors of the *Detroit Courier* expressed alarm about Michigan's future. They had recently returned from the territory's interior, and they were appalled by what they found. "Infidelity" and other vices had gained a "strong foothold" in western Michigan. "To drive these monsters back," they urged reformers to reshape "the moral and intellectual character" of the territory's settlers, and to transform Michigan from a gloomy and "desolate wilderness" into a land "like New England," which was "spread over with churches and schoolhouses, the steady witness to our happiness and prosperity."[1]

The *Courier* was not alone in its view of the frontier as a dark, savage land. Many Michiganians shared the newspaper's concerns, condemning not only the vice and wildness of Michigan Indians, but also the barbarism of the territory's white inhabitants, who violated the norms of genteel society and endangered efforts to build a peaceful and durable republic in the West.

This behavior, which seemed so wild to the *Courier* and its readers, grew out of Michigan's rich and complex history. Until the mid-nineteenth century, the Great Lakes region was the center of a lucrative fur trade, the location of fierce imperial rivalries, and the crossroads of several cultures. France conquered Michigan in the seventeenth century; England gained possession of it after the Seven Years' War; and the United States placed Michigan in the Northwest Territory after wresting it from British control in the American Revolution.

As Indians and Europeans mixed, they exchanged values, beliefs, and customs, producing a borderland or hybrid culture in Michigan that combined European and Indian elements. The territory's borderland culture persisted until the mid-1820s, when the completion of the Erie Canal and the proliferation of steamboats on the Great Lakes sparked a surge of migration to Michigan from New England and western New York.

These Yankee immigrants voiced great alarm at the mingling of French, English, and Indian ways. Like the *Courier,* they believed that rather than Europeans civilizing Indians, the reverse seemed to be occurring in Michigan. Many whites were adopting Indian ways: men refused to farm, preferring instead to hunt and live idly off the fat of the land. Women defied male authority, rejecting the traditional female roles of wife and mother. To make matters worse, many settlers seemed to have become as irreligious and sinful as their Indian neighbors. Rather than attending church and observing the Sabbath, they drank, gambled, visited prostitutes, and even engaged in criminal and violent behavior.

The *Courier's* view of Indians as drunken idlers and violent criminals was inaccurate. Michigan was occupied mostly by three tribes—the Ojibwa, Potawatomi, and Ottawa. In addition to hunting, fishing, and farming, all three supplemented their income by trading fur for European manufactured goods. Although they had stoutly resisted Anglo-American occupation of their land in the late eighteenth and early nineteenth centuries, they were not bloodthirsty savages. But Michiganians, like other Anglo-Americans, were deeply suspicious of indigenous people. Since the conquest of Ireland in the sixteenth century, the English and their American descendants saw cultural outsiders as barbarians who lived without ethical or hierarchical boundaries.[2]

To eradicate such savagery, the *Courier* and its allies sought to establish two types of boundaries in Michigan—first, formal legal boundaries, and second, informal cultural restraints. Both types of barriers would help to establish order and to stabilize group identity by distinguishing insiders from outsiders. When reformers contended, for example, that real men did not drink, they created borders that helped not only to define masculinity, but also to discourage behavior that threatened social stability.

Creating formal legal boundaries involved establishing representative government and the rule of law, as well as a host of such lawmaking and law-enforcing bodies as courts, local government, and rudimentary police forces. These institutions served to restrain what many Michiganians perceived as the wildness and despotism of unelected territorial officials. They also were designed to curb drunkenness, crime, prostitution, and gambling, and to segregate the territory's Indian and white residents.

But reformers realized that the law alone could not tame the savagery of the frontier. They would also need to win the hearts and minds of their fellow settlers by establishing informal cultural barriers. Religion and education were to be crucial in creating such boundaries. The *Courier* relied on the image of the ax to emphasize their importance. Just as pioneers had used that tool to fell Michigan forests and to transform empty wasteland into productive farms, so reformers would rely on schools and churches to eradicate the territory's borderland culture. These institutions would educate and Christianize Michiganians, permitting the "cheering rays of sun" to fall on the territory's soil, destroying "the darkness of ignorance and the evils of vice and infidelity."[3]

Schools and churches, however, were not the only institutions that reformers employed to establish boundaries. Like the *Courier's* editors, reformers also turned to newspapers to tame savagery and wildness. Lacking the settled communities and well-established social institutions that helped to maintain order and stability in the East, Michiganians relied heavily on newspapers and other forms of print culture to perform the same function in the West. Rather than depending solely on churches, families, and schools to teach lessons about civics and morality, Michiganians published advice columns, letters, diaries, fiction, and editorials to warn readers about the dangers of wildness.

Newspapers also performed another important function: they enabled Yankees to read and make sense of the strange new world they inhabited, one that, in the words of historian Christopher L. Tomlins, challenged their "conceptual categories," as well as their "imaginative and linguistic resources." Journalists transformed this alien and sometimes threatening landscape into one that seemed familiar and comforting. They created, as historian Kathleen Neils Conzen observes, a "story the new community would be able to tell about itself," providing "interpretive coherence" to the "chaotic to-ing and fro-ing" of the frontier. Michigan imprints therefore provide invaluable evidence in understanding how settlers perceived Michigan's hybrid borderland culture and the types of boundaries they employed to tame it.[4]

In establishing these boundaries, reformers sought not only to eradicate savagery and barbarism, but also to replace it with Yankee culture. They hoped, in the words of the *Courier*, to take a "desolate wilderness" and turn it into a land that, "like New England," was filled with "happiness and prosperity," by instilling Yankee values and beliefs in their wild and uncivilized neighbors. These included a steadfast commitment to a calling or vocation, as well as to sobriety, industriousness, thriftiness, and evangelical Protestantism. Yankees also sought to strengthen such character-shaping institutions as churches, schools, and families, which they viewed as crucial to creating a stable, orderly, and godly community.[5]

But transplanting Yankee culture to the West proved to be no easy task. Complicating the effort to civilize the frontier were profound social, political, and economic changes that shook not only Michigan, but also New England and most of America in the first half of the nineteenth century, transforming an agricultural and homogeneous society into one that was increasingly urban, industrial, and heterogeneous.

This transformation began in the early decades of the nineteenth century with a dramatic growth in population. By the middle of the century, America's population had risen to more than 23 million, from roughly 5 million in 1800. The United States also became more diverse during this period, as growing numbers of Irish Catholics and Germans flocked to its shores.[6] At the same time, America's economy expanded dramatically. The construction of turnpikes, canals, and railroads after the War of 1812 spawned the growth of markets and prompted manufacturers to rely increasingly on factories to meet rising demand for their goods. Accompanying these developments were acrimonious political debates over banking, currency, the government's role in the economy, the fate of Native peoples, the growth of universal white male suffrage, and efforts by evangelical Christians to cleanse the nation of drinking, slavery, and other sins.[7]

In Michigan, conflicts over these economic and social developments were closely linked to questions about how best to tame the wildness of the frontier. Michigan's temperance crusaders, for instance, often saw drunkenness as an Indian trait and condemned excessive drinking by Anglo-Americans as a symptom of Indianization. Similarly, Michiganians viewed economic development as a means of taming a savage land and conquering the wildness of Indians and the settlers who emulated their ways. Debates over suffrage and other questions in Michigan also were associated with disagreements over how best to conquer the wildness and savagery of the territory's borderland culture.

Exploring these national developments from the perspective of a fast-growing frontier community thus demonstrates that Westerners viewed social and economic growth differently than Easterners did and provides perspectives on the early national period that differ from those offered by works that focus mostly on the East or on the nation as a whole.

An examination of Michigan's frontier also offers new insights into borderland culture. Recently, scholars have published a growing body of literature on this phenomenon. Much of this work, however, focuses on the rise and nature of borderlands, rather than on the techniques that anxious elites used to subdue them. Historians also have produced a large body of work that explores the taming of the West. Much of this literature falls into one of two categories. The first group focuses on the formal legal boundaries used to civilize the frontier. The second body of work, produced by the new historians of the American West, concentrates on the informal cultural borders used to separate Anglo-American settlers from indigenous and other non-English peoples. Exploring both formal legal and informal cultural boundaries in Michigan builds a bridge between the literature on state formation and the "new western" history, and demonstrates the importance of multiple boundaries in taming the frontier and creating republican polities in the West.[8]

Both types of boundaries were essential in civilizing Michigan; indeed, informal customary borders established the foundation on which formal legal rules were constructed. By linking formal and informal elements of civic culture, settlers established law and order not simply by enacting laws and creating police forces, but also by relying on families, community groups, schools, and print culture to reestablish traditional norms in a new environment. Michigan's civic culture thus was rooted not only in political parties and elections, but also in efforts to create racial, gender, and other types of boundaries.

Boundary creation, furthermore, was often a deliberative and contentious process. Although many boundaries were established with little forethought, others involved a fair amount of planning as well as rancorous debates in which settlers argued not only about the type of borders that they should establish, but also, in some cases, about whether these barriers were needed at all.[9]

Scholarly accounts of early Michigan have largely ignored these questions. Although historians have published excellent studies of Michigan's public life, their work pays little heed to Michigan's territorial period. Nor does it explore the state's frontier origins, the relationships among its Indian, French, and American inhabitants, or shifting conceptions of manhood and womanhood. Instead this literature primarily examines elections and the rise and fall of political parties. Because of this focus on political rather than civic culture, these works leave largely unexplored that area of society that, in the words of David S. Shields, exists outside of government, yet "permits states to function peacefully."[10]

The first three chapters of this book explore the formal elements of Michigan's civic culture, examining economic and political development in the first four decades of the nineteenth century. The latter half of the book explores the informal restraints used to subdue wildness and eradicate Michigan's borderland culture.

The book's first two chapters underscore the importance Michiganians assigned to the Northwest Ordinance as a constitutional and boundary-setting document and demonstrates their disappointment at its failure to ensure the rule of law and to resolve their boundary dispute with Ohio.

Chapter 1 traces Michigan's constitutional development from the late 1810s through statehood, exploring the creation of legal boundaries that settlers hoped would establish the rule of law and protect their rights from unscrupulous territorial officials. This process began shortly after the territory was formed in 1805, when settlers began complaining about the shortcomings of the Northwest Ordinance. The Ordinance, which Michiganians believed served as their constitution, failed to protect them from unscrupulous officials who were more interested in enriching themselves than in obeying the rule of law. Settlers insisted that their transgressions were inciting a spirit of wildness, lawlessness, and disorder in Michigan. The ordinance provided no way to curb this "anarchy," because it failed to separate Michigan's three branches of government and permitted corrupt officials to judge their own conduct. Settlers, therefore, initiated a vigorous campaign to gain the right to a representative assembly, which ended successfully in 1823.

Efforts to ensure stable constitutional boundaries resumed in 1835 when Whigs and Democrats engaged in a heated debate over voting rights at Michigan's Constitutional Convention of 1835. Whigs opposed alien suffrage but favored black enfranchisement. Democrats resisted efforts to enfranchise blacks but supported alien voting rights. Whigs depicted aliens as a threat because they were ignorant of republican culture and might be under the thumb of foreign despots. Democrats highlighted the importance of race, portraying African Americans in much the same way that Whigs described immigrants. Each side in this battle sought to establish constitutional borders that would protect the polity from the wildness and instability created by violent and supposedly ignorant cultural outsiders.

Chapter 2 examines Michigan's conflict with Ohio over Toledo, highlighting the importance that settlers assigned to stable geographical borders in maintaining law and order. Much recent work on borderlands focuses on how territorial boundaries maintained racial or ethnic purity and deprived nonwhite groups of wealth and power. This chapter illustrates the importance of borders in guaranteeing harmonious relationships between states and in making sure that no state got so dominant that it could threaten its smaller neighbors.[11]

Initially, Michiganians hoped that the Northwest Ordinance, which established the boundaries of new western states, would help settle the conflict with Ohio. But the ordinance failed to resolve the dispute, because each side could use the document to bolster its claims to Toledo. Boundary setting, in other words, failed because of the ambiguities of rule. Uncertainty about Michigan's southern border also threatened to destabilize the polity. Not only had Ohioans invaded Michigan, but they also had stirred up anarchy, rebellion, and lawlessness in the southern part of the territory.

Michiganians sought to secure their southern boundary to calm internal disorder and to prevent rapacious Ohio from becoming so large that it could prey on smaller states in the region.[12]

Chapter 3 emphasizes the importance of economic development in civilizing the frontier and laying the groundwork for Michigan's political growth. It begins by tracing Michigan's transformation from a fur-trading to an agricultural economy in the 1820s and 1830s, demonstrating that many Michiganians viewed this change as critical to "civilizing" a savage land. Ignoring how lucrative the territory's fur trade was, they believed that Michigan was wild because Indians and French settlers were lazy and produced little or no wealth. Getting rid of the fur trade not only curbed the Indians' role in the economy but also reduced the possibility of cross-cultural contacts between whites and Michigan tribes. Economic growth became a means of civilizing Michigan. Replacing wild forests and fields with prosperous farms and villages not only enriched settlers, but also helped to tame a savage land.

The Panic of 1837 threatened to undo much of this civilizing work, and it also demonstrated that unregulated capitalism might unleash speculative frenzy and destabilize the polity. In examining the origins of the Panic, Michiganians, like many Americans, focused on banking. Whigs and Democrats debated whether a central bank was needed to check the greed sparked by the economic boom of the 1820s and 1830s. The two parties also battled over a new Michigan law, making it easier to establish banks in the state. Democrats defended the law as a blow against monopolies, while Whigs charged that the measure destroyed Michigan's economy by loosening controls needed to rein in the speculative fever that raged earlier in the decade. In this debate, Whigs linked Democrats to the wildness of unregulated capitalism, and Democrats portrayed Whigs as the defenders of the privileged few.

Michiganians also blamed the Panic on the wildness of settlers who engaged in reckless speculation during the boom of the 1830s. Fiction and advice columns in Michigan newspapers condemned such behavior and sought to strengthen the boundaries of the moral economy by condemning speculators (who were usually men) and spendthrifts (who were often women). Characters in these tales threw away money, endangering not only their families but also the state's economy. Some tales condemned wives who undermined their families by spending recklessly on trinkets and fashionable clothes. Others contrasted industrious, thrifty youths from poor backgrounds with wealthy young men who squandered their fathers' money. The former became wealthy, while the latter brought ruin to their families.

The book's final chapters focus increasing attention on cultural boundaries and their relationship to the law. Chapter 4 explores attempts to subdue the wildness of Michigan's Indians and to stop Anglo settlers from adopting their savage ways. It first examines Yankee views of Michigan tribes, asserting that Anglo-Americans saw Indians in much the same way that their English ancestors had viewed the Irish, that is, as savages who might convert a growing number of whites to their vicious ways. The chapter next explores legal remedies employed to tame Indians, including laws to stop them from drinking and treaties that either confined them to reservations or expelled them from Michigan. The chapter, however, demonstrates that these laws were only partially effective: they failed to prevent white settlers from adopting Indian ways and creating a hybrid culture that mixed traditional Anglo customs with those of indigenous people. To reinforce racial boundaries, local newspapers published captivity narratives that discouraged whites from fraternizing with Indians by depicting the incompatibility of Anglo and Native American cultures.

Chapter 5 examines efforts to civilize the territory's white inhabitants, many of whom seemed as savage as Michigan's Indians. It explores the efforts of antebellum reformers to curb drinking, gambling, and other vices. This behavior, which reformers believed was widespread in Michigan, violated Christian and bourgeois morality. It also threatened to unleash chaos and disorder and to destabilize the polity. Reformers enacted laws to cleanse Michigan of sin and also initiated a campaign to strengthen the family, an institution that they believed was crucial to creating a virtuous citizenry. To make families stronger, reformers relied on newspapers, Bibles, and schools to discipline women and children and to teach fathers how to govern their households more effectively. The campaign helped to curb the drunkenness of men, but it produced unintended consequences: a new class of educated women emerged who refused to cook and clean or to conform to traditional female roles.

Chapter 6 investigates the cultural responses to two cholera epidemics that ravaged Michigan in 1832 and 1834. The disease became a trope for the wildness and disorder that elites sought to eradicate. Talk about cholera also illuminated informal social boundaries that separated the urban and agricultural frontiers. During the epidemics of the early 1830s, the disease became closely associated with the filth, poverty, and disorder of city life. These episodes also revealed a division among Michigan elites over the kind of social and physical boundaries needed to stop cholera from spreading, with officials in the countryside often insisting the disease was contagious, and those in Detroit denying this claim. Detroit officials usually opposed borders that separated town and country, favoring instead class-based mechanisms that would increase surveillance and control of the poor. Their counterparts in the villages surrounding Detroit, in contrast, began establishing legal boundaries in the form of quarantines designed to prevent city dwellers from entering their municipalities.

In explaining the process of boundary setting in Michigan, the book touches on one of the oldest debates in American history: whether westerners created new cultures or simply transplanted those in which they had been raised. Unlike some histories of the American West, it contends that Michiganians neither created a totally new culture nor simply recreated the one in which they had been raised. Instead, they established a landscape that resembled, but was not identical to, that of the East. Settlers were relatively successful in reestablishing traditional boundaries in politics, economics, and law. Their efforts to curb the power of Michigan officials during the territorial period, for example, enabled them to draft a constitution that was similar to those of eastern states. Michigan leaders, however, found it more difficult to reestablish cultural boundaries in the West, such as those that would prevent settlers from adopting Indian ways or women from violating gender norms. In such cases, Michigan elites often disagreed on what constituted wildness and how best to subdue it. Consequently, boundary setting involved a process of conflict, negotiation, and in some cases, compromise. The hybridized boundaries laid out in Michigan therefore looked different from those in the East, engendering a local culture that embraced behavior, such as granting women a degree of autonomy and power that would have been frowned on in the East. The battle to contain wildness thus resulted, not in pure transplantation of eastern culture, but in the creation of new regional forms that differed somewhat from the Yankee norms on which they were based.[13]

1

The Rise of

Michigan's New

Constitutional Order

When Yankees began migrating to Michigan in the late 1810s and early 1820s, they found themselves in an alien political landscape, one that lacked the stability and constitutional safeguards that they had known in the East. Five unelected officials governed the territory, some of whom, settlers insisted, were incompetent and corrupt and violated the laws that they had sworn to uphold. Michiganians complained, moreover, that because they lacked the right to vote, they could not curb this misconduct by removing or threatening to remove dishonest officials from office. Worse, Michigan's government contained few of the checks and balances that enabled state and federal officials to curb official wrongdoing and limit each other's power.

One of the Yankee settlers' first goals in civilizing Michigan, therefore, was to establish legal and constitutional boundaries to restrain the wildness of local officials and create a republic that respected the rule of law and guaranteed individual rights. Settlers accomplished these goals in two stages: in the first, they established a representative government based on the rule of law. In the second, they created boundaries to safeguard this polity from dangerous men who could not be trusted with political power.

Stage one occurred between 1817 and 1823, after Michiganians began to voice concerns about a territorial government that they viewed as corrupt and lawless. There is no way to judge the accuracy of these charges. In all likelihood, some accusations were exaggerated to persuade Congress that Michiganians needed an elected assembly to protect them from avaricious and dishonest territorial officials. Such a body would give white men a measure of self-rule and reduce the power of unelected officeholders.

During this period, Michigan leaders expressed concern that growing doubts about the legitimacy of the statutes enacted by the territorial legislature and administered by the courts were producing an environment that encouraged disrespect for the law and, therefore, anarchy. They also voiced misgivings about the Northwest Ordinance. Although they viewed the ordinance as their constitution and criticized Michigan officials for violating its provisions, they condemned the document for depriving white men of the right to vote and for failing to establish adequate constitutional boundaries between Michigan's three branches of government.

Phase two of Michigan's constitutional development took place during the drafting of the state's first constitution in 1835, when Whigs and Democrats debated how best to protect the polity from dangerous cultural outsiders. At issue was whether to enfranchise aliens or blacks. Whigs opposed alien suffrage but favored black enfranchisement. Democrats sought to enfranchise aliens but opposed granting blacks the right to vote. Whigs viewed aliens, especially Irish Catholics, as a greater threat than blacks to Yankee culture, since they feared that these immigrants threatened not only republican ideas and values, but also Protestantism. Democrats called for racial purity, warning that nonwhites were wild, lawless individuals who would destroy the republic.

THE CAMPAIGN FOR AN ELECTED ASSEMBLY

Initially, however, efforts to tame Michigan's polity focused not on questions of race or ethnicity, but on the need for constitutional safeguards to protect settlers from officials who many believed were wild and lawless. Initially, a governor, a secretary, and three judges, all appointed by Congress, governed Michigan. In addition to their executive and judicial roles, these officials also comprised the territory's legislature, erasing barriers that separated the executive, legislative, and judicial branches in state and federal government.

Under the Northwest Ordinance, Michigan residents could not advance to the second grade of territorial government and elect a representative assembly until they gained a population of more than five thousand free men. But Congress eliminated this requirement in 1800, prompting Michigan residents to seek an elected legislature shortly thereafter.[1] Propelling this campaign for a representative assembly were concerns about the absence of constitutional safeguards in Michigan, as well as longstanding complaints about the territorial officials, several of which dated back to 1805, when the Michigan Territory was established.

At the time, Detroit was little more than a dusty, backwoods village, containing a fort, a church, a few stores, and the wooden homes of several hundred mostly French residents. Situated on the Detroit River, the town possessed a handful of streets, which were so small that horse-drawn carriages moving in opposite directions had difficulty getting through. A large fence protected much of the town from the wilderness.[2]

A chorus of criticism greeted newly appointed territorial officials who arrived in this western outpost in 1805. Settlers complained that President Thomas Jefferson had failed to name anyone from the West who was familiar with their problems. Later, settlers charged Michigan officials with profiting from shady land deals. They also expressed mounting dissatisfaction over failed efforts to establish a bank and criticized officials for delays in rebuilding Detroit after a fire had ravaged much of the city in 1805. Tensions heightened when territorial officials split into warring factions shortly after arriving in Detroit.[3]

The bitterest rivalry was between Michigan supreme court justice Augustus B. Woodward and Governor William Hull. A native New Englander, Hull was a Yale graduate who became a judge in Massachusetts before moving to Michigan. Although he cut a dashing figure and had served valiantly in the American Revolution, Hull was reputed to be an inept executive, who not only refused to compromise with his opponents but also had problems making decisions. In 1812, he surrendered Detroit to the British and was court-martialed after being replaced as governor by Lewis Cass when Americans recaptured the city in 1813.[4]

Woodward, who served on the territory's supreme court from 1805 to 1824, was a New York City native. He attended Columbia College before moving to Virginia in 1795, where he became a lawyer, as well as a friend and follower of Thomas Jefferson. Over six feet tall and slovenly in appearance, he was famous for such eccentric behavior as showering in the rain and seldom cleaning his disheveled office, which also served as his bedroom. Michiganians attacked Woodward for his odd ways and criticized him for being obsessed with theory and ideas while neglecting the reality of life on the frontier.[5]

The conflict between Hull and Woodward stemmed not only from differences in style and personality, but also from disputes over Michigan's militia and other policy questions.[6] Soon, many Michiganians voiced anger at both officials. Silas Farmer, a nineteenth-century historian, reported that "many of the doings of the Governor and Judges were so utterly devoid of justice and such a mockery of government" that many residents "were disgusted and enraged." Others agreed. John Gentle, a Scottish store owner in Detroit, became a vociferous critic of territorial officials because he believed that they had failed to compensate him adequately for his losses in the 1805 fire. Because Michigan lacked a newspaper at the time,

Gentle published a series of articles in the *Philadelphia Aurora and Pittsburgh Gazette* in 1807, criticizing the actions of "the governor and judges as legislators," and "also their court proceedings." He insisted, moreover, that they controlled "lots in the city" for their own personal gain.[7]

With such criticism mounting, settlers launched a six-year campaign in the late 1810s to obtain an elected assembly. This effort occurred in two phases. The first phase began in 1817 when the *Detroit Gazette,* the territory's only newspaper at the time, ran a series of articles attacking Michigan's government. It ended in 1818 when voters rejected a proposal to petition Congress for an elected legislature. Washington, however, did permit Michigan to send a nonvoting delegate to Congress in 1819.[8] The second stage began in 1820 with a new round of attacks in the *Gazette* on the territorial government. At the same time, residents petitioned Congress for an assembly.

During this period, *Gazette* correspondents raised questions about the Northwest Ordinance's role as a boundary-setting document. On one hand, commentators criticized the ordinance for depriving Michigan inhabitants of the right to vote and to live under a regime in which the power of government was limited by the separation of the judiciary, executive, and legislative branches. Such criticism extended beyond Michigan. Earlier in the nineteenth century, Ohio residents had expressed similar concerns about power that the ordinance granted to officials in the first stage of development.[9]

Despite these flaws, Michiganians relied on the ordinance as the territory's only constitution and criticized officials who violated its provisions. Writing in the *Gazette* in 1820, "Xenos" betrayed an ambivalence about the ordinance that was fairly common in Michigan, calling it "an excrescence—a fungus on the body of American policy—containing in the very terms of its enunciation, a complete definition of despotism." But he added that if the ordinance were "administered in the spirit and intention of its framers," it might provide Michigan with a decent government.[10]

One of the most common complaints reformers voiced was that Michigan's legislature frequently violated the ordinance's provisions when drafting legislation. Under the ordinance, the legislature was required to adopt laws from the original states rather than draft statutes of its own creation. But "Xenos" charged in 1820 that the legislature frequently disregarded this provision. The "Ordinance of '87, which is our Constitution, ever had been and still is continually violated in the making instead of adopting laws." The legislature often enacted laws "without referring to the statutes of the states whence they purport to be adopted—and where, in fact, many of their provisions do not exist."[11]

Others registered the same complaint, attacking the legislature for creating new laws rather than adopting old ones. "Balistarius" grumbled in 1820 that the board "drafted" laws "without examining and without reference to the original states, from which they are purported to have been copied."[12] That same year, "Old Man" echoed this complaint, noting that "the manner in which laws are adopted by the Legislative Board" was "irregular and should be remedied as soon as possible."[13]

In 1822, a meeting of Wayne County residents went even further, claiming that "many of the laws" that the legislature enacted "have been rendered . . . of doubtful obligation," because they were adopted "from the statutes of states not deemed to be original" members of the Union. Doubts about the constitutionality of Michigan statutes also stemmed from the "extraordinary manner" in which Michigan lawmakers joined "fragments of acts of different states" into "one law."[14] These violations of the Northwest Ordinance raised questions about the legitimacy of territorial statues and suggested that the law, which was supposed to quell unruliness and savagery, had itself become wild, disordered, and anarchic.

Michigan officials responded to these charges by insisting that they did their best to obey the spirit, if not the letter, of the ordinance. Finding laws from the original states that met Michigan's needs often proved challenging. Statutes required to solve problems on the frontier did not always exist in the original states. In these instances, Michigan legislators had to modify eastern laws to serve western purposes. If they did enact legislation that was unjust or ill advised, Congress could protect Michiganians by vetoing it.[15]

While defending their own conduct, government officials denounced the savagery with which their foes attacked them. Woodward, for instance, was shocked by their "violence and passion." Detractors not only insulted officeholders but also forced them to defend themselves against the "low animosities of turbulent, uninformed men." Officials could not "walk or turn a corner . . . without being assailed by the most vulgar and insolent abuse." One government opponent had even declared that he would "kick the government to hell" if it passed a law that displeased him.[16]

Such threats were not reserved for Michigan's legislature. Michiganians insisted that the transgressions of this body paled in comparison to those of the territory's supreme court, charging that it ignored precedent and legal doctrine and encouraged wildness and lawlessness by failing to punish outlaws sufficiently. Justice Woodward was one of the main targets of these attacks.

Opponents charged that Woodward abused his power by failing to recuse himself from cases in which he had an interest. In one case, reported *Gazette* correspondent "Michigan," Justice Woodward had "acted as an accuser, a prosecutor or party, as a witness and as judge!" In another, Woodward "appeared also as the complainant and judge." Such misbehavior caused "every reflecting man" to "shudder." A "judge who dares to violate the law, to trample upon the dignity of his office" deserves harsh punishment. "No American citizen should quietly stand by and see his liberties strangled in the grasp of such an arbitrary and unfeeling judge."[17]

Michiganians also criticized the leniency that Woodward and the court showed to criminals. A *Detroit Gazette* correspondent asserted in 1818 that there was "an unpardonable laxity" in the administration of Michigan's laws. How else to explain why "old offenders, having repeatedly committed the same crime, and having been as often prosecuted, still remain" free, "growing hoary and hardened in their iniquity"? In Detroit, the writer complained, criminals "have generally been treated with so much tenderness, when they repeat their offenses here, that they appear very contented, and manifest no inclination to leave the country."[18]

A correspondent calling himself "Cipher" was even more critical of the courts. Writing in the *Gazette* in 1818, he asked, "How many fair statutes have we upon record" that have been "enforced but in a few solitary instances?" Michiganians "daily see them evaded, or broken with impunity!" This "fatal lethargy" would "result in general depravity and the reduction of our morals to the lowest degradation." He blamed this problem on Michigan judges. Although they vowed to "support the authority of the laws," they had acted like "unconcerned spectators of its violation." Their failure to enforce the law was "so glaring, so familiar to everyone," that it would "not be questioned." Their habit "of winking at crimes, when the person happens to be a 'clever fellow' has poisoned the community."[19]

To illustrate the latter point, critics recalled a number of cases in which the court had let criminals off lightly. One of the most notorious of these involved an Indian named Petobig. In 1817, "Rousseau" looked back on the years before the War of 1812 and recalled that Michigan judges had refused to sentence Petobig to death, even though he had committed "a most atrocious murder" and been "convicted by a . . . jury."[20] Evidently, the court feared that such a sentence might provoke a violent reaction "from the hordes of savages" that surrounded "our settlements."[21] Nobody could "forget the indignant sensations, which ran through the community on account of the escape of the murderer from the hands of the executioner."[22]

Nor was the court's treatment of Petobig exceptional. Michigan inhabitants also were incensed by two other high-profile rulings. In the case of the *United States v. Henry Hudson*, Michigan's supreme court in 1817 overturned a Wayne County court conviction of Henry Hudson, who had been charged with "receiving stolen goods."[23] Although a lower court had sentenced Hudson to three years in prison, he was "now at liberty," fumed the *Detroit Gazette.* "At every court held in this territory since the year 1803, this scoundrel has been arraigned for some misdemeanor." Unfortunately, he "always had the good fortune" to avoid "punishment."[24]

A decade later, Michigan residents attacked a judge for refusing to convict a Detroit woman on charges of prostitution. Authorities had charged Molly Brown with "keeping a disorderly house." But the judge ruled that the evidence against her was based on "the general reputation of her house" and therefore was insufficient to convict her. The *Detroit Gazette* insisted that this "opinion was singular," differing from that of "almost everyone else" in the city: "It was a matter of astonishment to many of our citizens that the defendant should escape punishment, when it was known that an intelligent grand jury had found a bill against her, and when the character of her house was so notorious." It might be that "no greater misfortune" can "happen to a community than to have placed on the seat of justice an ignorant man, whose vanity and obstinacy are insurmountable obstacles to his improvement."[25]

Compounding these problems was the court's astonishing ignorance of the law, and its failure to adhere to precedent and the rules of common law construction. "Xenos" noted in 1820 that the judges failed to follow established rules of statutory construction when interpreting laws. Even when the legislature did adopt a law from one of the original states, the judges would "give constructions and decisions entirely at variance with the known and established constructions in the state whence it was taken." As a result, the court would "entirely alter the intent and operation of the statute."[26] In addition, the court often ignored precedent. The court's rulings, reported the *Detroit Gazette,* are, in similar cases, "so discordant that they furnish no guide to conjecture what will be their decisions on the same points in the future." They have "declared . . . that their own decisions shall not be obligatory as precedents." As a result of the court's flawed rulings, law in Michigan became "wild," unsettled and unpredictable.[27]

The court's ignorance of legal doctrine and its propensity to base its rulings on little more than "whim," thus created doubts about the legitimacy of its decisions. Wrote "Sidney," another *Gazette* correspondent, "Nothing appears to be known or settled by the court, not even the most common and elementary principles of law." The jurists "contested and argued" every issue "as though it were then for the first time to be passed upon by a court of law." After the court finally did issue its rulings, it was "impossible to ascertain the grounds or principles" upon which they were founded. On the rare occasions that the court was "pleased to declare the governing principles, its adjudications" appeared to rest on "whim, caprice, or anything else than the safe, well defined, and established rules of law."[28]

The effects of this judicial and legislative misconduct were devastating, inciting a spirit of wildness, lawlessness, and "anarchy" in Michigan, critics reported. After making this claim in 1817, "Rousseau" declared in the *Gazette* that Michigan had descended into a state of "anarchy," because residents questioned "the legitimacy of some of its rulers" and the need to obey the law that they created. Republics were "sustained by the virtue and good opinion of the people, by confidence in their rulers and sacred regard for, and implicit obedience to the laws." Only by displaying an "exemplary assiduity" in performing "their official duties" could authorities expect residents to respect and obey the law.[29] A few weeks later, "Rousseau" insisted that this had not been the case in Michigan, where the misdeeds of the legislature had rendered "property insecure" and created "confusion everywhere" due to the "doubtful obligation of the laws."[30]

"Sidney" made a similar argument, insisting that well-defined legal boundaries were essential to protecting people's rights. He argued as well that the court's failure to abide by precedent and correct legal doctrine undermined the law and threatened freedom. How "with such a court" could anyone in Michigan "ascertain his rights, or arrive at a satisfactory knowledge of laws established and founded in caprice and ignorance?" Nothing safeguarded "our lives, our liberties, or possessions, where all the most sacred and well established principles of jurisprudence are violated and trampled down by the highest judicial tribunal in the country." Could the "law of the land never be settled and known?" Would Michiganians "never possess the means" of discovering "the conditions, upon which most essentially depend the enjoyment of life, of freedom, and of every thing dear to us?"[31]

To remedy these problems, Michiganians sought the right to elect their own legislature. This would enable settlers to limit the power of Michigan officials, giving white male citizens the right to vote and separating the territory's judiciary and legislative branches. Critics also argued that in depriving Michigan men of the right to vote, the Northwest Ordinance had unmanned them and subverted their status. They were treated like children and other dependents who lacked the capacity to govern themselves. "Rousseau" in 1817 compared Michigan men to orphans who had been abandoned and placed under guardians who not only were indifferent to their well-being but also sought to keep them in perpetual subservience. In the states, "the most just and perfect equality prevails and . . . rights are secured throughout by clearly defined landmarks." But Michigan residents were bereft of rights "so consoling and exalting to their nature." They were "cast off like foundlings" or dependents (which, we will see in another chapter, included women and Indians). The federal government further eroded the status of Michigan men by consigning them to "guardianship of those who have no affinity to them, and who feel not for their political health or prosperity and have no kindred interests." These officials protracted "their nonage" and perpetuated "their dependence for unmerited rewards."[32]

Several *Gazette* writers agreed, castigating the ordinance for depriving Michigan men of their independence, a quality that was so important in nineteenth-century conceptions of manhood.[33] In 1822, "A Yankee" relied on language remarkably similar to Rousseau's, describing Michigan men as illegitimate children who had been robbed of their autonomy. By depriving them of the rights enjoyed by most Americans, the federal government had "cast" them "off like bantlings of a spurious love, to serve out a nonage of dependence upon those who are arbitrarily designated for their rulers."[34] Other reformers also emphasized the benefits of self-rule. A "Citizen" in 1822, for example, declared that there was "a moral influence in the exercise of self-government which promotes activity of mind and body." Nobody could "deny that there is among us a torpor (arising from political and other causes . . .) that it would be highly advantageous as soon as possible to remove."[35] One year later, a group of reformers echoed these sentiments, deploring their "vassalage" to the federal government, which controlled the "whole machinery of the territorial system."[36]

Reformers also emphasized the importance of voting in protecting people from arbitrary rule. "Rousseau" in 1817 underscored the importance of voting in preventing "misconduct and misrule," since the ballot would give voters the power to "censure" those who were "clothed with the authority to make and administer the law."[37] Five years later, "A Yankee" noted that "the rights of electing their own rulers is considered one of the most important of all rights guaranteed by the constitution." Yet the ordinance deprived settlers of this right. Instead, "the territories, in their first grade, may be and often are gratuitously supplied with exotics, ignorant of the interests of the people and unknown to the subjects of their control." Because "the voice of the people is not heard," Michiganians had to rely "almost entirely upon the moral soundness and political and legal intelligence of four men." If the rulers of the territory were just, this might not be a cause for concern. But in Michigan, the "defects of the Ordinance and the abuses arising from them are not, nor have they been altogether imaginary."[38]

At the same time, an elected legislature would curb the power of Michigan's justices by eliminating their dual role as judges and legislators. "Rousseau" noted that because judges served in both capacities, they wielded an inordinate amount of power. "The concentration of legislative and judicial powers in the same body is the most abhorrent despotism that can be imagined."[39] In federal and state governments, Rousseau observed, the judiciary remained "distinct and independent of the legislative department" and could overturn laws that violated the constitution. But what if Michigan's legislature passed an unconstitutional law, one, for example, that expanded "the jurisdiction of the Justices of the Peace to any sum exceeding twenty dollars"? It was unlikely that a plaintiff who challenged "the constitutionality of so outrageous a measure" would receive "a fair and impartial determination before the very persons that had enacted the law."[40]

In meetings and petitions to Congress, Michigan residents seconded these views, claiming that the merger of legislature and judiciary in Michigan endangered both their "rights and property." A meeting of Wayne County residents noted that the "union" of legislative and judicial "powers in the same persons, rendered rights and property insecure." The judiciary was as "a co-ordinate and independent branch—the palladium of the independence of the people"—which served as a "barrier" to prevent the "executive or legislative branches" from encroaching on the boundaries that protected their liberty. In Michigan, however, the judiciary provided no such "security." The territory possessed no "tribunal" that could "correct the acts of the Supreme Judges in their capacities of Judges or legislators."[41] Petitions to Congress too criticized the inordinate amount of power that the ordinance granted to judges. "In the theory of Governments," the mingling of the "Judicial with the power to make laws, is considered as obviously and essentially despotic, and is abhorrent to every principle of free government." Yet this situation prevailed in Michigan, and the effects had been disastrous, enabling the legislature to pass laws containing "unconstitutional provisions."[42]

The campaign to win an elected assembly ended successfully in 1823 when Congress responded to these complaints with legislation that permitted Michigan electors to pick eighteen candidates to serve in a territorial council. From this pool, the president of the United States would pick nine to sit in the legislature. As a result, Michigan's governor and three Supreme Court justices relinquished their legislative duties. But the governor retained his veto, and Congress continued to review all legislation passed by the council. In 1827, federal lawmakers increased Michigan's autonomy, permitting the territory's voters to elect their own thirteen-member legislature. As a result of these triumphs, Michigan residents stopped complaining about the deficiencies of the Northwest Ordinance.[43]

THE DEBATE OVER SUFFRAGE

But these victories did not end conflict over constitutional boundaries. Questions about the type of barriers needed to protect Michigan from wildness and savagery resurfaced during a debate over voting rights in 1835. The conflict began when Democrats unveiled legislation that year permitting aliens—any white man who had lived in Michigan for three months—to vote for delegates to a convention that would draft the new state's first constitution. Many of those whom the bill would enfranchise were Catholics from Ireland and Germany. They often supported Democrats, but accounted for less than 5 percent of Michigan's population.[44]

Still, Whigs objected to the legislation. They worried that Democrats, who already controlled Michigan politics, would guarantee their dominance for decades to come by using foreign voters to get their delegates elected to the convention and then include a provision on alien suffrage in Michigan's new constitution. The *Detroit Journal* observed that the bill would "enable" Democrats "to get such a delegation" as they wished so that they could "form such a constitution as the interests of the party requires."[45] Whigs, however, were unable to prevent Democrats from enacting the alien suffrage bill. Nor could they prevent Democrats from winning the vast majority of the constitutional convention's ninty-one seats.[46]

The battle over voting rights, however, did not end with the election. It continued at the constitutional convention, where Democrats fought to enfranchise aliens but adamantly opposed giving African Americans the right to vote. Whigs opposed alien suffrage but favored enfranchising blacks. Self-interest motivated both sides in this conflict, with each party seeking to enfranchise groups that were likely to vote for its candidates. But fear of cultural outsiders was also crucial.

These concerns were not confined to Michigan. During the first half of the nineteenth century, many states dropped property-owning requirements and, in some cases, tax-paying requirements for voting, thereby adopting white male suffrage. A number of western states also enfranchised aliens, while denying African Americans the right to vote.[47]

In Michigan, most Democrats insisted that the savagery of nonwhites posed a much graver risk to society than did foreigners. In contrast, Whigs and dissident Democrats dismissed the importance of racial purity and emphasized the importance of cultural homogeneity. Although important differences divided Michigan's African Americans from white New Englanders, Whigs believed that these divisions shrank in importance when compared to those that separated Yankees from Irish Catholics and other immigrants.

In opposing alien suffrage, Whigs insisted that foreign voters threatened to undermine Michigan's new republic. Immigrants had been socialized in monarchies and did not possess the habits or education that voters required. Consequently, they remained tied to foreign despots, who could use them to undermine Michigan's fledgling republic.

Aliens could not be permitted to vote, therefore, until they had absorbed the values and ideas of republican culture. William Welch of Kalamazoo praised the "bravery and patriotism" of the Irish. But he insisted that neither they nor "any other class of foreigners were, the moment they landed on American shores, entitled to all the political privileges of American citizens." The rights Americans "enjoyed were obtained by the labors and with the blood of our fathers . . . and we were bound to them from everything that might tend to endanger them." Were "persons from the arbitrary governments of the Old World—persons ignorant of our language and institutions" who had "no feelings in common with American citizens" to be trusted with "our political destinies?"[48]

Whigs who made this case underscored the importance of education in shaping virtuous citizens. David White of Monroe asserted that "education, habits, manner and customs had a powerful influence on the mind." No one can expect that " a man who has received his education under a government where the laws which govern the relations of life, are entirely different from our own . . . that such a man will be able to exercise the elective franchise with discretion." The immigrant should be placed on a "short probation," during which he could "lay aside his prejudices," and gain a "little time to study the genius of our institutions."[49]

The advantage of the federal government's naturalization law, Whigs asserted, was that it required foreigners to spend time learning U.S. customs and beliefs before becoming citizens. William Woodbridge, a Whig from Detroit, argued that in passing the law, Congress had insisted that foreigners "remain with us" until they "learned something of the nature of our institutions" and became "familiarized with our customs and habits and our forms of government." After proving themselves "worthy," aliens could enjoy "the blessings our fathers fought for." If a man "be unacquainted with our forms of government, and his habits of thinking and acting have not become settled and fixed upon an American model; it is neither wise nor safe to place our destinies in his hands." A man might be intelligent and devoted to liberty, but these qualities alone were "not sufficient to qualify any man for the performance of the high and responsible duties of an American citizen! His habits must . . . have been formed upon our model."[50]

Permitting immigrants who lacked these republican habits to vote would produce despotism, violence, and instability, opponents of alien suffrage claimed. Woodbridge, for instance, asserted that enfranchising such individuals would create the same kind of unrest that plagued Latin America. Like the United States, nations on that continent had hoisted "the standard of liberty and independence." In recent decades, however, the new republics had been "drenched in blood—in human blood." Their "political features" had "changed incessantly, with the seasons and with the flowers." They were in constant turmoil because their people were "strangers to the habits of freemen." The transition "from despotism to liberty was too sudden." They did not possess and "could not acquire the habits of freedom."[51]

But Whigs did not simply emphasize the need to educate aliens before enfranchising them. They also depicted foreigners in darker terms, as ignorant savages who lacked the independence and loyalty of the native-born. Relying on nativist rhetoric, they portrayed immigrants as unruly, immoral, and barbaric "hordes" who were overrunning the republic and threatening America in much the same way that the Huns had menaced ancient Rome. In 1835, the *Detroit Journal* charged that Democrats were permitting "the elective franchise, the dearest privilege of the American citizen . . . to be defiled and degraded by beings sunk in ignorance and besotted with vice."[52] In that same issue, the *Journal* printed an article from the *Journal of Commerce* that portrayed immigrants in similar terms: "Is it to be supposed that if hordes of emigrants continue as they have hitherto, to settle in this country, and the right of voting is extended to them . . . that they will not influence our institutions?" Enfranchising aliens amounted to "giving them our birthright." These immigrants were "the most ignorant, poor and mentally imbecile population of . . . Europe." Worse, growing numbers of these savages were arriving on American shores each year and threatened soon to outnumber its native stock. This "tide of immigration" threatened "to pollute our virtue and overturn" the nation's republican "institutions." Can such "ignorant foreigners . . . manage a republic?" This was unlikely, since Americans learned to govern themselves "by serving an apprenticeship . . . from birth," drinking "republican virtue from their mother's breast."[53]

Whigs focused their deepest suspicions on Catholics, who had been taught from birth to obey the dictates of a despotic and hierarchical church. The *Detroit Journal* asserted that Catholics represented "the presence of a powerful body . . . ready to obey the nod of an ambitious priesthood, imbued from infancy with the principles of despotism." Michigan must place "a check upon their inroads against the institutions of the republic." These men "opposed . . . our social system" and sought to convert all Catholics in Michigan to their "anti-republican doctrine." In the recent election for delegates to the constitutional convention, the church had subverted the democratic process, sending its "functionaries" to win support "for the cause of Van Buren." These priests had helped the Democrats triumph and could "now write home to their patrons in Europe . . . that the time is at hand when the reins of government will pass from the natives to the foreigners."[54]

Delegates at Michigan's Constitutional Convention also questioned the loyalty of the immigrants, expressing concerns that European tyrants could use aliens to take control of Michigan's fledgling republic. These rulers could easily manipulate foreign voters because they often lacked two masculine qualities that were vital to citizens: independence and loyalty to their adopted country. Woodbridge pointed to "the evils" and "untried dangers" that alien suffrage might introduce. "How easy . . . if some highly important measure were pending, in which some foreign power might take a deep interest, for an European monarch . . . to send among us a mass of voters whose casting might control the decision." Michigan was about to receive "two thousand" German immigrants. "By whom they are sent, what may their views be, and how long they may continue among us . . . we can only conjecture."[55] Some delegates even expressed classical republican fears that homegrown demagogues as well as foreign despots could use alien voters to advance their own interests at the expense of the public good and to thereby subvert the common good. Edward Ellis, a dissident Democratic delegate from Monroe and the editor of the *Michigan Sentinel,* warned that alien voters were "liable to become the mere instruments of dangerous and designing men, bent rather on their own personal elevation than any desire to advance the real interests of the public."[56]

Whigs also doubted that foreigners could be trusted to defend the United States, especially in a war fought against their native land. In that case, foreigners might become a fifth column and shed the blood of their fellow Americans. Randolph Manning reminded the convention that Michigan was "a border state" and needed to "strengthen" its hand "against the contingency of a foreign war." Because of its location, Michigan "should guard . . . against a multitude of foreigners, whose natural attachments to their own country" might well outweigh their allegiance to America.[57] Woodbridge agreed, recalling that not long ago, many of the foreign immigrants now in Michigan had fought against America. "How many are there, in resisting whom, the best blood of the country was poured out like water?" If war broke out again, no one could be certain that foreign immigrants would defend their new home: "He fights with a halter around his neck!" In arming these men, Michigan might be putting guns "in the hands of those who are bound by their oaths of allegiance to use them against us!"[58]

Democrats defended aliens, insisting that they were as loyal as many native-born Americans. At the convention, John Norvell recalled that those who had settled the thirteen colonies were America's original immigrants. Had they refused to fight for their new homeland, America "would have been, at this time, in the exclusive occupancy of Indian tribes. It would never have become the chosen and civilized abode of liberty." Aliens who immigrate to America "come from choice. They come to enjoy freedom and equal rights." In the past, they made up "a part of our most skillful and gallant soldiers," and did "not pause . . . to consider whence the invading enemy comes."[59]

Norvell insisted that in immigrating to America, aliens had severed ties to their native lands and adopted republican beliefs. He also asserted that, though immigrants were unfamiliar with American government, they knew enough to vote wisely. He admitted that "a portion of the foreign emigrants to this country [were] unacquainted with the forms and machinery of our government." This was also true of much of the native population. Yet, he said, "the wise and patriotic statesmen, who formed the constitution, knew that no peculiar knowledge" was required to understand its main ideas. "They knew that sufficient information on the subject would prevail among the people to qualify them to vote at elections."[60] He also refuted claims that aliens were not attached to republican institutions, wondering why foreigners had immigrated to America, if they were so devoted "to the institutions of their native country." They came to this country "because they were not wedded to those institutions; because they considered them arbitrary, and ours free and liberal." "They chose to change "their residence to this land of liberty and equality." Immigrants were "attached to our republican institutions and nearly the whole mass were their ardent supporters."[61]

Though mainstream Democrats dismissed concerns about cultural boundaries, they insisted on the need for racial barriers to protect the republic from the violence, unruliness, and barbarism of nonwhite people. These fears surfaced after dissident Democrats and Whigs sought to strike the word *white* from the suffrage provision of the constitution.

Ross Wilkins, a dissident Democrat and lay Methodist minister, began the debate on black suffrage by deconstructing the whole notion of racial barriers, arguing that the word *white* could not adequately describe or classify people. "There are men of every shade and complexion, white, sallow, brown, olive, yellow; how will you regulate the shade of him which shall entitle an individual to the privilege of a freeman?" Which of these individuals were white? "Paper is white and snow is white, and yet how many men were white as paper or as snow?" Judging by these standards, "many men at that convention would not be eligible . . . and might not be recognized as white at the ballot box." Many of his neighbors in Lenawee County "were neither Indian nor negro, nor of any connexion in color with either of these races, and yet who could not be called white."[62]

Wilkins reminded delegates, moreover, that neither the Declaration of Independence nor the preamble to the Bill of Rights, which then were being considered by the convention, made distinctions based on the color of a man's skin. "By the Declaration of Independence, which was generally recognized, 'all men' are declared 'Free and Equal.'" This same "principle, is placed in the front lines of the preamble of the Bill of Rights reported to this convention."[63]

Democrats who opposed black suffrage relied on two arguments. First, they predicted that black suffrage would create social disorder and political instability. Second, they insisted that the convention could justify withholding the franchise from some because voting was not a natural right. Those who made the latter argument distinguished between natural and conventional rights. Norvell explained that racial boundaries did not apply to natural rights, which included "the enjoyment of liberty, property, and the pursuit of happiness." Blacks as well as whites could enjoy "such rights."[64] Isaac Crary claimed that this was because natural rights were those enjoyed by all in "a state of nature." But the right to vote was different. Granting blacks the franchise was "a question of expediency." When the "good of government" was best served by "admitting them to vote, then admit them; if not, then exclude them."[65]

Democratic delegates argued, moreover, that enfranchising blacks would hurt rather than help the polity by producing higher rates of crime, disorder, and instability. Permitting blacks to vote would dramatically boost the group's political power in Michigan by increasing their migration to the state. Isaac Crary said that if Michigan enfranchised blacks, freemen would "be ready at once to find an asylum in the new state." He claimed they "will flock hither in hundreds and thousands; whole townships will be occupied by blacks, and, as a necessary consequence, we shall have blacks to make laws and blacks to execute them."[66]

This growth in Michigan's black population would cause chaos, because blacks supposedly by nature were prone to crime, violence, and disorder. In linking African Americans to wildness and savagery, Democrats characterized black men as overly masculine creatures given to violence and wrongdoing. John Williams reminded delegates that a black community already existed in "the vicinity of Detroit," consisting of renegades and "runaways." Enfranchising blacks would enlarge this community and increase crime. Almost "every gentleman" was aware of "the frequent disturbances and murders committed by blacks." Were Michigan "to be overrun" with blacks, "the consequences would be dangerous, or, to say the least, a state of society would be produced, by no means desirable." On one hand, Michigan residents would be threatened by growing numbers of black criminals. On the other, such criminals would have the power to elect officials who bowed to their lawless views.[67]

Worse, eliminating racial boundaries from the polity would lead to the erasure of social boundaries, destabilizing the family and other institutions on which society rested, or so foes of black suffrage prophesied. Such racial boundaries, Norvell insisted, were needed to protect society from a wild and "degraded cast of mankind" who were "injurious" and "a nuisance to the community." Whites would "not take" blacks "as equals, to our homes, to our tables, to our bosoms." Unless Michiganians "could consent to treat them as equals in all respects; until we could bring our minds to an association with them in private life, it would be . . . insulting . . . to tender to that class of persons . . . political rights and power."[68] Handing blacks political power would lead to the racial contamination of white families. Norvell urged delegates to apply the principle "of political equality to their social circle, to their families and fireside." Given "the sense of honor and respectability" that delegates "cherished for themselves, their wives, their sons and daughters," would they "suffer the negro to become an equal member in their families?" Such notions violated boundaries established by "nature," which men "had, in all ages, recognized and sanctioned."[69]

After defeating efforts to enfranchise blacks, delegates briefly considered granting Indians the right to vote. At issue was whether Indian savagery was rooted in race or culture. Delegates who favored enfranchising tax-paying Indians took the latter position. John McDonnell, for instance, asserted "that the word white was used in contradistinction to the black alone, and though the Indian was copper-colored, he was not to be classed among the latter."[70] The convention should enfranchise Indians who had adopted white ways, Williams said. "There were many of this race, who were employed in agriculture, had excellent farms, and were identified with the very soil of Michigan." Williams favored granting voting rights to these individuals.[71]

In the end, though, efforts to enfranchise blacks and Indians were defeated. Whigs, however, did not go home empty-handed. With the aid of dissident Democrats, they were able to restrict alien suffrage. The constitution did grant voting rights to aliens living in Michigan when the document was signed. But thereafter suffrage was limited to white men who had lived in the state for six months.[72] Though not a total Whig victory, this outcome fell short of the Democrats' initial aim of enfranchising any white man who had lived in Michigan for three months.[73]

Examining Michigan's long and difficult quest for republican government thus demonstrates that the state's political development encompassed more than the rise and fall of political parties. It also involved efforts to establish legal and constitutional boundaries that would rein in the lawlessness of territorial officials, and cultural outsiders. The Northwest Ordinance played a key role in the first of these battles. Although settlers criticized it for failing sufficiently to protect their rights, they viewed it as a constitution that laid the foundations on which to build a stable and orderly polity.

From the beginning of their quest for self-rule, Michiganians expressed concerns about despotism and the absence of the rule of law. Such concerns were voiced most forcefully in the years after the War of 1812, when Michiganians campaigned to win an elected assembly. At the time, settlers criticized territorial officials for violating provisions of the Northwest Ordinance that limited their power. Such behavior threatened the well-being of the polity in a number of ways. On the one hand, Michiganians contended that their rights could not be safe in a regime where government officials refused to abide by constitutional boundaries. On the other hand, they insisted that they could not establish a peaceful, law-abiding society when government officials violated the rules they had sworn to uphold, because doubts about the legitimacy of laws created by such a regime engendered a state of anarchy and rebellion.

Fears about violence and lawlessness also fueled the debates over voting rights. Whigs argued that alien voters could endanger the polity because of their savagery and lack of independence. Because foreigners had been raised in monarchies, they lacked the independence of native-born Americans and could easily become the tools of demagogues and foreign despots who sought to subvert the republic. At the same time, opponents of alien suffrage relied on nativist propaganda to portray immigrants as barbaric hordes whose unruliness could threaten the safety of Michigan residents and the stability of society. Opponents of black suffrage, meanwhile, relied on racist rhetoric to paint a similar portrait of blacks. They predicted that enfranchising African Americans would engender lawlessness by attracting a growing number of violent and unruly blacks to Michigan. This would destabilize society by producing growing crime and violence. It also would encourage disorder and instability by giving such criminals the power to place in office men who would do their bidding. In the end, these fears about the wildness of blacks outweighed concerns about cultural homogeneity, as delegates to Michigan's 1835 Constitutional Convention disenfranchised nonwhite voters but allowed some aliens to vote.

Ohio and the Battle

for Michigan's

Southern Border

In the summer of 1835, the *Michigan Sentinel* condemned the rapacity and ruthlessness of Ohio governor Robert Lucas, who, the editors claimed, was blinded by "lustful and repining ambition" and the single-minded pursuit of ever-greater amounts of power. In his "wild career" he desperately sought to boost the size and wealth of Ohio and was loath "to lean in the slightest degree to the most forcible dictates of conscience." Lucas behaved wildly because his impulses had steeled "his sensibility" from "the strong voice of reason" and prevented "his heart" from hearing the "appeals of oppressed humanity." Because of "blind zeal," he refused to waver "from his obnoxious purposes," even when his path was "blackened with crime."[1]

The *Sentinel's* condemnation of Governor Lucas stemmed from a long, bitter boundary dispute between Michigan and Ohio over competing claims to a tract of potentially valuable land that encompassed modern Toledo, Ohio. During this largely bloodless battle, both sides mobilized their militias and fought a heated war of words in Congress and in the press, with each side claiming that the Northwest Ordinance and other key documents proved their right to the disputed tract. The conflict not only delayed Michigan's entry into the Union by some three years but also ignited a brief armed confrontation between Ohio and the Wolverine State that came to be known as the Toledo War.

This conflict over Toledo, then known as Port Lawrence, occurred in three phases between 1832 and 1837. In each phase, Michiganians sought to guarantee boundaries set forth in the Northwest Ordinance and to ensure that no new western state became much larger or more powerful than its neighbors. Phase one began in 1832 with Michiganians debating the merits of becoming a state. Their focus, however, soon shifted to the conflict over Toledo, where violence erupted in the spring of 1835 after Ohio sought to take possession of the disputed tract without congressional approval. Both Ohio and Michigan mustered their militias, and Ohio sympathizers in southeastern Michigan rebelled against duly constituted authorities.

In Congress and the press, meanwhile, a debate raged over the standing of the Northwest Ordinance as a constitutional document. Ohioans denied that a document created by Congress, a mere legislative body, could possess constitutional properties. Michiganians, however, observed that in important respects, the ordinance resembled a constitution, because it protected settlers' rights and established the geographical boundaries of new western states. This argument also represented a strategy by which Michiganians hoped to defuse Ohio's efforts to win Toledo through its large and powerful congressional delegation. If the ordinance possessed constitutional properties, as Michiganians claimed, it meant that federal lawmakers lacked the authority to change the boundaries that the document established, thus nullifying the advantage that Ohio's large congressional delegation gave it over Michigan in the nation's capital.

Phases two and three in Michigan's quest for statehood both involved internal disputes in Michigan over how best to retain the Toledo Strip. In phase two, which occurred simultaneously with phase one of the crisis, Jacksonians, who dominated Michigan politics, battled Whigs over Democratic governor Stevens T. Mason's plan to establish a state government without obtaining prior congressional approval. Democrats backed the governor's scheme, contending that federal approval was not needed to create a state government, because the Northwest Ordinance granted territories the right to enter the Union once they achieved a population of 60,000. Whigs insisted that Mason's plan was unconstitutional. They charged, further, that the Democrats, like South Carolinians in the Nullification Crisis, were acting wildly and recklessly in defying federal authority.

The final phase of Michigan's battle to enter the Union occurred in the second half of 1836, after Congress hammered out a compromise to settle the boundary dispute with Ohio and permit Michigan to become a state. Before it became final, a convention elected by the people of Michigan had to "assent" to the settlement. In the campaign to elect delegates to the convention, Democrats backed the congressional compromise, while Whigs and dissident Democrats opposed it, urging Michiganians to hold out for a better deal. During this debate, each side accused the other of acting wildly and betraying Michigan's interests. Federal lawmakers soon replaced Ohio as the main villain in the battle for Toledo, with Whigs and their allies claiming to defend local rights from a boundary-busting Congress that had acted on the basis of "expediency" rather than justice. Although Michiganians initially sided with the Whigs and selected delegates who rejected the compromise, they soon changed their minds and elected a second convention that assented to the deal offered by federal lawmakers.

Michigan's three-phase campaign to join the Union thus raised crucial questions about the importance of boundaries in curbing the wildness of large states and ensuring internal order and stability. The crisis, at the same time, seems to have solidified and reinforced Michiganians' identity as an "imagined community" by providing them with both a common foe and a negative reference point. Because of the conflict over Toledo, Michiganians could define themselves in opposition to Ohioans, with Michigan's southern border representing the difference between two communities: Michigan, on one hand, was filled with peaceful, virtuous people, intent on defending their native soil; Ohio, on the other, was dominated by boundary-busting, power-hungry officials who were deaf to the promptings of reason and morality. Indeed, Ohio, like Philip the Great, seemed bent on conquest. How else to explain its efforts to take jurisdiction of Toledo without congressional approval, and to sponsor anarchy and disorder on Michigan's southern border?[2]

Such aggression demonstrated the importance of boundaries in preventing anarchy and disorder and in maintaining what Peter Onuf has described as the delicate "balance of power" that protected small states from their more powerful neighbors. If big states became too large, their leaders would grow drunk with power, gobble up small states, and destroy the federation. Michigan's conflict with Ohio was a case in point: ignoring the dictates of conscience, Ohio officials sought to increase their wealth and power at Michigan's expense. The conflict also forced the federal lawmakers and the nation to reexamine both Congress's authority to establish the borders of new western states and the Northwest Ordinance's status as a constitutional document.[3]

THE TOLEDO WAR

These questions became a source of growing concern as Michigan's population surged in the 1830s. By then, the arrival of steam-powered ships on the Great Lakes, the construction of more roads in Michigan, and the completion of the Erie Canal in 1825 sparked dramatic population growth and prompted Michiganians to discuss the possibility of becoming a state. Michigan's territorial legislature responded to these concerns by organizing a referendum on statehood, which voters approved in 1832.[4]

But Michigan's long-standing boundary dispute with Ohio soon impeded the territory's efforts to join the Union. Such conflict was not unheard-
of in the early republic. Similar battles over land had occurred in the late
eighteenth century between New York and Vermont and between Connecticut and Pennsylvania.[5] Unlike those earlier conflicts, the Northwest
Ordinance and the boundaries that it created played an important role in
the conflict over Toledo.

The ordinance had given Congress the option to create three or more
states in the Northwest Territory. If Congress chose to establish only three
states, their northern boundary would be the Canadian border. If, however, federal lawmakers decided to create four or five states in the territory,
then the northern boundary of Ohio, Indiana, and Illinois was to be a line
running due east from the southern tip of Lake Michigan. The ordinance,
though, was silent on one important issue: whether Congress could alter
the east–west line that was to serve as Ohio, Indiana, and Illinois's northern boundary.[6]

Further complicating matters was uncertainty about the location of Lake
Michigan's southern tip. This problem, which resulted from the inaccura-
cy of early maps of the region, was important because it might determine
whether Toledo and its potentially valuable harbor on Lake Erie belonged
to Michigan or to Ohio. Delegates to Ohio's constitutional convention of
1802, being aware of this confusion about the location of their northern
border, noted it in Ohio's 1802 constitution and, pending congressional
approval, claimed Toledo if it fell outside of the line designated in the
ordinance as its northern boundary. Congress never explicitly endorsed
Ohio's claim to Toledo. But because Congress accepted its constitution,
Ohio authorities asserted that federal lawmakers implicitly had agreed to
award them Toledo. Three years later, when Congress placed Toledo in
the newly created Michigan Territory, Michigan officials claimed that this
proved that Congress intended to make Toledo a part of Michigan.[7]

Over the next three decades, Ohio's congressional delegation sought unsuccessfully to win federal approval for its claim to Toledo. Congress, meanwhile, tried and failed to resolve the dispute by authorizing two surveys to
mark the border between Michigan and Ohio. The first was conducted in
1817 by William Harris, a surveyor who, following the instructions of his
boss, Edward Tiffin, the U.S. surveyor general and former Ohio governor,
placed the disputed tract within the Buckeye State. After furious protests
from Michiganians, Congress ordered a new survey. The second was performed in 1818 by John A. Fulton, a surveyor who followed the provisions
of the ordinance more faithfully than Harris had, locating the land in Michigan. The Harris and Fulton lines thus became the informal borders of the

roughly 468-square-mile disputed tract later known as the "Toledo Strip."[8]

The conflict over Toledo remained largely dormant for more than a decade but escalated dramatically after Michigan formally initiated efforts to join the Union in late 1833. Fearing the loss of Toledo, Ohio used its power in Congress to deny statehood unless Michigan relinquished claims to the disputed land. In January 1834, the *Free Press* printed a letter from Lucius Lyon, Michigan's nonvoting delegate to Congress, reporting that the House Committee on Territories was considering Michigan's request for statehood, but he added that the memorial had run into stiff opposition. "There is a good deal of difficulty about boundaries," he wrote. Ohio had "arrayed all her strength against us," he observed, and seemed "determined to take this opportunity to compel us to submit to her claims."[9] A few months later, the *Free Press* informed its readers that Congress had tabled Michigan's memorial on statehood. Ohio and its allies would continue to oppose "passage of a law for our admission," unless Lyon agreed to "yield the question of boundary."[10] Lyon refused to give in to Ohio, and Congress was initially unable or unwilling to resolve the dispute.

Leading Michigan in the battle with Ohio was its feisty governor, Stevens T. Mason. Only twenty-two when the crisis over Toledo began in late 1833, Mason was the scion of a distinguished political family. One of his ancestors, George Mason, had helped to draft Virginia's first constitution. Stevens T. Mason was born in Virginia but grew up in Kentucky, where his father, a lawyer, lost considerable sums investing in the iron industry and other ventures. President Andrew Jackson rescued the family from poverty in 1830, naming John T. Mason secretary of the Michigan Territory. When the elder Mason left Michigan on a mission to Mexico the following year, Jackson named his precocious nineteen-year-old son, Stevens T. Mason, to succeed him as Michigan's new secretary. Despite being greeted by protests from Michiganians who worried about Mason's youth and inexperience, the young Kentuckian displayed more political skill and dexterity than many older statesmen. When Michigan governor George Porter died in July 1834, Mason succeeded him as acting governor.[11]

During Mason's first year in office, the battle over Toledo intensified dramatically. After learning that Michigan planned to secure Toledo by establishing a state government without first receiving congressional approval, Ohio governor Robert Lucas, on February 6, 1835, urged his state legislature to enact a law taking possession of the disputed tract. Michigan passed the so-called Pain and Penalties Act six days later. It sought to prevent Ohio from gaining jurisdiction of the disputed tract by imposing a $1,000 fine or five years in prison on Ohio officials who tried to exercise authority in the area.[12]

On February 23, Ohio's legislature responded defiantly to Michigan's new law. Without waiting for federal approval, Buckeye State lawmakers took possession of the Toledo Strip by statute. In addition to extending Ohio's jurisdiction over Toledo, legislators authorized residents of the disputed tract to elect justices of the peace and other local officials to administer Ohio law. They also instructed a team of surveyors to re-mark the Harris line to encompass Toledo.[13]

As tensions between Michigan and Ohio mounted, President Andrew Jackson tried to avert violence. He asked U.S. attorney general Benjamin Butler to rule on Michigan's and Ohio's competing claims to Toledo. Butler upheld Michigan's Pain and Penalties Act and held that Ohio could not take control of the disputed land without prior federal approval. Still, Jackson's administration, which feared alienating the Buckeye State and losing its rich trove of electoral votes in the 1836 presidential election, told Michigan governor Mason to permit Ohio surveyors to reestablish the Harris Line. After Mason refused, Jackson appointed two commissioners—Richard Rush and Benjamin Howard—on March 24, 1835, to resolve the conflict peacefully. Despite an intensive effort, they failed to hammer out a settlement on which both sides could agree.[14]

Michigan newspapers, meanwhile, continued to attack Ohio for its reckless violation of legal, constitutional, and geographical boundaries. The *Michigan Sentinel* informed its readers in March that "this powerful and arrogant state" seemed bent on the "forcible possession" of Michigan's "soil—regardless alike of the justice of her claim or the consequences which must inevitably follow."[15] A few weeks later, the *Sentinel* accused Ohio lawmakers of undermining the republic by enacting a statute that was "without precedent in our history, and of a truly desperate character." By trying to countermand constitutional texts with new statutes, they defied not only "moral right and public justice, but even the laws and Constitution of our country."[16] Similarly, the *Democratic Free Press* criticized Ohio governor Lucas for "laboring under the strange" belief that "Michigan as a Territory" was "neither entitled to, nor [would] receive the . . . protection of the federal government." The governor seemed to believe that the "superior physical power of Ohio" would accomplish "his purposes, regardless alike, of the rights of Michigan, the justice of the case, and the laws and authority of the U.[nited] States."[17]

At the same time, Michigan governor Mason warned Ohio governor Lucas that Michiganians would not surrender Toledo without a fight. In a letter to Ohio's chief executive, Mason vowed that "no portion of the rightful jurisdiction of Michigan" would be "surrendered by her citizens" until the federal government had resolved the controversy. Nor was this "language" meant "for purposes of empty show or intimidation." Rather, Mason hoped that it would persuade Lucas to "desist for the present from any attempt to carry the law of [his] state into effect."[18]

Ignoring Mason's admonitions, Ohio proceeded with plans to seize Toledo. In April, Governor Lucas ordered the state's militia to the disputed tract and dispatched surveyors with an armed escort to establish the Harris Line as Ohio's northern border. In early April, Michigan supporters in the Toledo Strip elected local officials. A few days later, Ohio supporters in the strip elected officials loyal to the Buckeye State. Stevens T. Mason, meanwhile, sent his territory's militia to the Toledo Strip and ordered them to shoot Ohio officials who entered Michigan.[19] The *Michigan Sentinel* reported in March 1835 that Mason also "removed from office" all those in the Toledo Strip "favorably disposed to the claims of Ohio."[20]

One member of the Michigan militia, J. Wilkie Moore, recalled the enthusiasm with which Michiganians embraced Mason's position. In Detroit, the militia gleefully prepared for battle, parading and drilling on Campus Maritus. Although the troops were ill equipped—lacking uniforms, and training with "long broom handles" instead of guns—they enjoyed great popularity. "Crowds turned out to see us and the town was full of excitement," Moore observed. As the militia marched south to the front, farmers greeted them warmly because they "were fighting for Michigan." Though not explicitly stated, these sentiments suggest that the conflict with Ohio united territorial residents in a common cause and cemented their identity as Michiganians. This sense of purpose and togetherness also is reflected in the seriousness with which the militia greeted their task. Moore's commander was a "fine looking man . . . named Captain Fitzpatrick," who "kept us pretty steadily in motion." The troops, moreover, were "very much in earnest and expected bloodshed."[21]

Their expectations, however, proved to be illusory. Despite all of the bellicose rhetoric and angry posturing, almost no blood was spilled in the Toledo War. One of the few clashes that occurred came to be known as the Battle of Phillips Corner. It began when Michigan officials learned, in April 1835, that Ohio surveyors, ordered to re-mark the Harris Line, had entered Michigan, violating the Pain and Penalties Act. After organizing a posse and obtaining a warrant to arrest the Ohioans, Michiganians found the trespassers at the home of a man named Phillips, near Adrian, Michigan. According to the *Democratic Free Press*, two Michigan sheriffs left the posse and approached the house in which the Ohioans were staying, demanding that they "surrender."[22] The Ohioans initially refused. But when they saw the size of the Michigan posse, the *Michigan Sentinel* reported, they "took to their heels," surrendering after "a few guns" were "fired over their heads." Although the posse arrested nine Ohioans, four escaped to the Buckeye State.[23]

Such mayhem paled, however, when compared to the rioting and disorder that beset Toledo. Asserting that Michigan lacked authority in the

Toledo Strip, which now belonged to the Buckeye State, Ohio supporters increasingly defied Michigan authorities. The *Michigan Sentinel* reported in April 1835 that a deputy sheriff had arrested several Irishmen and was taking them to the magistrate when two Toledo inhabitants helped the prisoners escape.[24] A more dramatic instance of rebellion occurred in July of that year when Ohio sympathizers prevented two Michigan officials from executing an action for debt against Toledo resident Jeremiah Odel Jr. According to the *Free Press,* trouble began when Truman Hemmingway, a Michigan constable, held an auction to sell Odel's horses and wagon. After bidding opened on his steeds, a local "tavern keeper," J. B. Davis, "struck down Hemmingway," while others in the crowd "seized the horses" and stopped the auction. The "lawless mob" then proceeded to a nearby warehouse and "took from it the other goods seized from Odel for sale on the execution against him." The rioters also grabbed Henry Clark, the creditor who initiated the legal proceedings against Odel. Dragging Clark to the local magistrate, the crowd forced him to withdraw his complaint against Odel, threatening to "take his life, and quarter him," unless he entered "satisfaction in full for the judgment obtained against Odel."[25]

On July 15, Michigan deputy sheriff Joseph Wood went to Toledo to arrest Two Stickney, a leading Ohio sympathizer, whose eccentric father had christened his brother and him One and Two respectively.[26] Finding Stickney at a local tavern, Wood told the suspect that he had a warrant for his arrest. Stickney, according to the *Free Press,* replied that "unless the warrant had been issued under" the auspices of Ohio, "he should not answer to it." When Wood tried to arrest Stickney, the suspect wounded the deputy, stabbing him with a "large dirk knife."[27] Rather than condemning this act of violence, the *Free Press* reported, Ohio supporters applauded it, warning Michigan officials to "keep away" from Toledo, if they wished to avoid the "fate of Wood." They insisted, moreover, that they had "dirks sharpened . . . rifles loaded, and would resist Michigan and her officers to the last drop of their blood." Michigan sheriffs were unable to bring Stickney to justice, but they eventually captured others alleged to have instigated the riot.[28]

Despite these arrests, Michiganians expressed growing concern about the violence and disorder caused by the instability of their southern border. In a letter to U.S. secretary of state John Forsyth, Michigan governor Mason reported that "excitement" in the region was "exceedingly great" and worried that more "violence and outrage" might occur in the future.[29] Similarly, the *Michigan Sentinel* warned that the lawlessness of Ohioans and their Michigan supporters threatened to undermine order, stability, and republican institutions. In August 1835, the *Michigan Sentinel* asserted that a "very unhappy state of things" had disrupted the "peace and harmony" of Toledo; and unless "tranquility" was quickly restored, "something more serious may be apprehended." The savagery of Ohio loyalists bore "the mark of despotism" and indicated that the "moral state of society" was "disordered and . . . sickly." If remedies were not found soon, the polity might be "beyond the reach of recovery." Ohioans were seeking to "weaken or destroy the grand political edifice in which as freemen we all take shelter from the storms of despotism."[30]

These concerns about violence and lawlessness, however, proved to be exaggerated. Tensions in Toledo eased in the fall of 1835. In August, President Jackson dismissed Governor Mason, because his confrontational style exacerbated the conflict. As John Forsyth observed, Mason's "zeal" for what he considered the "rights of Michigan" had "overcome that spirit of moderation and forbearance" that was needed to preserve the peace. Mason's dismissal, nonetheless, had little effect on his career: Michigan formed a state government later that autumn, and voters elected him to his old post shortly after his dismissal. His departure, however, did restore calm to the region.[31]

THE DEBATE IN CONGRESS AND THE PRESS

Although rioting and disorder ceased in late 1835, the war of words between Michigan and Ohio continued, as each side sought to persuade Congress that its cause was just. Continually emphasizing the need to establish boundaries that would curb the lawlessness and rapacity of Ohio, Michiganians based their claim to the Toledo Strip on two principal arguments: first, they asserted, Washington needed to maintain a rough parity among states and not permit some, such as Ohio, to become more powerful than their neighbors. Second, Congress, they claimed, lacked the authority to change the boundaries that the Northwest Ordinance established.

This latter argument was based on their belief that the ordinance was a constitutional document co-equal to federal constitutional provision and off limits to congressional tampering. Michigan governor Mason stated this position in a letter to Virginia's governor in 1834, recalling that "the Ordinance fixed unalterably the southern boundary or boundaries of the state or states to be formed by Congress, north of an east-west line drawn through the southerly bend of Lake Michigan." Writers argued, remarkably, that once approved by Virginia, which had ceded the land that constituted the Northwest Territory, "the ordinance became a fixed and fundamental law of the land" and could be changed only "by all the contracting parties." Once Congress decided to form additional states north of the line that the ordinance established, "the rights of the people of Michigan" became "absolute and vested." Only through "common consent" could the federal government "alter the boundaries of this territory as prescribed" and not violate "an instrument as sacred and inviolable as the Federal Constitution itself."[32]

Others agreed. The ordinance, the *Detroit Free Press* said in 1834, was "our constitution—our only peculiar constitution," providing Michigan residents with "certain rights—among them the establishment of a Southern boundary" that had been "plainly marked out and defined."[33] Delegates to Michigan's constitutional convention reiterated this argument in 1835 in their appeal to the people of the United States. "Congress has no power to act upon this subject," they said. The ordinance "prescribed" Michigan's "boundaries," and the "national faith" put "the matter beyond the reach of the federal legislature." Congress's "power ha[d] been spent, and the most important political and territorial rights acquired by another party." Federal lawmakers, they warned, could as well "change the boundaries of any state of the union as those of this Territory."[34] Similarly, in an 1835 letter to Congress, Michigan's territorial legislature insisted that the ordinance represented "articles of compact between the people of the original states, and the people and states in the ceded territory." The ordinance "was forever to remain unalterable, except by common consent." Congress could neither repeal it nor "tamper with its provisions."[35]

Ohio officials claimed, on the contrary, that Congress had agreed to give them jurisdiction of the Toledo Strip when it approved the state's 1802 constitution. Governor Lucas said that Congress had agreed to this change "when they adopted our constitution and admitted Ohio into the Union." The boundary created by the ordinance, moreover, was entirely alterable. "This provision" granted Congress "discretionary power" in forming states. Lawmakers were not confined "to this line, as the special boundary of one or two states to be formed north of it." Had this line "been intended as the permanent boundary" of the three southern states in the Northwest Territory, "there would certainly have been some expressions in the Ordinance that would have indicated such intentions." Yet "we find no expressions of this character in the ordinance."[36]

Even Ohioans, who agreed that the ordinance possessed constitutional properties, interpreted its east–west line differently than did Michiganians. The ordinance, they insisted, guaranteed that all territory below the line belonged to Ohio, Indiana, and Illinois—the three states in the southern portion of the Old Northwest. But the document did not prevent those states from taking land north of the line.[37]

Congress, moreover, provided a precedent on this question. Governor Lucas recalled that Congress changed the boundary, which Michigan insisted was unalterable, when "the states of Illinois and Indiana were admitted." The boundaries for both states extended "considerably north of the southern extremity of Lake Michigan and if these states had the right to extend their boundaries north" of the line established by the Ordinance "Ohio undoubtedly had an equal right."[38]

In Congress, meanwhile, Ohio representative Thomas J. Hamer contended that the Northwest Ordinance lacked the weight of a constitutional document. Unlike a constitution, the ordinance was simply a law passed by federal lawmakers, and no Congress could pass a law that bound "their successor and their country through all time." But this was the notion that Michigan advanced. "The ordinance is an act of Congress. It is no compact, as to the country north of the line named, whatever it may be, as to the rest." Compacts required "two parties," but in this case, "there was but one."[39]

But Michiganians did not rely solely on the ordinance to make their case for retaining Toledo. They also argued that Michigan should retain Toledo because Washington needed to ensure that states were approximately the same size. This argument dated back to the earliest days of the republic and arose in part from concerns about preserving internal peace and stability. Since the American Revolution, battles between large and small states over land, power, and other questions had troubled the new republic. Such conflict, early American statesmen feared, might endanger the Union. In Europe, they noted, states that became too large dominated or destroyed their smaller rivals. This same problem might plague the new American federation, with large states dominating or swallowing their neighbors. When federal lawmakers drafted the Northwest Ordinance, therefore, they sought to ensure that new western states were roughly equal in size. This parity not only would prevent large states from dominating smaller ones and destroying the republic, but also would stave off the armed conflict and deadly rivalries that characterized international relations. Borders were thus crucial in dividing wealth and power equitably between states, and preserving peace and stability.[40]

Implicit in this argument was the notion that poorly drawn geographical borders would lead to the creation of states that violated legal and constitutional boundaries, such as those needed to ensure the rule of law, political stability, and republican institutions. In making this argument, Michiganians insisted that power already had corrupted Ohio officials, leading them to become wild and lawless boundary-busters who were deaf to the dictates of reason. The only remedy for this threat was to establish borders that limited their power and prevented them from destabilizing the Union.

These concerns surfaced repeatedly during debates in Congress, as Michigan officials urged federal lawmakers not to make Ohio, already a large state, any bigger. Michigan's congressional delegate Lyon predicted in 1834 that Toledo was likely to become a prized port on Lake Erie. Once the Wabash and Erie Canal was completed, the town would "grow up a place of considerable commercial importance." Ohio was already larger and more powerful than Michigan. If federal lawmakers bowed to Ohio's demands, it would make a bad situation worse.[41] Echoing these sentiments, the *Michigan Sentinel* observed that Ohio was "already sufficiently extensive, as it regards extent of country resources, and natural agricultural and commercial advantages." Taking "from our soil an additional district," the *Sentinel* claimed, would weaken "us in point of numbers as well as in natural advantages."[42]

In an 1834 speech to Congress, Lyon enlarged on this point. Michigan contained about half as much arable land as its southern neighbor. Michigan's climate was more "unfavorable" and its population much smaller than Ohio's. Taking land from Michigan and giving it to Ohio would "only increase the present disparity in population and advantages and tend to make the weak weaker and the strong stronger." This reallocation of resources would contravene "the ends of political justice, as well as the intention of Congress and the state of Virginia at the adoption of the ordinance." Both Congress and Virginia sought "to equalize the size and apportion the advantages of the different states to be formed in the North-west territory."[43]

Because of its great size, Ohio already had become one of the menacing behemoths that the drafters of the ordinance feared, Michiganians observed.[44] The Buckeye State, they said, was not only wildly barbaric and avaricious, but also a boundary-buster determined to conquer smaller, weaker neighbors and threaten the federal system. In making this argument, Michiganians borrowed ideas and imagery from classical republican thinkers, who relied heavily on the metaphor of trespass to describe how government officials violated constitutional and legal borders to increase their power at the expense of the people's rights.[45]

Relying on similar imagery, Michiganians suggested that its southern border was not the only boundary at stake in its dispute with Ohio. Rather, Michigan's southern border became a symbol of the legal and constitutional boundaries safeguarding the republic, and journalists characterized Ohio as a despot that had readily trampled the law and Michigan's sovereignty to increase its wealth and power. One *Detroit Journal* correspondent, for instance, compared Ohio's behavior to Philip of Macedon and his "encroachments upon weaker but smaller neighbors." Employing sexual imagery, he compared Ohio's conduct to that of others who had subverted republics, noting that its behavior brought to mind "the lust of power which distinguished the whole history of the Roman commonwealth" as well as modern Italian states.[46] Other correspondents portrayed Ohio as wild, despotic, and irrational. The Buckeye State, said one, "exhibits to the world a lively specimen of the actings of our nature, when uncontrolled by reason, justice and morality." Greed "keeps pace with her growth in wealth and resources. Not content with a large and fruitful territory and with a great proportion of the southern coast of Lake Erie . . . she also has laid her insatiable grasp upon a proportion of our comparatively small territory, and right or wrong seems determined to cling to it."[47]

Journalists were not alone in issuing these warnings. Delegates to Michigan's constitutional convention in 1835 also emphasized the importance of the federal government in enforcing the rule of law and controlling large and bellicose states, which threatened not only smaller, weaker ones, but also the republic. The past demonstrated "that ambition is not the infirmity of monarchies alone, but that it frequently operates with decisive energy in republican governments." How would the nation protect "the political rights and even the political existence" of "the smaller states of this union . . . if the principle is once practically established that each member of the confederacy may, at any time, proceed without obstruction to its forcible possession"? Coercion endangered the very existence of the federal system. It was "not difficult to foresee" that states would fall one after the other and that "consummation would be found in the establishment of one single consolidated government."[48] In these conquests, Ohio was portrayed as a predator that would stop at nothing to satisfy its lust for power. Michigan was gendered female and depicted as a helpless victim who depended on the masculine power of the central government for protection.

The *Michigan Sentinel* echoed these views in 1835, depicting Ohio as a threat to the republic: Ohio officials were a "few factious and nullifying hotheads" who had violated the Constitution. They broke "the peace-bands of society" and endangered "both the lives and property of those" who lived near Toledo merely to obtain "by force" a piece of land "which their ambitious speculators chance to covet." Neighboring states would not back Ohio in these endeavors. Preserving the Constitution was now and always would be their "first and prevailing object." To violate that document, "which binds the confederacy together . . . is but opening a door" to "anarchy—and hence a dissolution of the union must . . . be the consequence." So far, the American republic, "whose walls, reared by the magic hand of her illustrious founders, and consolidated by the wisdom of her institutions, has remained unshaken by the invader or nullifier." Let wild Ohio be indulged "but for one short season in her mad career," and the great "chain that so strongly binds these United States in harmony together" would be destroyed, "rent asunder by a rebellious separation of one of its members. Ambition and anarchy in proud stubbornness and sober determination, will exult at beholding the criterion by which each of these twenty four links may in succession be rent and scattered to the four winds in broken fragments."[49]

Lyon said that another important reason to make Michigan stronger was its vulnerable position on the Canadian border. Ohio, he observed, already was larger than the authors of the Ordinance had intended. Early maps had placed Lake Erie "twenty to thirty miles" south of its true location and gave Ohio far more territory than the framers of the Northwest Ordinance had intended. "What reason or justice, or propriety, then can there be in now giving that state a portion of Michigan, when she is already so much larger than was intended at the time of her formation?" Congress, however, had good reason to make Michigan larger. Michigan would "remain in a very exposed situation on the frontier, and for a long time to come, must be in the immediate vicinity of a powerful and warlike tribe of Indians." Consequently, it made sense to strengthen Michigan "as much as possible" and reject a measure that would do "so much to weaken it."[50]

THE CONFLICT BETWEEN MICHIGAN
DEMOCRATS AND WHIGS

The struggle to retain Toledo, however, was not the only conflict that the crisis over statehood stirred. Michigan's efforts to join the Union also sparked heated debate between Michigan's two political parties. Although Michigan's Whigs and Democrats agreed on the need to maintain possession of Toledo, they disagreed on how to attain that goal. After Congress thwarted Michigan's efforts to become a state in 1833 and 1834, Democrats, the territory's dominant party, passed legislation in January 1835 enabling the territory to establish a state government without receiving congressional approval. Whigs contended that establishing such a government without obtaining congressional approval was unconstitutional.

This battle over Michigan's right to create a state government was a classic contest between those asserting the claims of national power versus those claiming states' rights, with Whigs defending and Democrats opposing Congress's authority to admit new states. Citing Tennessee's entry into the union in 1796 as precedent, Democratic officials asserted that Michigan did not need Congress's permission to become a state. Instead, the Northwest Ordinance granted Michigan the right to become a state once its population contained more than 60,000 free men. Michigan governor Mason contended in 1834 that the ordinance required "only 60,000 free inhabitants, to entitle Michigan to admission into the Union as an independent state." Once that happened, the "only discretion left for Congress to exercise, is to determine that our constitution is 'Republican.'"[51] Similarly, "A Friend of the West," writing in the *Free Press* that same year, insisted that all Michigan needed to do to become a state was to draft "a constitution . . . and demand admittance into the Union."[52]

Whigs charged that creating a state government without congressional approval violated the Constitution. They stated that the Constitution, which superseded the Northwest Ordinance, granted Congress the authority to regulate the territories and admit new states. The *Detroit Journal* said that if the ordinance "contained any provisions that were repugnant" to the Constitution, they "were of course superseded and rendered void."[53]

Whigs also alleged that in ignoring Congress, Michigan officials were acting lawlessly and endangering the Union, as had South Carolinians, who a few years earlier had claimed that states possessed the power to nullify or overturn federal laws. In early 1836, the *Journal* opined that Democratic officials were offering a "new and refined system of nullification . . . to the favorable consideration of the people of Michigan." The violent "severing" of ties between the "territory and the general government, precipitating the people of Michigan into a state of revolution." Such a policy would not "give any greater security in the settlement of the boundary question."[54]

Whigs also placed greater faith in Congress to let Michigan enter the Union and retain the Toledo Strip than did Democrats. The *Journal* claimed that if Michigan simply had waited a "few months," federal lawmakers would have given their assent and "opened the door of admission" to them.[55] The speaker at a Whig meeting in Wayne County reiterated this assertion in 1835. If Democratic officials had not acted rashly, the admissions bill then in Congress "would have passed . . . and Michigan become a state."[56]

Democratic officials ignored these views, partly because they believed that becoming a state as quickly as possible gave them the best chance of keeping Toledo. Governor Mason contended that once Michigan became a state, it could take its dispute with Ohio out of Congress, where the Buckeye State with its large congressional delegation had a great advantage over Michigan, and place it before the United States Supreme Court. "As a territory," Governor Mason complained in an 1835 speech, "we have but little weight in the deliberations of Congress, on subjects connected with our vital and permanent political rights." Federal lawmakers, he added, decided these questions by relying on "principles of expediency, with a view to other interests" than those of Michigan. In a letter to Michigan lawmakers that same year, Mason elaborated on this point: "Congress, if brought to the test," he explained, "will decide the question against us." Michigan's only chance of "success," therefore, was to keep the question of its southern boundary out of Congress. After becoming a state, it could "appeal for justice" to the nation's "supreme judicial tribunal."[57]

THE COMPROMISE

But Mason's strategy of sidestepping Congress failed. That body hammered out a compromise in the middle of 1836 that awarded Toledo to Ohio. Federal lawmakers had begun considering legislation to end the dispute over Toledo in December 1835, shortly after Michigan established its new state government. As details of what became known as the "admissions bill" emerged in early 1836, Michiganians were shocked to learn that Congress was likely to rule against them. In March of that year, the *Free Press* reported that federal lawmakers had "decided in favor of Ohio" on this question. In ignoring the "ordinance of 1787," Congress had based its decision on "expediency, that great innovator of the day, which threatens to undermine all the existing safeguards of popular rights."[58]

In March 1836, the *Free Press* reprinted a congressional report on the boundary dispute that explained Congress's decision to give Toledo to Ohio. Written by the Senate Judiciary Committee, it dismissed Michigan's assertions that Congress lacked the authority to rearrange boundaries in the Northwest Territories. In the act ceding the Old Northwest to the United States, Congress had insisted that Virginia grant it this power, to ensure that states in the region had access to resources needed for economic development. Lawmakers also found that the legislation creating the Michigan Territory had established temporary, not permanent, boundaries. More importantly, the authors of the Northwest Ordinance had intended Ohio to have Toledo. Senators arrived at this conclusion after perusing maps from the late eighteenth century, which placed the southern tip of Lake Michigan much farther north than it was actually located. "Mitchell's map . . . so lays down this lake and the adjacent country, that a line drawn due east from this point" placed Toledo in Ohio. Both Congress and the people of Ohio thought "that the new state of Ohio, would comprehend not only the territory in controversy, but a much larger tract of country lying north of it." As a result, "the intention of both . . . parties to this compact has been defeated by a mere mistake as to a single fact" of geography.[59]

Rather than simply giving Toledo to Ohio, though, Congress worked out a compromise to sweeten the deal for Michigan. In return for relinquishing its claims to the disputed tract, Michigan could enter the Union and annex a sizable portion of the Upper Peninsula, a large tract of land that was situated on the south shore of Lake Superior and north of Michigan's Lower Peninsula. Initially, the *Free Press* reported the compromise was to become final after the "authorities of Michigan" gave their "assent" to the "altered boundaries." Some in Congress, nonetheless, insisted that Michigan's legislature lacked the authority to agree to such a change because it altered Michigan's constitution. Indiana Democrat John Tipton asserted, for instance, that Congress could not "clothe the legislature of any state or territory with authority to alter or amend any portion of its constitution." In the end, federal lawmakers amended the bill to require that Michiganians elect a "convention of delegates" to "assent" to the deal. President Jackson signed it on June 15, 1836. In turn, a special July session of the Michigan legislature enacted a law enabling voters to elect delegates in September to a convention that was to assemble later that month in Ann Arbor and decide whether to accept the congressional compromise.[60]

THE TWO CONVENTIONS

Initially, Democrats and Whigs both denounced the settlement. In March 1836, Detroit Whigs attacked Congress for manifesting "an extraordinary disregard of the dictates of wise policy." Four months later, Michigan's Democratic governor, Mason, expressed similar sentiments, charging that federal lawmakers who awarded Toledo to Ohio had violated "every principle of justice" and had established a "precedent" that would "work evil of the utmost magnitude" to the nation's "civil institutions."[61]

Despite this criticism, Democrats eventually backed the compromise, asserting that Michiganians could not hope to regain Toledo by rejecting Congress's offer. In August, a writer assumed the identity of one of America's fiercest critics of despotism, "Common Sense," and pointed out in a series of articles in the *Detroit Free Press* that Michiganians were not voting on whether to surrender the Toledo Strip to Ohio. A tyrannical federal government already had decreed that they "must give up the disputed ground to Ohio." Congress did not ask Michigan residents "to assent to this surrender of territory." How could Michiganians "expect to retain, against the laws and power of the United States, the disputed ground which those laws" had given to Ohio? No "enlightened man" could "anticipate any such result from a rejection of the proffered terms." Other Democrats echoed these views. The *Free Press* reprinted an article from the *Tecumseh Democrat* that noted that voting against the settlement "restores not the boundary and yields not the slightest glimmering of a hope of a future restoration."[62]

Indeed, Democrats predicted that spurning the compromise could only foster "anarchy," chaos, "bloodshed," and disorder. "Common Sense" forecast that if Michiganians rejected the compromise, they "would incur the odium . . . of a fruitless opposition to the laws of the Union." Rejecting the compromise might even encourage Michiganians to defy Washington in an effort "to maintain possession of the usurped portion of their soil." This would lead irresistibly to bloodshed. A deep stain would, in all likelihood, follow. In addition, "a deep stain would be inflicted" on republican institutions, and the "union of the states would be endangered." Similarly, the *Constantine Republican* prophesied, in an article reprinted in the *Detroit Free Press,* that rejecting the compromise would be "little short of political suicide" it surely would lead to "anarchy, confusion, treason, and blood-shed." Was it not "humiliating and degrading" to lose Toledo? Merely be-cause "our hair is scorched and our garments smell of fire, it would be extreme madness to plunge into a furnace."[63]

Democrats also reminded Michiganians of the benefits to be gained by agreeing to the compromise. "Common Sense" contended that the only chance Michiganians had of recovering the Toledo Strip was to approve the compromise and file suit; as a state, they might "possibly . . . be en-abled to bring the subject" before the United States Supreme Court. If, however, Michiganians remained "out of the union," they would not "be recognized by that court as a legitimate party" to any suit.[64] Statehood, meanwhile, carried economic rewards in its train. The *Free Press* reprinted an article from the *Constantine Republican* that reminded readers that once it entered the Union, Michigan would receive 5 percent of the revenue that the federal government earned from the sale of public land within its borders, Michigan's share of the federal government's surplus revenue, as well as the land the new state would obtain from Washington to con-struct public buildings, schools, and a university. This assistance, the *Free Press* predicted, would reduce taxes and increase immigration. Democrats also argued that the Upper Peninsula might turn out to be quite valu-able. The *Free Press* in August 1836 printed a letter from H. R. Schoolcraft, Michigan's Indian agent, who reported that although the Upper Peninsula had "little or no value" for farming, it might provide minerals and other natural resources.[65]

Whigs and their allies, who rejected these arguments, emphasized the importance of territorial integrity in attacking the compromise, arguing that the loss of Toledo would undermine Michigan's power, wealth, and status. They also denounced federal lawmakers who had assumed Ohio's role as an aggressive and lawless boundary-buster. In March 1836, for in-stance, a Whig meeting in Detroit accused Congress of "dismembering this territory."[66] The *Michigan Sentinel,* a Democratic newspaper that sided with the Whigs, used similarly graphic language, denouncing the com-promise as the "dismemberment of the state"; soon, other critics came to label the settlement the "dismemberment bill."[67]

Additionally, writers elaborated upon earlier arguments, charging fed-eral lawmakers with violating the Constitution and the Northwest Ordi-nance to assuage Ohio's powerful congressional delegation. In April 1836, the *Sentinel* charged that in passing the admissions bill, Congress satisfied the "unlawful demands of Ohio" by robbing Michigan of a "very valu-able portion" of its Territory.[68] In doing so, lawmakers had violated both "the ordinance of '87" and the "Constitution of the United States."[69] Similarly, a September meeting of the settlement's opponents in Detroit alleged that in changing Michigan's boundary, Congress had "infringed" on the "rights guaranteed to the . . . states" in the northern portion of the Northwest Territory.[70]

Whigs denied Democratic predictions that rejecting the settlement would mean any permanent loss of federal largess: in their view, any reduction in such revenue would be temporary. Writing in the *Detroit Journal* in August 1836, "Amicus Republicae" doubted that Michigan would lose its share of revenue from Washington. "Its reception may be retarded; we may be disappointed the present year, but we will eventually receive it." Even if rejecting the compromise meant losing federal bounty, however, the "high-minded citizens of Michigan" were not "prepared to barter their birthright for a mess of pottage." Nor were they willing to agree to "their own dismemberment and humiliation for any sum which Congress might" offer. "Every patriot in Michigan, every citizen in whose veins flows the blood of a free American will indignantly answer no."[71]

Whigs predicted, moreover, that if Michiganians refused to surrender Toledo, federal lawmakers surely would reverse their decision and permit the new state to keep the disputed tract. The *Michigan Sentinel* argued in June 1836 that in giving Michiganians the power to veto its decision, Congress demonstrated that its resolution of the boundary dispute was not final. If Congress had given Michiganians no "redress but by force of arms," there would be no point in trying to retain Toledo. But federal lawmakers had "only" proposed to give Toledo to Ohio "with our consent." Michiganians were not obliged "to sign" their own "death warrant"; anyone who did so "must be a traitor to our laws and institutions." Agreeing to the compromise, predicted the *Detroit Journal*, would make Congress's mistaken policy permanent, "forever" fixing Michigan's "boundaries to the inconvenient shape" that federal lawmakers had proposed. Even if Congress refused to restore Toledo to Michigan, voting against the compromise would probably tempt them to compensate the new state with land in the newly organized Wisconsin Territory.[72]

These arguments seem to have been persuasive. When Michiganians went to the polls on September 12, 1836, most of the delegates they elected opposed the compromise. The *Free Press* reported in September that though returns were coming in slowly, it seemed certain that a "majority of the candidates supported by dissenters" had prevailed. Many dissenting delegates were Democrats; if enough of them "united" with their fellow party members, they would constitute "a decided majority in the convention." It still was possible, in other words, that the convention might give the "necessary assent" and permit Michigan to enter the Union.[73] It required only that Democrats toed the party line. Shortly after delegates assembled in Ann Arbor, however, these Democratic hopes were dashed. On September 27, delegates elected as convention president an opponent of the compromise ; three days later, a majority of the forty-nine delegates ignored Democratic appeals and rejected the congressional settlement by a seven-vote margin.[74]

After the Ann Arbor convention adjourned, Democrats criticized its decision to reject the compromise, calling for a second assembly that would agree to the terms that Congress had established for entering the Union. The *Free Press* in late September printed a letter from "A Gentleman at the West," who asserted that "darkness and gloom" pervaded Michigan's future. He insisted that the convention's decision was not final, because the "great body of the people" had been "deceived." They had voted for opponents of the compromise because they had been tricked into believing that Michiganians would enter the Union "without opposition" and "retain possession of the disputed territory by rejecting the terms proposed." Governor Mason echoed these sentiments, asserting that the people had been "represented by unfaithful agents" and "misled by the distorted representations of designing men."[75]

In late October, the Democratic Party of Wayne County recommended that a new convention be called and charged the delegates in Ann Arbor with acting wildly. The actions of the Ann Arbor convention had been "little short of nullification and incipient steps towards an illegal and violent resistance of the laws of the United States." They expressed concern about the "spreading evils and dangers which a refusal to go into the Union" had "brought upon the people of Michigan," and they urged other Democrats to convene meetings "in every county of the state" to call for "another convention" that would give the "assent required by Congress."[76]

Soon other Democrats joined the campaign for a new convention. The party made the elections for the state legislature that November into a referendum on the compromise. Partisans insisted that the overwhelming victory of "assenters" in those contests demonstrated that the people were behind them. The *Free Press* observed in December that the recent election indicated that a "large majority of the citizens of Michigan" were "dissatisfied with decision of the Ann Arbor Convention." Those opposing the compromise had nominated candidates to the Michigan Senate "in every district," and "with but one solitary exception" they all had been defeated. Even worse, dissenters had elected only twelve of their candidates to Michigan's fifty-member House of Representatives. Democrats also reminded Michiganians of the federal funds and land that Ann Arbor delegates had relinquished by rejecting the compromise.[77]

Despite calls for a second convention, Governor Mason declined in

November to have the state legislature pass another bill authorizing such an assembly. The executive branch, he asserted, did not possess the authority to "issue a proclamation recommending the election of delegates to another convention." Instead, Mason invited Michigan residents to "take the measure into their own hands" and elect delegates to a second convention. In making this case, he pointed to the example of Pennsylvania during the American Revolution, which relied on "county committees" to draft a constitution after breaking with Great Britain.[78]

Heeding Mason's advice, General John R. Williams, a former Detroit mayor, and other prominent Democrats urged Michigan counties to elect delegates in early December to a second convention that would meet in Ann Arbor on December 14. When elections for delegates took place in most counties, assenters won a huge victory. The second Ann Arbor convention agreed to the compromise. Despite Whig protests that these proceedings were illegal, Congress approved and President Jackson signed a bill on January 26, 1837, permitting Michigan to join the Union.[79]

Michigan's long and bitter dispute with Ohio over Toledo thus can be read on two levels. Most obviously, the conflict was simply a battle over property that seemed likely to become a major Great Lakes port. On another level, though, the conflict illustrates the importance that Michiganians assigned to boundaries in dividing wealth and power in the early republic, thereby preventing large states from becoming dangerous new powers that could threaten not only their smaller neighbors, but also the nation. Americans believed that republics were fragile entities, easily subverted by those seeking to increase their power at the expense of liberty. Typically, historians have argued that Americans in the early national period viewed the federal government in Washington as the main threat to the republic. The conflict over Toledo, however, suggests that they were also concerned about the potential threat that large states, such as Ohio, posed to the rule of law, political stability, and liberty. The Toledo War demonstrates, too, the key role that they attached to boundary maintenance in the face of the culture of wildness. It illustrates, moreover, the important role that defending Michigan's boundaries played in state building: the battle with Ohio not only united Michiganians against a common foe but also reinforced their sense of belonging to an "imagined political community."

In addition, the conflict with Ohio shows the faith that Michiganians placed in the Northwest Ordinance as a constitutional, boundary-setting document. During the first phase of their battle with the Buckeye State, the territory's Democratic officials relied heavily on the ordinance to justify retaining Toledo claims and fend off the rapacity of their boundary-busting neighbors. This phase began when voters narrowly approved a resolution to apply for statehood. Michigan officials soon learned, however, that Ohio's large congressional delegation would prevent them from entering the Union unless they relinquished their claims. In battling for Toledo, Michiganians contended that the ordinance was a constitutional document, and that Congress, a mere legislative body that could be easily swayed by the rich and powerful, lacked the authority to revoke or to change the terms of the ordinance.

During the second phase of the crisis, Democrats relied on the ordinance to justify forming a state government without congressional approval. Whigs condemned this reading of the document. In thwarting federal authority, they charged, Democrats not only violated the Constitution but also incited anarchy, rebellion, and lawlessness.

In the final phase of the conflict, Whigs continued to rely on the ordinance in opposing the congressional compromise that awarded Toledo to Ohio. They argued, as Democrats had earlier, that the deal that federal lawmakers hammered out was unconstitutional, because they lacked the authority to change the boundaries established by the ordinance. They also insisted on the need to preserve Michigan's territorial integrity, labeling the congressional compromise the "dismemberment bill." Initially, Michiganians supported this argument, electing a convention that refused to agree to Congress's settlement. Before long, however, Michiganians seemed to have changed their minds, and in December of 1836 they convened a second convention, of questionable legality, which assented to the compromise. The Whigs' failure to win the day suggests that by the late 1830s, classical republican concerns about the corrupting nature of power lacked resonance. In the final months of 1836, as a banking panic and depression settled over the nation, Michiganians seem to have been more concerned with the economic benefits to be gained from joining the Union than with the danger posed by powerful states such as Ohio.

Nor did Congress seem overly troubled by such fears. In working out a settlement on Toledo, federal lawmakers seem not to have been overly concerned about the threat that powerful states such as Ohio posed to the republic. Instead, they seem to have given far more weight to Ohio's argument that since the ordinance was drafted by the Continental Congress, it lacked any standing as a constitutional document. In the end, therefore, the battle over Toledo confirmed Congress's authority to establish borders and to determine how to divide wealth and power among the states.

Economic Development

and the Panic of 1837

During the first half of the nineteenth century, Americans completed one of the most ambitious construction projects in their history. They built thousands of miles of turnpikes, canals, and railroads that linked once isolated towns and villages, in remote corners of the republic, into a vibrant transportation network stretching from New England to Louisiana. These projects dramatically reduced freight costs, enabling businesses to sell their goods more widely than ever before. The growth of markets in turn sparked the rise of manufacturing, the commercialization of agriculture, and the development of cities, transforming America from an overwhelmingly rural nation into one that was increasingly commercial, urban, and industrial.[1]

Americans responded to these changes by splitting into warring camps, with workers and small farmers opposing and businessmen embracing the rise of a market economy. The latter insisted that the commercialization of American life would enhance the republic by offering individuals the possibility of achieving greater prosperity and more upward mobility. Workers and their allies, however, viewed economic development with great suspicion, fearing that the growth of markets would increase the gulf between rich and poor Americans and greatly boost the power of the former.[2]

These divisions over the rise of a market economy also existed in Michigan. But not all Michiganians fell into these categories. Many viewed economic development differently than easterners did. Between the mid-1820s and mid-1830s, many Michiganians saw economic development as a means of taming a savage wilderness. The ability to develop what they viewed as a prosperous economy was an important marker of civilization: in their view, Indians, the French, and other early settlers were barbaric because they either refused or were unable to improve the land—failing to establish commercially successful farms, banks, or canals, or to undertake other projects to create wealth. Indians' failure to undertake such projects indicated, moreover, that they were incapable of achieving progress, another crucial sign of civilized peoples. Lacking history, they lived in the same barbaric conditions as had their distant ancestors. The French and other early European settlers who resided in Michigan, meanwhile, had relinquished the civilization of their ancestors, converting instead to the savagery of their aboriginal neighbors.

Initially, both Whigs and Democrats favored the rise of farming and industry as a way to civilize Michigan and its allegedly primitive inhabitants. Replacing the fur trade with a vibrant agricultural society not only got Indians off the land and out of Michigan's economy but also reduced contact between local tribes and the territory's white inhabitants, diminishing the potential for cross-cultural contamination.

Attitudes toward economic development changed dramatically during the Panic of 1837, one of the worst depressions in the nation's history. After the economic boom of the 1830s ended, Michiganians focused less on economic development as a civilizing force and more on it as a source of instability, wildness, and disorder. Michigan's Democrats and Whigs expressed growing alarm about a currency that seemed increasingly worthless and an economy that was veering out of control. To explain these economic woes, Michiganians focused on problems connected with two types of boundaries.

The first problem was linked to the formal legal boundaries established to control banks and regulate the amount of currency that they issued. On the national level, the parties debated the need for a central bank. On the state level, they disagreed about a new law that made it easier to open banks in Michigan. In both cases, Whigs and Democrats offered conflicting explanations of why these devices had failed and what might be done to make them more effective.

The second problem, the reckless and almost drunken speculation and spending in which Michiganians had engaged during the boom, involved the violation of informal customary boundaries that controlled the way individuals worked, saved money, and spent money. When discussing problems connected with these informal boundaries, the two parties largely agreed, blaming the Panic on individuals who refused to be sober, frugal, and industrious and, above all, to maintain self-control. Democratic and Whig newspapers printed fiction, editorials, and advice columns that castigated men who had speculated too heavily in land and stocks. These writers saw the Panic as just punishment for those who had gambled on get-rich-quick schemes. They also chastised women whose lavish spending on luxury subverted the household economy.

THE ECONOMIC BOOM OF THE 1830s

Before the Panic, such issues preoccupied neither Whigs nor Democrats. During the boom of the 1830s, Michigan's population and economy grew rapidly. This growth was due primarily to the opening of the Erie Canal in 1825 and the arrival of steam-driven ships on the Great Lakes.[3] Consequently, Michigan became a magnet that drew increasing numbers of eastern immigrants in the 1830s. During the first seven years of that decade, its population mushroomed, growing from 31,640 in 1830 to 174,543 in 1837.[4]

Caroline Kirkland, who lived in Michigan with her family for six years around this period, observed the effects of this surging population on Detroit in her autobiographical novel, *A New Home: Who'll Follow? Or, Glimpses of Western Life*. When Kirkland and her family moved to Michigan in 1837, she found the "western fever" at its height, with "thousands" of easterners streaming into Detroit daily. "Every tavern of every calibre was as well filled as ours, and happy he who could find a bed any where." Immigrants paid fifty cents for "six feet by two of the bar-room floor. The country inns were thronged"; and "your horse's hay cost you nowhere less than a dollar per diem."[5]

This increase in population sparked a growing demand for land. Between 1830 and 1834, sales of public land spiraled from roughly 147,000 acres to almost 500,000 acres. In 1835, land sales in Michigan totaled more than 1.8 million acres and accounted for a significant portion of all such transactions in the United States. Speculators made many of these purchases, buying large tracts of inexpensive government land and then making sizable profits by selling it to eastern seaboard and European immigrants at higher prices.[6]

These changes transformed Michigan from an economy based primarily on the fur trade, in which Indians played a central role, to one devoted increasingly to agriculture. Despite some misgivings, many Democrats and Whigs warmly embraced these developments and saw them as harbingers of a bright future. Not only would the growth of population and farming create wealth, but it also would reduce Indians' role in the economy and help to tame a wild land.

Michigan boosters linked such changes to the spirit of "improvement" and the march of progress. Byron Cutcheon, for instance, touted the territory's "material development," insisting that it reflected the "intellectual and moral advancement of a people."[7] In 1834, the editor of the *Detroit Journal,* Michigan's main Whig newspaper, emphasized this point: "To one used to the gradual progression of older settlements, the rapidity with which the country advances in population and improvement is striking indeed." Throughout the countryside, "thriving villages" had sprung up "on the soil yet hardly under the dominion of civilization." Michigan residents transformed "the wilderness" into "populous towns, busy with all the avocations of a cultivated life."[8]

In 1829, the *Western Emigrant,* an Ann Arbor newspaper, ran a letter from an Ypsilanti resident that also applauded economic development as an antidote to wildness. In the previous five years, Ypsilanti had become an increasingly popular destination for people from Canada and the East, and these immigrants had transformed the town. Once it had been "a dreary wilderness, the haunt of savages" and the "home of wild beasts, with no sound but that of howling wolves." Recently, it had become a "place of business."[9]

A decade later, the *Pontiac Courier* echoed these sentiments, recalling that just a "few years since" all of Oakland County had been "wild and uncultivated," a place where the "dusky sons of the forest" wandered "unfettered and free." Now this land was home to "civilized man" and "surrounded by evidences of his industry." Growing villages occupied land, "where but a season since was seen the rude cabins of the Aborigines, with its ruder inmates." Fields in which wild animals "but lately fed, now yield to the husband man the rich productions of a genial soil."[10]

Economic development thus seemed to tame wildness. Writers in the *Courier* and *Emigrant* especially flirted with the dual meaning of *wild:* as an antonym, on the one hand, for domesticated or cultivated and, on the other hand, for something that was savage or uncivilized. The Ypsilanti author highlighted this point: in his view, undeveloped lands were wild because they had not yet been domesticated and produced no wealth. But they were also wild because "savages" and "wolves" inhabited them. Such land became not only an obstacle to development, but also a trope for darkness and danger, since it threatened to devour those who set foot on it. Developing the land would tame wildness by putting it to productive use and freeing it from "savages" and "wild beasts."[11]

Whig newspapers also fulsomely praised bank credit. The *Detroit Journal,* for instance, emphasized the important role credit had played in settling and civilizing Michigan. It had curbed savagery by stimulating commerce, getting rid of Indians and other "beasts," and disciplining young settlers. "What is it but credit that has built up a rich and populous country in the west, where forty years ago, the Indian and the wild beast roamed unmolested?" Additionally, credit was "the great moral stimulant" that encouraged "youth, when commencing in life, to aim at establishing a reputation for moral integrity and industrious habits."[12]

Whig editors were not alone in praising the boom. Democratic journalists also applauded Michigan's surging economy. In the spring of 1832, the *Detroit Free Press* proudly reported an increase in immigration to Detroit along with a "rise in the price and value of Real Estate." Such good news "could not be anticipated, were it not that the business of the country is constantly increasing, and our advantage becoming more and more realized at home and better understood abroad." But Detroiters ought not to rest on their laurels. They should do more to turn the city into a center of manufacturing. "The manufacturing interest is one which had proved the permanent support of many of the wealthiest towns—as will eventually be the case with our own." City residents needed to establish textile factories, "paper mills," and other "flourishing establishments."[13]

Democrats also asked Congress to increase funding for internal improvements in Michigan. The petitioners observed that "important objects" had "been secured to the nation by the spirit of emigration." Settlers had "changed the frontier wilderness, into a well cultivated region of the country." Yet little had been done "to develop the great natural advantages of these regions. The commerce of the Mediterranean Seas, which has increased greatly since the year 1815, is yet in its infancy." Given the richness of the region's soil, shipping on the Great Lakes likely would double within five years. To encourage that possibility, the federal government ought to "provide a ship canal to connect the navigation of Lake Erie, [Lake] Huron and [Lake] Michigan with Lake Superior." Congress should help fund the construction of railroads, the opening of copper mines, and the improvement of Michigan's roads.[14]

Democrats even applauded speculators for aiding western settlement. In the fall of 1836, the *Free Press* reprinted an article from the *New Orleans Times* that lauded these investors for attracting migrants to the West. They traveled "with a guide and pack horse," visited "uninhabited forests," and selected "some beautiful tracts of virgin soil." Once a speculator had purchased a tract, he met "the tide of emigration, and endeavor[ed] to direct it toward this spot of his predilection." Those who succeeded could earn "in a short time, a ten fold profit." Yet speculators deserved these huge gains. "It is doubtful whether our western wilds would be colonized half so fast, without speculators," opined the writer. Not only did speculators "seek out and find favorable places for making settlements" that otherwise might "remain undiscovered," they helped subdue wildness by directing European emigrants "to the cultivation of soil" and preventing them from becoming "vagabonds in our cities."[15]

THE PANIC OF 1837

These views began to change after the economy soured in 1837. At the time, British bankers began to call in their American loans. The inflation that had fueled the boom of the 1830s ended, as specie grew increasingly scarce and prices plummeted. To protect their reserves, Michigan banks, along with those in the rest of the nation, temporarily stopped redeeming their notes for gold and silver in the spring of 1837.[16] By 1837, Michigan newspapers reported that the state's citizenry experienced severe hardship. Although much of this evidence comes from Whig papers, which had political reasons for exaggerating the effects of the Panic, the details they provide suggest that misery indeed prevailed.

In 1837, the *Detroit Journal* reported that Michigan's overgrown currency was "contracting." As a result, "temporary embarrassment was producing many failures and many transfers of property and much distress among laborers."[17] One year later, the *Journal* reported that the economy had not improved. "Complaints of the times are universal and in the main well founded"; they came "from all classes and characters. The industrious and patient complain scarcely less than the idle and uneasy." Nor was Michigan's economy likely to improve anytime soon.[18] A few months later, the *Journal* observed that great distress and "unparalleled suffering" existed "in all parts of the land," complaining that it was "not limited in its extent to particular classes, or sections of the country." Rather, it "falls equally upon the merchant, mechanic and . . . laborer."[19]

The editor of the *Michigan Whig* of Adrian too was horrified by the state's economic woes. "Never . . . have the times appeared so appalling in Michigan as at present."[20] Local merchants were unable to purchase goods from their eastern suppliers on credit and could no longer replenish their inventories: nearly half "of our store keepers have now nothing to present to their former customers but empty shelves."[21]

In Oakland County, the *Pontiac Courier* reported, "our suffering is intolerable." New York suppliers "are calling upon our merchants and traders for their dues." The merchants in turn called "upon farmers and citizens— and our farmers and citizens are calling upon each other. 'Money—money,' seems to be the never ending cry." But because currency was in short supply, "the times" were "daily growing harder."[22]

Unemployment rose dramatically in Detroit. The *Journal* noted that as demand for labor fell, "vast numbers of workmen" were "thrown out of all employment" and had to live on their savings. But few if any laborers were able to put away much money for a rainy day. "Add to this the expenses and privations of a northern winter," and it became clear why their condition was "truly wretched."[23]

By 1838, hard times were so pervasive that settlers began to reconsider long-held assumptions about poverty. The *Detroit Journal* asserted that it was strange "to speak of any distinct class as the poor." Earlier in the decade, no group "could be properly regarded as subject to real poverty, much less actual want." There always had existed some who were poor because of "misfortune or vice," such as "the orphan, the widow, the diseased and those whom vicious habits had reduced to pauperism." But because of the depression, poverty oppressed a "very different class of persons." The "healthy, the industrious, and the temperate" felt its gripping "hand."[24]

In searching for the causes of the Panic in Michigan, observers pointed to the decline in immigration to the state and the indebtedness of Michigan businessmen to eastern creditors. The depression had sharply reduced immigration to Michigan, and immigrants had represented an important market for Michigan producers, stated a report written by delegates to a bank convention that met in Ann Arbor in the spring of 1838. When the number of easterners coming to Michigan dropped, many Michiganians lost income they had relied on to pay for the agricultural and manufactured goods that they imported from the East. Because Michigan lacked any "article of export," the bankers observed, the nation's economic woes had "fallen with a peculiar severity" on the state.[25]

THE DEBATE ON BANKING

But the lack of exports was not the only factor responsible for the Panic. Whigs and Democrats also blamed the depression on problems in banking. At issue was how to establish boundaries that could limit the power of banks, which were seen as encouraging speculation and other forms of wildness that helped to destroy Michigan and the nation's economy.[26] This debate focused primarily on two key issues: first, Democrats and Whigs battled over Michigan's recently enacted free banking law and whether it was compounding the effects of the Panic. Second, the two parties fought over Jackson's destruction of the Second Bank of the United States, disagreeing on whether this move had helped to cause the crash.

In this debate, Whigs portrayed state banks, and Democrats depicted the Second Bank of the United States, in frightening terms. They relied on such metaphors as "storms, floods and tornadoes" to describe their destructive power and worried that if banks were not controlled, they could destabilize the polity. Both parties connected banks to the threat that an ever more commercial society posed to the republic, which was based on values that emphasized the sacrifice of one's individual interests for the common good. But the two parties associated this threat with different institutions.

Not surprisingly, Whigs blamed the Panic on state banks; Democrats pointed an accusing finger at the Second Bank of the United States. Democrats actually split into two groups: the first consisted of those who opposed all banks; the second, those who disliked the national bank but supported state banks.[27]

This last group supported President Jackson's decision to kill the national bank, arguing that states could best establish the boundaries needed to control banks and the amount of currency they issued. In addition, they contended that the national bank was a monopoly that threatened the republic and helped to cause the depression. Whigs, on the other hand, saw the need for some central authority to establish boundaries to control state banks. In killing the national bank, Jackson had eliminated the only authority that could set boundaries and discipline these institutions. In killing the bank, removing government deposits from its vault and placing them in "pets," Jackson had compounded the problems, greatly enhancing the destructive power of these institutions.

The *Detroit Journal* was one of several Whig newspapers that blamed the Panic on "the destruction of the United States Bank," which led to an increase of state banks, and the expansion of the paper system, stimulating unprecedented speculation and overtrading.[28] A few weeks later, the *Journal* elaborated on these views. The destruction of the bank created "a vacuum" that was "immediately filled by hundreds of state banks." They "maddened the spirit of enterprise, which could not be gratified without an almost unlimited expansion of the circulating medium. The formidable excess of paper issues, over and above the specie on which it was professedly based, resulted in the dreadful embarrassments which now rest upon the land."[29]

The *Pontiac Courier* also condemned Jackson's policies, using images of an uncontrollable "flood" to depict the damage he had wrought. Its editor asserted that one of the main causes of the Panic was President Jackson's decision to destroy the United States Bank, remove the government deposits from its vaults, and distribute them to "State pet banks." The effects of this policy were disastrous. After receiving public money, the state banks unleashed "a Flood of paper money" and "deluged the land from Maine to Georgia and from the shores of the Atlantic to the Valley of the Mississippi." No one could deny that this "flood of paper money now abroad, irredeemable worthless rags called money, is the result of the 'Glorious Experiment.'"[30]

The *Detroit Daily Advertiser* also railed against Jackson's custodial skills, depicting the former president as a cruel father who had deprived his family of shelter. It reprinted an article from the *Constantine Republican*, which argued that the United States Bank had protected the people from the destructiveness of state banks. Jackson should have known that destroying the bank would lead to "a multiplication of State Banks," exorbitant issues of paper currency, and "inordinate speculation." He should have realized, too, that most people "would suffer dreadfully from the multiplied embarrassments it would bring on the whole community." In depriving Americans of a national bank, Jackson had committed an "offense of nearly the same nature as pulling down the houses which shelter our heads from the storm." No one could blame Jackson for the "excesses and follies" of men. But as president, Jackson was obliged "to protect society against the consequences of these excesses and follies."[31]

The *Journal*, the *Courier*, and the *Advertiser* used biblical imagery to emphasize the power as well as the wildness and destructiveness of state banks. These institutions symbolized concerns about the growing power of money in the early republic and the threat that commercialization posed to the nation. The *Advertiser* relied on the trope of the storm, and the *Courier* used the image of the flood to depict the devastation wrought by these institutions, which quite literally were deluging the nation with currency. This imagery suggested that the state banks' ability to issue paper money gave them almost godlike power. Their control of currency resembled God's power over nature; like God, they could unleash terrible destruction. The nation, meanwhile, was depicted as relatively weak and passive, a helpless victim at the mercy of the banks.

Whig papers portrayed the national bank as the only institution that could check money's growing dominance and prevent it from destroying the nation. The *Courier* framed the relationship between the national banks and the pets as hierarchical and insisted that some such central authority was needed to control these unruly institutions and prevent them from subverting the republic by drowning it in money. Destroying the national bank had deprived the republic of this protection. The *Advertiser* relied on family imagery drawn from sentimental literature to make this case, portraying Jackson as a callous father and the nation as the family that he had victimized. The national bank was the home that protected the nation from the growing power of banks and commerce. When Jackson destroyed the national bank, he erased the boundaries needed to control this destructive force. Like an uncaring father, he had robbed his family of the only shelter that could protect it from the elements.

The *Journal* evoked similar concerns but relied more specifically on figures of madness and the loss of self-control to explain the destruction that Jackson's policies wrought. As in the *Courier*, journalists emphasized the hierarchical relationship between the Bank of the United States and state banks but also suggested that money possessed the power to cast a spell over people, inducing a lust for wealth that made them lose sight of all else. These drives were dangerous not only because they seemed insatiable, but also because they produced temporary "mania." By destroying the institution that could set boundaries needed to rein in these drives, Jackson permitted state banks to seduce and destabilize the nation, maddening spirits that could not be satisfied.

Democrats not only denied that the United States Bank could have prevented the Panic but also asserted that the irresponsible policies of the national bank had helped cause the economy to crash. They insisted that establishing some quasi-governmental, central authority to oversee state banks betrayed republican principles and that the best way to control the flow of paper currency was for states to limit the quantity of bills in circulation.

Democrats agreed that the nation needed to control the size of the money supply. But rather than relying on a central bank, they insisted that this problem should be handled at the state level and offered several proposals to limit the amount of currency that banks could issue.[32] In 1837, for instance, the *Free Press* ran an article from a Baltimore newspaper that praised Missouri for including in one of its banking charters a provision limiting the supply of paper money to "two dollars for every one dollar in gold and silver actually possessed by the bank."[33] That same year, the *Free Press* advocated a proposal, first advanced by Jackson to prohibit banks from issuing bills smaller than twenty dollars. Instead, minor transactions, "heretofore glutted with paper of all denominations," would be made in gold and silver. Such a plan would "introduce as far as practicable, a gold currency, by the prohibition of small notes."[34]

Democrats said that their proposals for controlling the money supply were superior to the Whig plan for reestablishing a central bank, because the latter violated republican principles. In the summer of 1838, the *Free Press* reprinted the extract of an article from the *Democratic Review* that relied on classical republican ideas to frame the argument over the national bank as a contest between liberty and power. Journalists equated state banks with the people, and the national bank with the menacing power of a "moneyed aristocracy." Whigs threatened liberty because they believed that state banks could not "manage their affairs prudently" and needed a national bank "to control" them. But this constituted "an argument against popular government itself! The people constitute the governing power of the United States, and it is by their authority that . . . state banks are created." Whigs assumed that the "people" could not "check and control a class of institution which they create." They believed that "a new agent, unknown to the state and irresponsible to them or the people" was needed to rescue them "from the disastrous consequences of their own acts."[35]

These views, supposedly similar to those espoused by monarchists, comprised the "leading argument in favor of monopoly and absolute power." The crowned heads of Europe exercised "absolute dominion" because they believed that their subjects could not "act wisely and protect themselves against the evil consequences of their own ignorance and error." Even if state banks failed to control the amount of currency they issued, establishing a central bank to govern them would not be "a republican remedy." It denied that the people could "be trusted to amend their own institutions, and that we must have an irresponsible corporation to prevent these evils." But state governments that "created these institutions were fully competent to modify and reform them and impose all those checks and restraints . . . which the banking system" needed.[36] Like Whigs, Democrats also feared the wild destructiveness of state banks, agreeing that "checks and restraints" were required to limit their power. But they raised the question of who best could be trusted to establish such boundaries. Removing such decisions from the people and placing them in the hands of a remote and powerful corporation smacked of monarchism.

Democrats also denied that the United States Bank could have prevented the Panic, had it existed in 1837. The *Free Press* noted that the Bank of England was a central bank that served much the same purpose; indeed, the Bank of England enjoyed "a capital" and exercised "an influence tenfold greater than the U[nited]. States Bank ever did." Yet the Bank of England had been unable to stop the growth of banks and paper currency. "The joint stock and private banks in England have increased, within two years in a ratio much greater than here, from precisely the same causes—the general prevalence of a spirit of gambling speculation."[37]

Some Democrats took this argument one step further, insisting that the United States Bank deserved much of the blame for earlier as well as the current economic crisis. The *Free Press* charged that the bank not only had failed to "restrain the spirit of over trading and speculation" that had caused earlier Panics but had "largely encouraged" this behavior.[38] Democrats also observed that the bank still existed as a state institution and in that capacity had acted irresponsibly. The *Free Press* charged that the bank had "contributed very largely to the excessive speculations in lands and trade, which have brought the country" to the edge of collapse. "If it has done so as a state bank, it would have done so as a national institution."[39]

A meeting of Jackson County Democrats in 1837 was even more vehement in denouncing the bank, comparing it to a despot that spread "pestilence" and induced "mania." Attendees insisted that the bank was "more to be dreaded than the veriest tyrant whose brow is stamped with the ensigns of royalty—yea more than the deadly sirocco or the desolating pestilence." The bank had "failed to regulate the currency or render any important service to the public in the present crisis." It also had helped "to promote the general mania for speculation, which has swept like a tornado over our fair country, proving . . . that a gigantic moneyed institution, subject to the direction and supervision of frail humanity, will ever prove a curse, rather than a blessing."[40]

Just as Whigs blamed state banks for the nation's currency woes, Democrats argued that the national bank was the source of the problem. In some respects, the Democratic critique of the national bank was similar to the Whig attack on state banks. Democrats argued that the national bank, instead of safeguarding the nation, had terrorized and destabilized it, causing tornadoes and spreading pestilence. While Whigs associated state banks with increasing commercialization, Democrats linked the national bank to the growing power of money in an economy that was increasingly dominated by the cash nexus of trade and a "moneyed aristocracy." In this guise, it could infect people with a "mania" or madness that caused them to lose self-control and become obsessed with acquiring ever greater amounts of wealth.

The destruction of the Bank of the United States was not the only source of conflict between Michigan Democrats and Whigs. Between 1837 and 1839, the two parties also struggled over the state's general banking law of March 1837 that permitted investors to establish banks without first obtaining a special charter from the state legislature. Whigs attacked the bill on several grounds. They argued that in loosening state control of banking, lawmakers had compounded the effects of the Panic by filling the state with a greatly depreciated currency. Whigs also asserted that the new law exposed Michigan residents to fraud. They labeled the new banks established under the law "wild cats," because those who ran them sought to cheat the people out of their hard-earned money.[41]

Democrats insisted that they had gone to great lengths to protect Michiganians from such problems. The banking law protected Michiganians from fraud, they asserted, by placing stringent requirements on the amount of capital and specie each bank possessed, as well as limits on the size of loans and the amount of currency the banks could issue. Bank notes, furthermore, had to be backed by mortgages on real estate or personal bonds. Finally, the law required that the banks formed under the law contribute to a safety fund established in 1836, which would redeem the bills of failed banks; consequently, the institutions formed under the new law came to be called safety fund banks.[42]

Despite these provisions, Whigs lost little time in attacking the measure. They initially criticized it for dramatically increasing the number of banks in Michigan and failing to provide bill holders with adequate security. In November 1837, the *Detroit Daily Advertiser* denounced the statute for failing to protect Michiganians from fraud and alleging that the new banking system was a great "deception upon the whole people." It did not provide enough security for those who held notes of the new banks, because it failed to guarantee that the banks had enough specie to redeem their bills: "Good banks may start up under the law, but this depends more upon the honesty of those concerned in getting them up, than upon the goodness of the law itself."[43]

A few weeks later, Michigan legislator Jacob Howard emphasized that lawmakers, by eliminating the charter system, had failed to recognize the importance of the state's role in overseeing banks and establishing boundaries that protected residents from swindlers. Legislators "lost sight . . . of their duty." They passed legislation that allowed "anybody and everybody, honest or dishonest, to convert all his capital into a banking establishment, and thus created corporations indefinite in number without subjecting them to the wholesome and necessary supervision of the legislature." This constituted "a sin—a political sin . . . against their constitutional duties."[44]

Whigs also expressed alarm about the sudden mania for banking that seemed to be sweeping through Michigan. Because of the general banking law, the number of banks in the state almost tripled in one year, climbing from slightly more than one dozen in 1837 to forty in 1838.[45] Whig publications questioned the qualifications of those who ran these institutions and expressed concern that they were focused primarily on making profits and not serving the people. In 1838, the *Journal* expressed shock that in the last year, banks had "sprung into existence like mushrooms." So great had been "the mania" for banks "that no village . . . is without the institution"; almost everyone "you meet is an officer or at least a stockholder in some new bank." Nor did the sudden popularity of banking seem very different from the rage for speculation in land that recently had yielded such sad consequences. The previous year, "every man owned a village; this year, he owns a bank." These men failed to understand "the object of banking" and were more interested in enriching themselves than in aiding the community.[46]

As the number of banks in Michigan increased, Whig newspapers called for an investigation of these new institutions. They reported that as skepticism about the soundness of new banks grew, the value of their currency had declined. According to the *Detroit Journal,* businesses hesitated to take "these bills and in some cases they were wholly refused and sales actually broken off, because payments could be made in no other money." People who had already received these bills were "anxious to pass them away as soon as possible." Michiganians had become more and more apprehensive about the solvency of these banks, as rumors continued to circulate "that in many instances the grossest and most palpable evasions of law had been practiced in their establishment."[47]

To illustrate the dire effects of the "wild cats," the *Detroit Journal* presented an anecdote about a German worker's unsuccessful efforts to buy flour with their currency. After the German completed his task, his employer "pulled out a wallet full of 'wild cats,' of every bank and denomination," and told the German to take what he wanted. When the German went to buy flour with these bills, the merchant told him that his money "was good yesterday, but not today." The worker visited many stores and returned home "down-hearted at the necessity of passing the Sabbath without a mouthful of bread." He returned to his employer, got new bills, and then spent several hours "in the useless attempt to buy flour."[48]

Such suffering was not confined to Detroit. Caroline Kirkland's novel *A New Home* described similar scenes of misery in the countryside. "The distress among the poorer classes of farmers," which was the main consequence of the "Bank failures, was indescribable." Individuals who have witnessed "only a city panic, can form no idea of the extent and severity of the sufferings on these occasions." Many farmers came to towns from the "deep woods many miles distant where no grain had yet grown," journeying "two or three days and nights, with a half-starved ox-team, and living on a few crusts by the way." Imagine their dismay when they offered their "splendid-looking bank-notes . . . hard-earned all, for the flour which was to be the sole food of wife and babes through the long winter," and discovered that these "hoarded treasures were as valueless as the ragged paper which wrapped them." To punish the "heartless adventurers" who were responsible for such suffering, Kirkland suggested that they be compelled to "behold at one glance all the misery" they had caused.[49]

Democrats responded to these attacks by blaming Michigan's currency woes on Whig efforts to undermine confidence in safety fund banks. They also applauded the new banking law as a measure that would free banking from the iron grip of monopolies. Delegates to the Jackson County Convention lauded the measure as an antidote to monopolies. It represented "the dawning of a new era in the march of liberal and enlightened principles," and a victory "over the pernicious doctrine of monopolies and exclusive privileges."[50] Similarly, the *Free Press* applauded the statute as "one of the greatest improvements of modern legislation," one that would provide "equal rights and privileges to all."[51] In a speech before the Michigan legislature, Democratic representative Samuel N. Gantt echoed those views. He insisted that the general banking law would aid "the poor as well as the rich" and make "banking just what it ought to be—as common a pursuit as mercantile, manufacturing, farming or any other kind of business."[52]

At the same time, Democrats denied that the plummeting value of Michigan currency stemmed from problems with safety fund banks, blaming the crisis instead on a Whig conspiracy to destroy these institutions by raising doubts about their financial soundness. The new banks were as safe as or safer than chartered banks. Depicting Whigs as wild and lawless, Democrats alleged that they conspired to undermine the state's economy and impoverish its people for their own political advantage. In the winter of 1838, Detroiters had organized a meeting to call attention to the declining value of the state's money. The *Free Press* charged that the meeting was the "denouement of a grand federal scheme, which had long been on foot to prostrate, the general banking system of this state for political purposes." Some time ago, the "federal junto" ordered "that the general banking system must be destroyed," and charged upon the democracy with flooding Michigan "with an irredeemable bank currency."[53] Whigs sought to crush the safety fund banks "so that a mechanic or laborer" who had their "bills in his possession will not be able by Saturday night to buy provisions enough to last his family over Sunday."[54]

Despite such rhetoric, mounting opposition to the new banking system compelled Michigan lawmakers to authorize an investigation of the banks. In 1838, the probe revealed widespread fraud. Alpheus Felch, a Democrat who had opposed the new banking system, later recalled that many of the new banks possessed little or no specie and had no way to redeem their notes. "The Bank of Sandstone, for instance, never had any specie," even though its liabilities amounted to more than $38,000. The Exchange Bank of Shiawassee had issued more than $22,000 in currency, yet it had "only seven coppers and a very small amount of paper" in its safe. In another case, an unnamed bank had loaned $18,000 to one individual and $6,000 to another without ever recording the transactions or obtaining security on the loans. Worse, the bank had issued $13,210 in notes, even though it possessed less than $100 in specie.[55]

Such instances of fraud were fairly widespread, Felch asserted. Until the investigation of 1838, bankers had devised ingenious ways to fool Michigan's bank commissioners into believing that they possessed enough specie to redeem their notes. In some cases, Felch remembered, they would substitute for specie "a kind of paper denominated specie certificate." In other instances, bankers played a shell game, moving specie from institutions that bank commissioners had already examined to those they next were scheduled to visit. In still other cases, bankers tricked commissioners into believing that they had more specie than they actually possessed by placing a thin layer of "silver dollars" over a box filled "with nothing but glass and nails." Caroline Kirkland's *A New Home* described this same phenomenon, reporting that the vault of a wild-cat bank in the fictitious town of Tinkerville contained a "heavy charge of broken glass and tenpenny nails, covered above and below with half-dollars, principally 'bogus.'"[56]

After these findings became public, Whigs more frequently depicted the new banking system as wild, because it had enabled criminals to victimize Michiganians. In 1838, the *Journal* reprinted a letter from an Ann Arbor resident to the *National Intelligencer,* insisting that easterners did not realize the "misery" that Michigan suffered because of "Wild Cat misrule." These "wild-cat" bankers had valued the lands used to secure their notes at extremely inflated prices, purchasing land from the government "at the minimum price" of one dollar and twenty-five cents an acre and then listing it "as security at ten dollars an acre."[57] Friend Palmer, another Michigan resident prominent in banking circles, agreed, recalling that the lands that the banks used as the "basis of their capital were appraised at fabulous prices."[58]

Others also complained about the rapacity of the safety fund banks, comparing them to looters who had "plundered" Michigan. In 1839, the *Journal* recalled that Michiganians had been "swindled over and over again by a few speculators who went headlong into a most outrageous and unnatural . . . system of banking." This system relied on "fictitious capital—upon paper promises to pay—upon broken glass and ten penny nails—upon fraud, robbery and perjury." Though Democrats had defended the new system as a way to give everyone an equal opportunity to become a banker, the experiment had produced very different results. "A few hundred bankers" were allowed "to swindle two hundred thousand free citizens, farmers, mechanics, merchants," and workers. Democrats had permitted Michigan residents to be "plundered," so that they could advance "'the hallowed principle of equal rights.'"[59]

In 1839, the *Advertiser* also linked Michigan Democrats to the greed of the "wild cats." In its view, Democrats had transformed the state's currency "into wild cat trash," much of which lay in "the vaults of broken pet banks."[60] That same year, the *Advertiser* reprinted a speech made by a leading Whig, William Woodbridge, in which he outlined the devastation the "wild cats" had caused. Merchants stood behind their counters "with greatly diminished business, brooding over their sorrow," and waited to hear about "suits for debt" that they could not pay. Though they had "chests full of money," they were filled with the "bank bills of those swindling shops" that the Democrats created.[61]

Whigs at the Grand River District Convention echoed these sentiments, passing resolutions in 1838 that condemned Michigan's wild-cat banks. Michigan's banking system was "fraught with incalculable mischief to the prosperity," they insisted, and had been "productive of the "most disastrous consequences to the credit and the financial relations of the state." Eliminating the state as a gatekeeper had "opened the way for the indiscriminate admission of the dishonest with the unworthy to meddle with the currency." It had placed beyond the "reach of supervision or enquiry the characters of those seeking to avail themselves of its proffered privileges" and "facilitating the operation of knaves and swindlers." These individuals had flooded the "state with vast quantities of paper" money that was "worthless" and "irredeemable."[62]

THE MORAL ECONOMY

To stop this behavior, the state rescinded the state banking law in 1839.[63] The decision shifted the discussion on the causes of the Panic from the destructiveness of banks to the wildness and irresponsibility of Michiganians who had become addicted to luxury and had invested recklessly in land and stocks. Such conduct, increasingly common during the boom of the 1830s, violated the boundaries of the moral economy and the customs and values that governed economic behavior and formed the foundation on which a sound economy and banking system rested.[64] These conventions taught individuals to shun luxury and speculation and instead to practice frugality, industriousness, and self-control.

In Michigan, critics targeted two groups as violators of these norms. First, they criticized women who were obsessed with fashion. They symbolized the new consumer culture in which individuals, usually females, bought goods not because they needed them, but because of the pleasure or status derived from owning them. These women had become addicted to luxury and threatened the household economy by spending prodigious sums on inessential goods. Second, critics chastised speculators: men who, they insisted, shunned work and wasted hard-earned money, often their fathers', on wild-eyed schemes that produced bankruptcy. These attacks on speculators and women addicted to consumption reflected pre-industrial opposition to a modernizing economy and a fear that capitalism could unleash greed and rapacity.[65]

These concerns surfaced in Michigan during the end of the boom and increased during the Panic. In these years, both Whig and Democratic newspapers were filled with editorials and fiction that linked the economy's decline to the immoral behavior that Michigan residents displayed during the recent spurt of economic growth. Prosperity, they held, had induced Michiganians to become wild, engaging in "reckless," foolhardy ventures.

In 1838, the *Journal* recalled that in the "season of speculation, the general habits of the people underwent a marked change." They engaged in "more daring enterprise than formerly" and also exhibited "less industry, economy, sobriety and general steadiness of character" than had their forebears. They abandoned "the old household virtues by which our fathers became in due time rich and even independent" and replaced them "with a bold reckless spirit which ventured all at a single throw."[66] In describing speculators, the *Journal* relied on images associated with wildness, such as drunkenness, recklessness, and gambling. The newspaper also framed Michigan's economic problems as a conflict between generations, in which younger Michiganians had rebelled against their elders, rejecting "sobriety" and the other virtues that had enabled their elders to become wealthy.

Democratic newspapers also railed against speculators and accused them of playing a large role in the economy's collapse. In 1837, the *Free Press* ran a letter from a New York correspondent, who insisted that "speculation in real estate and overtrading" had "produced the present alarming crisis."[67] A few weeks later, the editor of the *Free Press* expressed similar views. "In the train of causes which have produced . . . disastrous consequences . . . the first and most prominent were overtrading and speculation."[68] Stevens Mason, Michigan's Democratic governor, also emphasized the problems caused by speculators. The Panic, he said, ought to "teach us . . . to avoid . . . the seductive career of apparent, but unreal prosperity, which the nation has lately pursued, and which has brought us ultimately to the very verge of general bankruptcy." These problems grew out of the "evils of our overtrading and speculation."[69] Mason's use of the word "seductive" linked speculators to the wildness of sexual predators, who used cunning and charm to ruin young women, in much the same way that speculators had employed notions of easy money to beguile and devastate the nation.

Journalists also criticized speculators for laziness. In 1839, the *Journal,* a Whig paper, published a letter that criticized a plan for debtor relief that would aid speculators by forcing creditors to accept land in the payment of debts. Such a scheme would reward those who, for two or three years, had "plunged headlong into every scheme for growing rich without hard work." They purchased "thousands of acres of wild land, and now when the rage is over find themselves over head and ears in debt, with the land dead upon their hands." It was unfair to permit such slackers to "rid themselves of their load by throwing it upon the shoulders of others, who have been working hard while they were growing rich by speculation." It would compel "prudent and hard working people . . . to take wild lands at the speculating price in payment of their just dues, and . . . pay their own debts in money or else lose their character."[70]

Democratic newspapers also railed against speculation, linking it to the growth of cities, the decline of farming, and the erosion of traditional values. The *Detroit Morning Post,* published by the agrarian wing of the party, contrasted the virtues of hardworking farmers who created real wealth with the vices of urbanites who wasted money on "mad" schemes that produced no lasting benefits. "If the people of our cities, instead of rushing into mad speculations, buying and selling fancy stock in Wall Street and fancy villages in Michigan, had attended to agriculture, the present embarrassments would not have occurred." This "rage for making fortunes through financial legerdemain, instead of acquiring it, as the Almighty intended 'by the sweat of the brow,'" had destroyed Michigan. On one hand, the *Post* condemned speculators for relying on trickery and deceit to make money. On the other, the paper played on the dual meanings of "rage," which refers both to a "fad" and to "violent anger," to highlight the wildness of speculators, linking their idleness to their fury at God and efforts to thwart his designs. This rebelliousness had "produced panic upon panic" and "hurled the rich from his proud elevation, and his fall has crushed the poor."[71]

Michiganians also blamed the depression on the nation's growing fondness for luxury and expressed alarm that this taste for the "finery" of Europe was subverting the nation by creating a huge debt and robbing Americans of their independence and industriousness. The *Detroit Post* reprinted an article from the *Albany Argus* that linked the Panic to a decline in the number of farmers in America and a growth in "the number of consumers." This development had forced Americans to import food from Europe. Given America's growing dependency on Europe, it had seemed likely that Americans would reduce their consumption "of foreign finery." Instead, they had searched "every foreign country . . . for all that luxury could wish, until a foreign debt of some seventy five million" fell like a "deluge upon a country whose immediate resources" were "exhausted." Americans searched for precious metals to pay this debt. But from "whence shall they come?" Nobody could expect "that money should be plenty." It was "only strange" that it was not "more scarce." Americans could not "prosper when such a fearful balance of trade" was "impressing upon" them. To solve this problem, Americans had to make "a great change" in their "habits of industry and business." They ought to "stop the importation of gee-gaws from Europe and go to work in good earnest in a faithful and diligent cultivation of the soil."[72]

Democrats, moreover, voiced concerns about the corrupting effects of luxury, expressing concern that it would undermine the republic by inducing aristocratic tastes and feminize the people. To survive, republics needed virtuous, manly citizens who were hardworking, thrifty, and sober. An addiction to luxury could enfeeble them, making them easy prey for despots.[73] The *Post* echoed these fears when it recalled that President Jackson had warned the nation against its growing attraction to speculation and consumerism and urged Americans to change their ways. America could "retrieve its character" only by "encouraging domestic manufactures, instead of the gee-gaws of Europe." Merchants should "follow the plough—and the artizan, who left his tools to become a gentleman-speculator, roll up his shirt sleeves and go back to the workshop." America possessed the resources to be great. But the people must "return to their former simplicity of life." The aristocratic tastes of Europe had "corrupted" and "vitiated" republican values, as Americans "acquired a childish fondness for nice broadcloths—London tailors—diamond rings—gold chains—balls—fetes—dashing carriages—livery—servants—kingly residences and titles."[74]

Whig newspapers also condemned luxury's effects, fearing that the elite's addiction to these goods would soon infect the lower orders. The *Detroit Advertiser* linked the taste for such goods to the pride of the wealthy and insisted that by making the "acquisition of gain" their sole aim in life, too many businessmen had "condemned themselves to . . . a cart-horse way of life." They "lavish their thousands on luxuries of dress and equipage, which only minister to sordid vanity." This behavior set "a bad example for the weak and vain and excites an absurd emulation" in those who had less money. Such men "counteract all the good effects of their industry by the bad example of a display of luxury."[75]

The *Detroit Journal* evoked animal imagery to condemn the acquisitiveness that had enthralled so many Michiganians. Writers condemned the "money getting" that was "absorbing all the energies of men" and added that such behavior was only "acting out the instinct of the chip-monk and other hoarding animals." Though hoarding in men required intelligence, "it is intelligence subordinate to animalism. It is intelligence diverted from its high destiny, and made the slave of mean desires and instincts."[76] Acquisitiveness thus represented the loss of self-control and the triumph of base drives over higher faculties, transforming men into wild animals who become the captives of their lowest and most selfish impulses. Like chipmunks, they become solely devoted to hoarding and consumption.

These concerns about Michiganians' growing taste for wealth and speculation were reflected in novels and short fiction that appeared in Michigan newspapers. Kirkland's *New Home,* for instance, satirized Tinkerville, a village that Mr. Mazard, a speculator, created. Advertised as a bustling metropolis that featured "canals and railroads," as well as a "steam mill" and "wind mill," the village was actually situated in a "woody swamp" and contained few if any amenities. Angry "lot-holders" insisted that they were quite "satisfied that there was an abundance of water there to duck a land-shark, if they could catch him near it."[77]

Other tales contrasted characters who obeyed the dictates of the moral economy with those who rebelled against it. Like Horatio Alger, the former rose from humble beginnings and were able to avoid the seductive lure of speculation and consumer culture. The latter had inherited wealth and frittered away their fortunes on luxury goods and worthless investments. The stories often depicted those who inherited great wealth as aristocratic and feminized males, since, like women, they focused more energy on spending money than on earning it. While the stories condemned those who violated the boundaries of the moral economy, they applauded individuals who, through industriousness and thrift, were able to cross class barriers. They demonstrated the hazard of straying from the path of righteousness in a society where an individual's status was no longer fixed.[78]

One such tale contrasted two boys—Jeremiah, who came from a wealthy family, and Theodore, who came from humble beginnings. Initially, the wealthy Jeremiah ridiculed Theodore, who possessed only sixpence. But Theodore worked hard, saved his money and became a very successful merchant. He used his sixpence to buy fruit that he sold in the corner of his uncle's shop. Because of Theodore's "thrifty and withal honest" ways, his uncle took Theodore into his store as an assistant, allowing him to trade sundry specified articles on his own account.[79]

Theodore then established a business of his own and gained success "in the India trade." He "at last married a fine girl, whose fortune was a little inferior to his own." They lived in an "elegant mansion . . . and yet attended as usual to his business." Soon, Theodore received an unemployed visitor, a "thin, squalid figure," wearing a "threadbare suit of black" and "an old hat." It was Jeremiah who had ridiculed Theodore as a child. Destitute after spending all of his family's fortune, Jeremiah acknowledged the error of his ways. "I have not forgotten the little ragged boy, with his silver sixpence. Had I been half as careful of my thousands as he was of his pence, I should not have been here friendless and pennyless today."[80]

Other stories sounded a similar theme. One tale, which appeared in at least two Michigan newspapers, contrasted a father, who rose from an impoverished childhood, with his wealthy son, who destroyed the fortune his father left him by embarking on a career in speculation and conspicuous consumption.[81] Peter Bingham, the father of the story, started life with one penny, yet rose in Boston to become "a merchant of the utmost integrity," who "maintained a most enviable reputation during his long mercantile career." After retiring, the "elder Bingham" left his store, which was filled with "a large stock of goods and perhaps the best set of customers of any dealer in Boston," to his son, who was also named Peter Bingham. The junior Bingham soon acquired "the spirit of improvement" and spent freely. Tearing down the "old store," he built a new "elegant one, with a granite front, and of great depth to accommodate his business." When Peter asked his father how he liked the changes, the old man replied, "The store is too long."[82]

Despite this criticism, Peter continued to expand, becoming the "importer of teas and coffee" and marrying Julia Wentworth, a wealthy heiress. Peter then bought an "elegant mansion and . . . fitted it up in great splendor, becoming the high circle in which his beautiful wife would move." As a house-warming gift, Peter's father gave his son mirrors. "A golden tablet" crowning each mirror said, "Peter, the store is too long."[83]

Again ignoring his father's advice, Peter went wild, falling "into the speculating mania which seemed to have possessed the people of the age." Peter was "making fortunes in stocks—and was there any earthly reason he should not?" Because "cotton speculation was all the rage," he went into the "adventure as a matter of course." He gambled on property, too, buying $20,000 worth of land in "the intended city of Hamiltonia, the most beautiful site . . . in all the teeming empire of the mighty west." At first, Peter's investments paid off handsomely, but then his luck ran out and Peter's investments collapsed. "As a last resort," Peter visited his father "to solicit funds to help him through the pressure" and avoid bankruptcy. After surveying his son's "affairs," the old man gave his son "one penny," the amount he had possessed when he arrived in Boston.[84]

Both stories function on several levels. Most obviously, they serve as cautionary tales depicting the fate of men trying to establish themselves in a world of rapid change and unstable social boundaries, one in which individualism and social equality were replacing rank and hierarchy.[85] In such a society, no one's status was fixed. The authors greatly exaggerated the possibilities of social advancement to warn the sons of wealthy or middle-class families that industrious poor could usurp their positions. As an advice columnist in the *Western Statesman* warned, it was the "greedy appetite for wealth" that led boys to speculation and then to "bankruptcy and ruin."[86]

To avoid this fate, young men must attend to boundaries established by the moral economy and maintain habits of thrift and industriousness. Those who violated these norms and invested recklessly, like Jeremiah and the younger Bingham, were destroyed. The stories suggest, moreover, that poor boys had an advantage in this race for success, because, like the elder Bingham and Theodore, they were less vulnerable to the corrupting power of money and status. In each story, the poor character remained true to the old-fashioned virtues, while their wealthy counterparts strayed from and, in some cases, rebelled against these values.

The story about Peter Bingham, meanwhile, contains oedipal themes and warnings about the hazards of social mobility. In giving the store to Peter, the elder Bingham established a competition with his son. The elder Bingham's repeated assertion that "the store is too long" has obvious phallic implications: Peter's businesses failed because he sought to best his father. The story thus depicts the rage for speculation as an unwise, wild effort by rebellious sons to cast off the teachings of their fathers, portraying the Panic as just punishment for such disobedience. The tale, further, cautioned readers about the dangers of trying to climb too high on the social ladder. Rather than being satisfied with his father's store, the younger Bingham sought to expand it, cross class borders, and move into a more exclusive social circle. His fall resulted from efforts to best his father and to improve his standing by speculating, expanding his business, marrying an heiress, and buying a palatial home.

Much of this literature also condemned the rise of consumer culture. A story entitled "Samuel Slick—The Clock Maker" satirizes a salesman who relied on deceit and trickery to persuade people to buy products that they did not need.[87] The narrator begins by asking Samuel how he sold "such an immense number of clocks (which certainly cannot be called necessary articles) among a people" without much money? Samuel demonstrated his technique on a visit to Deacon Flint and his wife. Praising the Flints' farm, Samuel insisted nobody in Connecticut would believe that such a homestead existed "away down East here in Nova Scotia."[88]

Samuel said that he was on his way back to Connecticut and had just stopped by to say farewell to the Flints. Deacon Flint asked Samuel if he'd sold all of his clocks, and the salesman replied that he had one left, but that he had promised it to neighbor Steel's wife. This statement piqued the interest of the deacon's wife, who asked to see the clock. "Mr. Slick . . . yielded to these entreaties, and soon produced the clock—a gaudy, highly varnished, trumpery looking affair." Though the Flints thought the clock "was a handsome one," the deacon said that he had no need for such an item. He "was a prudent man," and since he owned a watch, "he had no occasion for a clock."[89]

Samuel explained that the clock was not for sale, because he had promised it to Mrs. Steel. But the salesman said he would leave the clock with the deacon until he returned from Connecticut. After leaving the Flints' home, Samuel explained that the clock was as good as sold. "Mrs. Flint will never let Mrs. Steel have the refusal, nor will the deacon learn, until I call for the clock, that having once indulged in the use of a superfluity, how difficult it is to give it up." People "can do without any article of luxury" that they have never enjoyed. But once obtained, luxury is addictive: few would "surrender it voluntarily." Most of the clocks sold, Samuel explained, "were left in this manner." When Samuel called for them, his customers "invariably bought them."[90]

Other stories linked the rise of consumer culture to women, portraying them as spendthrifts who subverted the household budget and, with it, the national economy. In the *Detroit Gazette*, "Rusticus" complained about his difficulty in stopping his wife and daughters from spending. After a talk with the women in the family, "many good resolutions" were made "to retrench our family's expenses and I have been fain to encourage these little beginnings in economy in hopes of finally extending them to more important branches." But his hopes were "dashed" when a stylish cousin came to visit. Several weeks later, his wife presented "Rusticus" with a list of garments that she wanted to buy. "To avoid a long argument," he placed the list in his "trunk, without one word of comment and resolved never again to mention the word economy in [his] family."[91]

Several tales presented women in a similar light. A story called the *Tale of Two Bankrupts* contrasted two women, the wives of business partners whose firm had gone broke. One woman spent recklessly, and the other was thrifty. Leonard Delmorton's wife, Eveleen, was portrayed as selfish and uncaring. After losing his business, Leonard went over the household items "assigned to his creditors" and explained to Eveleen that they had to surrender all these goods. "You cannot desire to indulge an idle fancy at the expense of your husband's reputation?" Leonard asked. She insisted that "a mosaic center table" would do little to satisfy his creditors.[92]

Leonard refused to keep the table. It was wrong "to retain the most petty superfluity, when those who have confided in me, cannot be indemnified, even by the most unreserved surrender of my property." Leonard then blamed his spendthrift wife for his financial difficulties. "You were frequently forewarned of my impending insolvency; yet you persisted to outrage prudence by every species of extravagance, in defiance of my gentlest remonstrance." It hurt "to think how entirely vanity" had "supplanted affection" in her "callous heart."[93]

Randolph Clifford was Leonard's business partner, and the behavior of his wife, Septima, was quite different. Before learning of her husband's financial problems, the "magnificently attired" Septima sat at home, waiting to attend "an evening party." When her husband got home, he explained "his folly in maintaining the most extensive establishment, even while conscious of its ephemeral nature." After learning that Randolph's business had failed, Septima began to remove from "their several localities the splendid gems that adorned her person," giving up everything except her wedding ring. Septima insisted that "she would never profane the symbol of love by contact with baubles of fashion. This alone of all his gifts no power on earth could tempt her to resign." She then gave him the key to her wardrobe and urged her husband to "select every costly article convertible into cash." She had replaced her gown with "the simplest in her possession, and instead of the superb chain worn at his entrance, she had thrown a neat one of his hair around her neck." Her husband, though "bankrupt in fortune," was "opulent in felicity."[94]

The story offers contrasting visions of women. Septima exemplifies traditional female virtues. A dutiful and subservient wife, she sacrificed her own needs to help her husband, gladly agreeing to give up her fancy gown to aid him, and even agreed to be chained to him with strands of his hair. In contrast, Eveleen represented women's attachment to consumer culture. She represented a subversive, wild force who put her attachment to commodities above her husband's welfare. Despite her husband's admonitions, she refused to renounce her profligate ways that had brought her husband to ruin. Even when the wolf was at the door, she refused to surrender her trinkets.

Both Democrats and Whigs believed that the failure of the moral economy to restrain speculative "mania" and the acquisitiveness of "wild-cat" women played a key role in causing the Panic. These customs, which emphasized the importance of thrift, industriousness, and self-control, established informal boundaries that formed the base on which a stable economy and banking system were built. But the heady growth of the boom had eroded these boundaries and led individuals to act wildly, becoming addicted to luxury and investing huge sums on worthless investments in land and stock. To restore those boundaries, both Democrats and Whigs relied on fiction, editorials, and advice columns to preach the importance of industriousness and self-control.

These developments suggest that greater consensus existed among Democrats and Whigs on economic issues than previous scholarship indicates.[95] In part, both parties located the roots of the Panic in the wild greed and rapacity sparked by the prosperity of Michigan's boom years; to ensure the state's survival, both believed as well that it was essential to reestablish the informal boundaries of the moral economy.

But Democrats and Whigs parted ways on the question of what formal legal boundaries were required to control banks and currency. In Michigan, this debate revolved around two issues: first, Democrats and Whigs disagreed about the wisdom of the state's free banking law, and second, on whether a central bank was required to establish boundaries that would prevent state banks from issuing too much currency. In arguing for a national bank, Whigs insisted that some central authority was needed to check the power of state banks. In making this case, they portrayed Jackson's destruction of the bank as a blow against the masculine authority that was needed to check the unruliness of feminine (that is, profligate) state banks and prevent them from flooding the nation with currency. Democrats, on the other hand, equated the national bank with tyranny, pestilence, and the growing power of money in an economy increasingly dominated by large and impersonal markets. The two parties disagreed, too, on the formal boundaries required to control banks in Michigan. Democrats initially favored a law that made it easier to establish new banks in Michigan, arguing that this would give more Michiganians the opportunity to become bankers and strike a blow against monopolies.

Whigs who attacked the bill asserted that loosening the boundaries on state banks was a critical mistake, because it exposed Michigan residents to the wildness of confidence men who lacked the specie needed to redeem the paper currency they issued.

Whigs and Democrats thus violently disagreed over the type of legal boundaries that were required at the state and national levels to protect people from the power of banks. For the most part, though, they agreed on the type of informal boundaries that were needed to control individual conduct and prevent Michiganians from falling prey to the corrupting power of money. Before the Panic, both parties saw economic development as a way to tame wildness, because it removed Indians from the land and greatly reduced their importance to the economy. After the Panic, however, they viewed capitalism more suspiciously, expressing concern that it unleashed rather than tamed wildness by engendering greed and rapacity in Michiganians, especially in confidence men and spendthrift women. This lust for wealth induced them to speculate, consume recklessly, and erode the boundaries established by the moral economy.

Some scholars believe that such values were largely a thing of the past by the Jacksonian era. Gordon Wood, for instance, asserts that by the early nineteenth century the "fear of luxury that had bedeviled the eighteenth century died away." But this was not the case in Michigan, where newspapers railed against men and women who destabilized society by rebelling against dictates of the moral economy.[96]

Two of the main targets of these attacks were speculators and women of fashion. Karen Halttunen asserts that opinion makers in the early republic believed that speculators were one of several types of confidence men. Like gamblers, demagogues, and strangers who seduced youth into a life of vice, they used guile and deceit to gain their ends. As a result, confidence men and women of fashion were among the most despised figures in antebellum America. This condemnation arose from the Victorian belief that hypocrisy represented "a major social threat." Both women of fashion and confidence men were "archetypal hypocrites." By undermining social confidence among men and women, they threatened to reduce the American republic to "social chaos."[97]

4

Taming the

"Savagery" of

Michigan Indians

In 1827, Michigan governor Lewis Cass pub-
lished an article in the *North American Review* responding to British critics
who charged that the United States treated American Indians inhumanely.
In defending U.S. Indian policy, Cass depicted Native people as drunken
savages who were addicted not only to liquor, but also to violence and cruelty. Whenever Indians could obtain liquor, they abandoned themselves
"to its indulgence, with the recklessness of desperation." Whether young
or old, male or female, chief or warrior, all surrendered to the "most bru-
tal intoxication." Indians also were bloodthirsty: like wild animals, they
lacked the ethical boundaries needed to curb their murderous "passions"
and were "urged forward in their career of blood by all around them,"
behaving "like the bear, and deer, and buffalo." Like his ancestors, the
Indian "lived in a succession of listless indolence and vigorous exertion to
provide for his animal wants or to gratify his baleful passions."[1]

Cass, who served for eighteen years as Michigan governor, played
an important role in shaping the territory's Indian policy. A native of
New Hampshire, he was born in 1782 and moved with his parents to
Ohio in 1800, where he established a successful law practice before serving in the War of 1812 and being appointed governor of Michigan in
1813. Cass, like many nineteenth-century statesmen, viewed Indians
with great suspicion, believing that they lacked the ethical and spiritual
boundaries needed to restrain their darker impulses.[2]

Many Michiganians shared Cass's Yankee roots as well as his hostility to Indians. They had moved to Michigan from New England and

western New York in the late 1820s and early 1830s and often viewed Indians as savage and inhuman, the very antithesis of civilization. This animosity stemmed from several factors: Anglo-Americans hoped to establish an agricultural economy in Michigan, and Indians, who possessed most of the territory's land, represented an obstacle to these plans. Yankees also viewed Indians as backward, because they equated civilization with a boundary that separated agricultural societies from those that relied on hunting.[3] Underestimating the productivity and importance of Indian agriculture, Yankees viewed indigenous people as hunters, who represented an earlier, more primitive stage in evolution. Viewing Indians in this way helped to stabilize Yankee identity, enabling New Englanders to define themselves in opposition to Indian barbarism. Michiganians also suspected Indians of disloyalty, fearing the ease with which local tribes crossed international boundaries and maintained close ties with British officials in Canada. Further fueling antagonism to Indians were long-held fears of cultural outsiders.[4]

One of the most important elements in taming Michigan's frontier, therefore, was the effort between the late 1810s and early 1850s to pacify Indians and strengthen the boundary between civilization and savagery. When the campaign was at its height in the late 1820s and 1830s, Michigan contained roughly 8,000 Native inhabitants and some 30,000 white settlers. Most Natives spoke Algonquian and belonged to the Ojibwa, Ottawa, or Potawatomi tribes. They engaged in hunting, fishing, and agriculture, supplementing their income by trading fur for European manufactured goods. Yankee leaders viewed local tribes as savage and feared that they threatened white communities in two ways. First, they worried that any drunken and violent behavior of Indians could destabilize the new order they sought to establish on the frontier. The specter of violence not only represented a threat to the safety of settlers, but also could deter easterners from immigrating to Michigan and could thus hamper the territory's economic development. Second, Michigan leaders expressed concern that growing numbers of settlers were violating racial borders by adopting Indian values and customs and maintaining the hybrid culture that their French predecessors established in the seventeenth century.[5]

Michiganians established legal, geographic, and cultural boundaries to defuse these threats. Initially, federal and local officials enacted largely ineffective laws to prevent Indians from drinking. They also confined indigenous people to reservations, where boundaries would protect them from the evil influences of both the forest and the city. The wilderness, Yankees feared, would lure indigenous people back to their savage ways; the metropolis would expose them to unscrupulous whites who sold them liquor. This policy sparked a debate over the ability of boundaries to tame savagery.

Reformers who thought savagery was a cultural trait believed that reservations could civilize Indians. Critics viewed savagery as a biological attribute and insisted that the restraints established by reservations could not tame Indian wildness. They urged that Indians be expelled from Michigan.

In the end, Michigan adopted both policies, confining some Indians to reservations and sending others to new homes in Kansas. Although these programs reduced Indian drinking and crime, they failed to prevent whites from emulating Indian ways. Yankees established cultural barriers to solve this problem, publishing numerous captivity narratives in Michigan newspapers. On one level, the narratives were simple adventure stories describing how whites who were captured by Indians managed to survive their ordeal. But on another level, the tales allegorized hybridization and boundary crossing, warning whites about the incompatibility of Indian and white ways and demonstrating the need to maintain barriers between Indian and Yankee cultures. In the end, however, creating boundaries that eradicated savagery and separated Indian and Anglo-American identity proved to be more difficult than Yankees expected. Rather than re-creating New England norms in the West, Michiganians established new hybridized boundaries that differed somewhat from those in the East.

INDIAN DRUNKENNESS AND VIOLENCE

This, however, was not the outcome that Yankees expected after initiating efforts to civilize Michigan Indians in the 1820s. At the time, settlers voiced growing alarm about the perceived drunkenness, violence, and unruliness of the territory's Indians. These concerns were not new. During both the American Revolution and the War of 1812, Indians allied with the British had raided American settlements in the West. Although the latter marked the last major Indian conflict in Michigan, Yankees complained that relations with Indians were far from peaceful.[6] During the 1820s and 1830s, they accused Indians of engaging in subtler forms of resistance to white occupation than they had in the past, committing a broad range of crime—from petty theft to murder. Settlers expressed growing concern about such behavior, which, they believed, stemmed from the absence of spiritual and ethical boundaries in indigenous culture and from Indian drunkenness.

The link between Indians and alcohol grew out of the fur trade and the exchange of liquor for pelts, long the key to success in the industry. Ironically, it was European traders who got Indians hooked on alcohol. Because other trade goods, such as pots and pans, lasted for years, interest in these items diminished as Indians acquired more and more of them. Indians usually ran out of liquor quickly, however, forcing them to continue trading pelts to replenish their supplies.[7]

Contrary to white perceptions, not all Indians drank alcohol. Indeed, many viewed liquor as a symbol of Europe's devastating effects on indigenous people. Like a foreign invader, alcohol had breached the boundaries protecting Native culture, destroying countless families and communities. Not surprisingly, Indian revival movements made temperance reform a central element in their drive to reinvigorate Indian culture by purging it of European contaminants. Before the War of 1812, Tecumseh and Tenskwatawa, or the Prophet, led one such pan-Indian crusade, urging tribes to get rid of alcohol as well as other European goods and to unite against Anglo-Americans. This message found a receptive audience in Michigan. Two of the territory's Native leaders—Le Maigouis, an Ottawa warrior, and Main Poche, a Potawatomi shaman—became followers of Tenskwatawa and persuaded numerous Michigan Indians to join their ranks.[8]

Although this movement ended after the War of 1812, indigenous opposition to alcohol persisted. Simon Pokagon, a Potawatomi chief, voiced this outrage in his autobiographical novel, *Queen of the Woods* (1899). Written in both English and Algonquian, it depicts the destruction that liquor wrought on Michigan tribes. At the beginning of the novel, an old Indian wakes the young narrator, Simon Pokagon, asking him how he "can sleep when he recalls how awsh-kon-tay ne-besh (firewater), that alluring jan-gend-ji-ged (enemy) brought among us by the whites, is destroying kwi-wi-zens and osh-kin-äw-e (our boys and young men) as well as our ak-i-wes-i (our old men), and laying waste qua-notch win (the fairest) of ki au-kee (our land)." Simon's sleep symbolizes his blindness to the evils of drink, and his awakening represents his growing awareness of this social ill.[9]

Anglo-Americans, however, viewed Indian drinking differently, seeing it as a symbol not only of Native American savagery, but also of their propensity to violate the boundaries needed to establish a stable, peaceful, and godly community. While acknowledging the role of unethical whites who peddled liquor to Indians, Michiganians blamed Indian drinking primarily on Native Americans' laziness and lack of self-control. A *Detroit Gazette* correspondent asserted in 1822 that drunkenness, so common to Indians, was the "natural consequence of their indolence and inactivity."[10] In 1820, another *Gazette* correspondent observed that Indians possessed an "unaccountable propensity for intoxication, to the gratification" of which they sacrificed all. "The universal prevalence of the vice among them is a moral phenomenon—for no consideration is sufficiently strong to restrain them from its indulgence."[11]

Drunken Indians, settlers believed, violated both legal and ethical boundaries. They broke the former by becoming violent and criminal and infringed on the latter by turning into lazy, weak, and pathetic figures.

Settlers were particularly amazed at the great quantities of liquor that Indians consumed. Jesse Turner, a resident of western Michigan, recalled an incident in 1833 in which drinking had the latter effect. Roughly one hundred Indians had obtained enough liquor "for a big spree," and only "two or three" of this large group remained "sober." The rest became so intoxicated that he "saw for the first time" Indians who were "too drunk to raise a cup to their lips." To aid these drunken men, Indian women "would fill their mouths with whiskey and squirt it into the mouths" of their besotted companions.[12]

Michiganians recalled other instances in which alcohol incapacitated Indians, transforming them into objects of pathos and ridicule. Mrs. E.M.S. Stewart, whose family had settled in Detroit in the 1820s when she was young, recalled that "a drunken Indian" had broken into her childhood home and refused to leave, despite her mother's pleas. The intruder lay on the kitchen floor "muttering to himself" until the sheriff seized him by the collar and "pitched him into the street."[13]

But liquor also could have the opposite effect, prompting Indians to engage in crime, settlers claimed. Inebriated Indians often pestered settlers for food and engaged in petty thefts. Jesse Turner remembered attending a dinner in the early 1820s at which the host planned to serve pork and potatoes. Before the meal, the host "asked a long and reverent grace." But he soon discovered "that his pork was gone for the d—d Indians had stolen it." At the time, losing "one's supply of pork was a serious enough thing to make even a good man swear."[14]

Heavy drinking sometimes led to more serious crimes. Between the 1810s and 1820s, the *Gazette* reported a number of incidents in which Indians violently attacked settlers in southern Michigan. In 1819, for instance, Indians demanded bread from a settler. When the settler refused, the Indians gravely wounded him and his companion.[15] A decade later, a band of about a half dozen Potawatomi broke into the house of a settler near Monroe, Michigan, "dragged him from his bed, stabbed him with their knives in several places, beat him with sticks and then left the house."[16]

Nor were whites the only victims of such alcohol-induced violence. Throughout the 1820s, the *Gazette* informed its readers that Indians periodically attacked each other after a bout of drunken carousing. In 1821, one Indian killed a companion who refused to share his alcohol. The victim's father then seized the perpetrator "by the throat, bore him to the ground," and stabbed him repeatedly "with a short knife."[17] Similarly, Indians stabbed three of their companions after a night of "drunken socializing" in 1826. A local editor who commented on the slayings opined that Indians "were determined not to be exterminated by the use of whiskey alone, but that the tomahawk shall also have its share in their destruction."[18] Such incidents, settlers contended, underscored the self-destructiveness of Indians. Although writers condemned Indians for attacking settlers, the 1826 passage suggests that they were equally shocked by the violence that aboriginal people visited upon each other.

But not all violence stemmed from drinking. Sober Indians also attacked whites, according to Henry Rowe Schoolcraft. A New York native, Schoolcraft explored and wrote about Michigan and other parts of the West after the glass-making business he established in the East failed in 1817. He was widely regarded as an authority on Indian language and culture after being appointed U.S. Indian agent in Sault Ste. Marie in 1822.[19] Many years later, Schoolcraft recalled two instances in which Indians had killed unsuspecting whites seemingly for sport, but there is no way to determine the accuracy of Schoolcraft's recollections. In 1821, an Indian shot and killed a white settler who had hired the Indian to guide him from Green Bay, then part of Michigan, to Chicago, where the settler's family lived. As the victim lay dying, he wondered why his guide had shot him, noting that he had never done this or any other Indian "any injury": "To kill me, too, when I was just returning to my wife and my little child, which I have never seen! It is more painful than death."[20]

Three years later, Schoolcraft helped to prosecute Indians involved in an even bloodier crime. An Ojibwa war party, headed west to attack the Sioux, came across four traders camping in the north woods. The Indians promised not to hurt the whites but changed their minds after one of the warriors insisted that when he "went out a-hunting, he did not like to return without killing something." The Indians then killed three of the traders and murdered the fourth as he tried to flee, cutting off the "unfortunate man's head, for the purpose of scalping it." The senselessness and brutality of such slayings seemed to prove the barbarism and inhumanity of Indians, suggesting that indigenous people lacked the discipline required to control their dark, violent impulses. Such bloodlust also demonstrated that Michiganians could not establish a peaceful and godly community until they strengthened the boundaries separating civilization from such savagery.[21]

Making the alleged ferocity of Indians even more frightening was the Native American's ability to subvert international boundaries such as the one that protected Michiganians from the British in Canada. In the War of 1812, English officials had used liquor and other gifts to induce local tribes to act as their proxies and attack Michiganians. After the war, this friendship between Michigan Indians and the British continued, prompting Anglo-Americans to question the loyalty of local tribes.[22] A *Detroit Gazette* correspondent wondered why in the 1820s the British continued to bestow "such a vast amount of presents" on "Indians living in our territory," expressing concern that the British again might be using Indians as a fifth column to strike Michiganians from inside their own borders. Unfortunately, there seemed no easy way to sever this link between the British and Indians and to prevent new rounds of bloodshed.[23]

Such carnage represented not only a threat to settlers' safety, but also an obstacle to Michigan's development. The territory's prosperity was linked to population growth, which depended on attracting immigrants from the East. Michigan leaders expressed concern that as news of Indian violence spread, it would deter easterners from seeking new homes in the territory. In 1822, for instance, Michigan executed two Indians who were accused of killing a white settler. Word of the hanging sent shivers through Michigan, where residents feared that Indians would soon seek revenge against white settlers.[24]

At the time, the *Gazette* published an article by an eastern writer who mentioned the execution of the Indians and warned his neighbors against migrating to Michigan. If the territory's tribes were angry and vengeful, it would be "madness for you to venture on your ruin," he asserted. "I will remain where I am, where I at least enjoy personal safety and where my wife and children will have nothing to fear or suffer from savage cruelty."[25] Michigan writers admitted that such sentiments were common in the East. "The intended emigrant" saw no reason to leave the "land of civilization and peace," where he lived "with tolerable ease and perfect safety," to settle in the "wilds of Michigan" and make himself vulnerable "to the scalping knife and tomahawk or rifle of the savage," declared one local scribe in 1822. Easterners saw no reason to "exchange security for danger" or to expose their wives and children to the "perils and terrors" of Indians, just to "increase [their] wealth."[26]

ESTABLISHING BOUNDARIES TO PREVENT
DRUNKENNESS AND CRIME

Responding to these concerns, federal and local officials created legal boundaries to curb Indian drinking and crime. In the late eighteenth and early nineteenth centuries, Congress passed a series of laws to prevent fur traders from peddling alcohol to Indians. Two of the most important were enacted in 1815 and 1822. The 1815 statute banned alcohol production on Indian land, fining violators $5,000. To prevent the smuggling of liquor to Indians, seven years later Congress empowered federal officials to inspect the belongings of traders and to rescind the licenses and confiscate the goods of those who violated the law.[27]

Local governments enacted similar laws during this period. In 1812 and

1815, Michigan passed statutes that banned the sale of liquor to Indians in its jurisdiction and fined violators up to $100. Neither local nor federal legislation proved effective. Traders largely ignored the laws, because they feared that if they stopped selling liquor, Indians would take their business elsewhere. The statutes also were notoriously difficult to enforce. Traders usually operated in the wilderness, far from the purview of those charged with policing them. Local officials, meanwhile, often failed to crack down on traders who violated the law, because they feared that doing so would hurt the fur trade, which was the backbone of Michigan's economy until the late 1830s.[28]

Settlers reacted angrily to this state of affairs. Their concerns peaked during the first half of the 1820s. In those years, the *Gazette* contained several letters in which residents complained bitterly about Indian drunkenness and merchants who continued to sell them liquor. In 1821, an anonymous *Gazette* correspondent reserved his harshest comments for those who knowingly violated the law. These individuals "are destitute of shame and are unworthy of the appellation of American citizen," he noted. After witnessing the scenes in "our streets that so often disgust," one would think that the sellers of liquor "would withhold it from Indians."[29]

Laws to stop Indian drinking were not the only boundaries that federal officials established to tame Indians. They also devised two more effective methods of quelling perceived Native barbarism: first, they placed Indians on reservations where they could be civilized; second, they removed them from Michigan. These policies were not restricted to Michigan. During the first half of the nineteenth century, the federal government confined eastern tribes to reservations or moved them to land west of the Mississippi River, now known as Oklahoma. Andrew Jackson's eviction of the Cherokee from the Southeast in the early 1830s stirred great controversy and constituted the darkest chapter in the saga of Indian removal, resulting in the Trail of Tears, a forced march in which many Indians died on the journey from Georgia to Indian country.[30]

Efforts to "civilize" Michigan Indians began with a series of treaties, most of which U.S. officials negotiated between 1817 and 1838, in which local tribes ceded much of the land that now makes up Michigan and were forced to live on reservations or leave the territory. In 1819, for instance, Governor Cass negotiated the Treaty of Saginaw, in which the United States paid a lump sum of $3,000 and an annuity of $1,000 to the Ottawa and Ojibwa for some six million acres of land in eastern Michigan. These pacts accomplished two goals. First and most familiarly, they enabled the federal government to transfer millions of acres of land from Indians to Anglo-Americans. Second, they permitted Cass and other officials either to remove Indians from the territory or to confine them to reservations, creating new boundaries that could pacify and control the supposed disorder associated with an alien race.[31]

Reformers who sought to tame Indians emphasized the importance of the boundary that separated civilized from savage society and the need to contain or, if possible, eradicate barbarism. Relying on agriculture for subsistence, civilized society was believed to be morally, spiritually, and intellectually superior to its savage counterpart, which depended on hunting. Theorists such as Comte de Volney compared hunters to wild beasts who sought merely to satisfy such basic needs as the search for food, shelter, and procreation.[32]

Evidence of such backwardness abounded in Michigan, Yankees believed. A *Detroit Gazette* correspondent in 1822 declared Indians to be "lazy and indolent to excess." Their life was spent primarily in repose. "They lie down and dose away an inactive life in a smoky hovel." Not only were they "satisfied with the most disgusting food," but they also displayed "an uncommon degree of insensibility to all the advantages with which God and nature have surrounded them." They typically planted just a few acres of crops in their villages and "in such a wretched manner" that they obtained "little increase from them." Nor were they interested in improving their living conditions. It was astonishing "to see with what carelessness, and strange indifference to all the comforts of life," they lived, even though they resided "in a country, whose spontaneous productions for the happiness and good of man, are many, and which needs but little cultivation to cause it to produce in abundance, all that his convenience can require."[33]

Instead, the *Gazette* correspondent continued, Indians preferred to live indolently, like unruly beasts. Relying on "the abundance, which nature in her wild state produces," they contented themselves with the copiousness of "game, and the pure waters, which glide by their wretched villages, with almost every variety of fish." Instead of laboring to increase nature's bounty, they slept "away the seasons of spring, summer and autumn, regardless of any thing future." In winter, they ventured out only "to procure what their immediate necessities require[d]." They then returned "to their former inactive and indolent habits, until aroused again by a recurrence of the same extremities." Such a lifestyle suggested that Indians were less than human. For it did not seem possible that "a creature wearing a human shape and features" could remain "deaf" to nature's "invitations" to toil.[34] What is more, Indian society lacked the boundaries necessary to separate the wealthy from the indigent and those who were lazy from those who worked hard: "Go among them and it is difficult to discover who is the richest or who the poorest or who is industrious & who idle."[35]

This inattention to what Yankees considered good order was also reflected in Indian government, which tended to extremes, another *Gazette* writer asserted in 1823. In some cases, Native peoples lived under tyrants who evidently were not bound by any rules. In others, they existed in a seemingly lawless state of anarchy: "Their government, if government it may be called, is one of opinion only." No individual or institution exerts "direct authority . . . and their war expeditions are composed of volunteers."[36] But Indians could also be tyrannical. This was particularly true of a chief named Kishkauko, who ruled over a community of Ojibwe in Saginaw. On one occasion, a member of his tribe killed another Ojibwa. The tribal council had permitted the perpetrator to live, because his family had agreed to provide gifts to the relatives of the man he had slain. As the two parties began to shake hands and light "the pipe of conciliation," Kishkauko struck and killed the slayer with a single blow. The Indians were "much astonished" and asked the chief why he had prevented "the operation of their old law." He replied, "The law is now altered."[37]

The absence of sound legal principles, Yankees averred, reflected the backwardness of a society lacking the ideals that motivated those in the civilized world. Ebenezer Reed, an editor of the *Detroit Gazette*, whom Governor Cass commissioned to study Indians in western Michigan, asserted in 1829 that Indians' backwardness could be seen in their language, which was far more primitive than European or Asian tongues. It was difficult to believe that any group, "however low in the scale of improvement," could be totally "destitute of words equivalent to ours of praise, honor, glory [and] worship." But rigorous investigation purportedly revealed that this was true of the Indians' language.[38]

Other writers shared this belief in Indian backwardness. In 1820, the *Detroit Gazette* reprinted a series of articles on pre-Columbian civilization from the *Western Review and Miscellaneous Magazine* that were based on this misconception. The author claimed that the ancestors of Native peoples were far too primitive to have created the enormous earthen mounds that the Hopewell and other early Native societies built in the Mississippi River Valley. "The manner and customs of our present North American Indians are so totally incompatible with the characteristics displayed in these laborious contructions that we cannot suppose their ancestors" built them. "Our Indians are almost exclusively devoted to hunting, a mode of life which precludes a numerous population." Therefore, they possessed few of the "civilized arts that ancient relics display."[39]

Worse, Indians lived in spiritual darkness, possessing few if any of the spiritual and ethical boundaries needed to control their darker impulses. Instead, they followed the dictates of shamans who seemed more like sorcerers than religious leaders. Rev. Abel Bingham, who founded an early mission at Sault Ste. Marie, declared that on questions of faith Indians were "uniformly in a very dark and ignorant state." They worshiped medicine men who practiced "a kind of sorcery" and "exerted much influence over their adherents." Their religious ideas were so confused "with their medical system that they were inseparable." They often used "their heathenish ceremonies" on the sick. Indians believed in an afterlife, "but in relation to the resurrection of the body, and most of the other doctrines of the Christian religion, they were as dark as night."[40]

To eradicate such pagan beliefs and rituals, Michiganians sought to confine Indians to reservations, where missionaries could civilize them, instilling in them the boundaries needed to control their savagery. Their campaign to do so, however, sparked a debate about the ability of boundaries to tame Indian wildness. At issue was the vexing question of whether Indian "savagery" was due to culture or race.[41]

Michiganians who backed reservations viewed wildness as a cultural trait that missionaries could erase with the aid of boundaries. Trying to tame Indians who lived in the forest was useless. In this environment, they would revert to savagery. Nor could reformers educate Indians in cities and other corrupted locations where unscrupulous merchants sold them liquor. The greatest obstacle to civilizing Indians, noted a *Gazette* correspondent in 1820, was the "depravity and disgraceful avarice" of some whites. "For a paltry acquisition to their purses," they did not "hesitate to instill into the minds of Indians the most erroneous and mischievous ideas."[42]

The reservation, however, established borders that protected Indians from unscrupulous whites and the savagery of the forest. On reservations, a *Gazette* correspondent observed in 1820, missionaries could prompt "red children of the forest" to leave their "shades and hunting grounds and partake of the comforts and blessings of civilized life."[43] Under the influence of goodhearted whites, Indians could learn to become "wealthy and respectable farmers"; they could possess "all the conveniences of life" and devote themselves to "agricultural pursuits with a skill that would do honor to a citizen of Massachusetts or Connecticut."[44]

To accomplish these goals, the government established mission schools and model farms. The latter were vocational schools wherein Indians learned agriculture as well as carpentry, blacksmithing, and other useful trades. Mission schools taught Indian children reading, writing, and arithmetic and also provided religious and vocational instruction.[45]

In a report on one such Michigan school, run by Baptist missionaries on the St. Joseph River, Judge John L. Leib of Michigan noted the progress made by Indian students. Writing in 1824, Leib said that the Indians had learned about "letters which enlarge the sphere of happiness and knowledge" and about "agriculture, which dispels all fears of a precarious subsistence." More importantly, the school was teaching them about Christianity, ensuring to those who observed its "commandments interminable happiness." From these beginnings, he expected to see "the Indian progressively reclaimed from a vagrant and savage state."[46]

One of the students was a fifteen-year-old Indian boy named Luther Rice. "When he entered this institution," wrote Leib, he "was wild from the woods, acquainted with no language but his native Indian." But Rice was "making rapid improvement in reading, writing and arithmetic." The school also benefited Indians who lived nearby. "The tribes surrounding" it evinced the most "conciliatory disposition" and sought to become "acquainted with letters, religious and agricultural instruction." Soon the Indians would make the land near the school into a "gradually growing settlement." Educating Indians, however, could occur only "in places remote from the white population"; the state would have to prevent Indians from having intercourse "with traders," especially "those unprincipled men, who disregarding all legal and moral restraints, debased them more and more by introducing among them ardent spirits."[47]

Leib then urged Governor Cass to help the school, arguing that efforts to civilize Indians were likely to be more successful than in the past, because the pupils were less likely to resist white culture than they had been in the 1810s. If the government supplied missionaries at the institution with "adequate means," their efforts and enthusiasm "would provide gratifying results." Some critics, he acknowledged, disagreed with such experiments, objecting that "efforts have already been made" to educate the Indian "without effect." Those efforts, however, had been undertaken decades earlier, when "the Indians were a formidable and independent people—sole lords of the forest, when they could command everything necessary to their mode of life." They even wildly took up arms and "broke up" a nearby settlement. But the Indian's plight had changed dramatically since then. "What can exceed the present humiliation of the Indian? His dependence is complete."[48]

Despite such optimistic assessments, opponents of reservations urged that Indians be expelled from Michigan. Some critics argued that Indians should be sent west because the boundaries that reservations established were unable to protect them from the pernicious influence of whiskey peddlers and other unethical whites. Others insisted that savagery was biological, arguing that missionaries could not eradicate it.

Edward Barber, who had spent his youth in early Michigan, recalled that it was impossible to try "to fill the Indian with our thought and culture" and "to induce him to adopt civilized modes of life." It was "like attempting to fill a tube that is open at both ends with water—for fast as it poured in at one end it runs out at the other." Though the Indian could learn in school, he refused to work, and "productive labor is the primary and essential factor of progress."[49] Melvin D. Osband, another settler, asserted years later that the Indian's "persistent intractableness rendered nugatory all efforts for a higher culture." Europeans "brought to him civilization and a higher manhood. But he would have none of it. He rejected it. He fought it and it sealed his doom."[50]

Aiding settlers who viewed savagery this way were mounting problems that the program to civilize Indians encountered in the 1830s. One of the first obstacles that beset reformers was the Indians' refusal to move to reservations. Initially, officials were not alarmed by this intransigence, because they believed that growing numbers of eastern immigrants would purchase the parts of Michigan that formerly belonged to Native Americans, forcing Indians off their homeland. But after the Panic of 1837, this surge of immigration failed to materialize.[51]

Officials also had difficulty finding qualified individuals to operate the program's model farms, which paid poorly and were situated in remote locations. Similar woes plagued Michigan's mission schools. Run by Presbyterian, Baptist, Methodist, Episcopalian, and Catholic missionaries, the schools initially suffered from low enrollment. In 1837, for instance, only seventeen students lived at the school in Sault Ste. Marie. Mission schools in other parts of Michigan did not fare much better. Low enrollment and other problems stemmed primarily from the schools' inability to attract teachers.[52]

These disappointing results prompted several prominent Michiganians to advocate removal. Governor Lewis Cass was one of the best-known champions of this position. While serving as Andrew Jackson's secretary of war from 1831 to 1836, he gained notoriety for helping to remove the Cherokee and other tribes from the East. But Cass had not always been an enthusiastic supporter of removal. He adopted that stance after becoming increasingly frustrated with efforts to civilize Michigan Indians.[53]

This disillusionment with efforts to tame Indians was evident by the late 1820s. During that period, Cass published an article asserting that despite two centuries of contact with Europeans, Indians persisted in their primitive ways. Though they had adopted some European technology—"our arms and ammunition . . . and many of our instruments of iron and steel"—their morals and manners remained barbaric. Lacking the "principle of moral improvement" that seemed "inherent in human nature," the "savage" remained tied to barbarism.[54] Three years later, Cass stated that Catholics and Protestants had established numerous missions to educate and Christianize Indians. Yet these efforts produced little, if any, success. "Year after year sanguine anticipations have been formed, to be succeeded by disappointment and despondency."[55] Such disappointing results left officials with only one alternative—removal.

H. R. Schoolcraft agreed. After initially opposing removal, he was backing the idea by the late 1820s. In part, this change was due to Cass's influence. In 1820, Schoolcraft had accompanied Cass on an expedition exploring the northern Great Lakes. Since then, Cass had become not only Schoolcraft's close friend, but also a mentor and father figure to the younger man. Additionally, Schoolcraft came to see removal as the only way to protect indigenous people from whites who sought to take advantage of them and profit from their demise.[56]

Removal's growing popularity had devastating consequences for the Potawatomi. Under increasing pressure from local and federal officials, tribal leaders signed the Treaty of Chicago in 1833, agreeing to sell their land in southwestern Michigan and move to Kansas, despite vigorous protests from many Indians who opposed the pact. After the pact became law in 1835, the government began transporting Potawatomi to their new homes. But many Potawatomi refused to leave after learning that Kansas was dry and inhospitable. In 1840, the federal government sent in the U.S. Army to force the Potawatomi out of Michigan.[57]

Edward Barber recalled that troops led by Gen. Hugh Brady "scoured the woods to collect" the Indians for "removal." The Potawatomi, meanwhile, "scattered like a flock of blackbirds." Some "fled north, far into the forest," but they were slowed by the presence of a "sick squaw." The Indians eventually sought "refuge in a dense swamp," where the army surrounded them and forced them to surrender.[58]

In *Queen of the Woods*, Simon Pokagon narrates this incident from the Potawatomi's perspective. Early in the novel, Simon's mother-in-law, Kobunda, recalls the terror that swept through Indian communities when the army arrived. A white neighbor boy ran into Kobunda's home, reporting that the army had "all the Injuns in the church tied together with big strings, like ponies, and are going to kill all of um." As Kobunda fled, she learned that the "whole country was alive with white warriors" seeking to "kill [Indians] or drive them toward the setting sun." To escape, she hid for a week in a "desolate swamp." Later, another character describes the treatment the Potawatomi endured as troops, "armed with guns and bayonets," forced them to leave Michigan. "Some they drove like cattle, and others they tied like sheep for market, and carried them in wagons." Many Potawatomi "died on the way, and were eaten by win-an-geg (vultures) and by maw-in-gwan-og (wolves)."[59]

As a result of these strong-arm tactics, Michiganians succeeded in removing most Potawatomi from Michigan. In the end, however, neither those favoring nor those opposing removal won a complete victory. Some Michigan Indians were confined to reservations, while others were banished to new homes in Kansas.[60] This strategy greatly reduced the presence of Native peoples in Michigan.

HYBRIDIZATION

Yet this success did not entirely quiet Yankee concerns. Michigan leaders had long worried that rather than whites civilizing Indians, the opposite would occur: Indian culture might prove so attractive that growing numbers of Anglo-Americans might adopt primitive ways, prompting Michigan's elite to worry that settlers might be reversing cultural evolution. Indeed, memoirs and fiction from the period suggest that many settlers did just that, subverting racial boundaries and adopting alien customs.

This borrowing of Indian customs had been common among Michigan's French inhabitants, many of whom seemed to be more barbaric than civilized to Yankees, who began streaming into Michigan in the 1820s. The French dressed like Indians, hunted like Indians, spoke the Indians' language, and in some cases had even married Indians and produced mixed-race children. Thus, wildness became a genetic as well as a cultural problem; by commingling with Indians, the French had erased racial boundaries and produced a population that was neither white nor Indian. As Gov. Lewis Cass stated in 1827, Michigan's French population seemed to bear out what the Marquis de Denonville had observed in 1685. France had sought "to mingle with the Indians in order to Frenchify them." But just the opposite had happened: "Those with whom we mingle do not become French, but our people become Indians."[61]

Yankees condemned this hybridization, asserting that the blurring of racial and cultural boundaries had transformed even the purebred French into savages. Indeed, New Englanders expressed alarm that their French neighbors seemed to have more in common with Indians than with their fellow whites. One settler remembered that when an Indian broke into her family's childhood home in Detroit in the early 1820s and her mother called for help, several Frenchmen refused to come to her aid. When informed of their response, the sheriff told her that these black Frenchmen "would never molest any Indian whatever he may be doing."[62]

In other ways as well, the French seemed to have taken on Indian traits and blurred the boundary between civilization and savagery. Anglo settlers condemned the French for being nearly as economically backward as were the Indians. Rather than creating a vibrant agricultural economy, the French, like Indians, seemed content to earn their living from the fur trade. French settlers who did farm cared little about their vocation: they refused to adopt modern farming techniques. Relying instead on antiquated methods developed by their ancestors, they employed equipment that was out-of-date, and they failed to fertilize their land effectively.[63]

The French settlers also seemed to have acquired the morals and deportment of Indians. Jesse Turner recalled that in western Michigan in the early 1820s, "a good many French" lived among the Indians. "One we used to call Mossau was a perfect Indian in all but color and he hadn't much advantage in that respect, for he was nearly as dark as any of them." Though Mossau's "squaw" was the daughter of a white man, "she was the most persistent beggar among the Indians."[64] Turner's description of Mossau and his squaw underscores the fear that Indianization evoked in Yankee settlers, because it demonstrated the ease with which the boundaries that distinguished Indians from whites could be crossed. In the process, European traits were obliterated. Turner described Mossau as white; yet in the next breath, he asserted that he was almost the same color as the Indians with whom he lived, suggesting that at least figuratively he had destroyed the physical boundaries that defined race. He emphasized, too, that like the Indians, Mossau and his squaw had become subhuman and pathetic figures who lived by begging rather than by labor.

Other settlers also believed that the French had regressed, crossing the boundary between civilization and savagery. Some of the French were "so shiftless," one settler recalled, that they "depended on outside sources for the very bread they ate." The French, like Indians, rarely aspired to anything more than the "possession of a canoe, a spear and a few hooks for fishing, with a rifle and a half dozen dogs."[65] Worse, observed another resident, "the roving, unsettled, uneducated wood ranger, fur hunter or 'voyageur'" led "a careless dissipated life."[66] Governor Cass echoed these sentiments, claiming that for two hundred years "in the depths of the American forest," the Frenchman had "associated with their rude tenants, and, as he could not elevate them to his own standard," he had "descended to theirs."[67]

Yankee disapproval of the French was spelled out in greater detail in *Shoepac Recollections: A Wayside Glimpse of American Life* (1856), a novel set in the Detroit of the 1820s and 1830s. Written under the pen name "Walter March" by Orlando Bolivar Willcox, the novel depicted Detroit before the massive influx of New Englanders as a multiracial society in which Indian, French, English, and American residents mixed freely; it satirized the Yankees' disapproving response to Detroit's syncretic culture.[68] The Shoepac—footwear developed by the French in North America that was part shoe and part moccasin—symbolized this blending of European and Indian culture.[69]

Willcox described Detroit in the early 1820s as a place where "Indian, Frenchman, Briton and American commingled harmoniously together, and there was room enough for all and to spare."[70] It would be difficult to "imagine a pleasanter state of feeling than mutually existed" between these individuals. At the time, the city's streets were filled with "motley groups, consisting of French, Americans and Indians" who together smoked "social pipes" and enjoyed conversations consisting of "words, nods, shrugs and the impenetrable 'Ugh! Ugh!' of the taciturn red man."[71]

This freewheeling community horrified New Englanders. As more "Bostonians" arrived in Michigan, "it gradually came to light that our lively little community were scarce a grain better than the wicked, nay than the very heathen," noted Willcox laconically. The fiddling and dancing that occurred on Sunday nights dismayed the easterners. On these festive occasions, "the prettiest and most mischievous-eyed French girls" danced "for dear life with good-looking frank-mannered *voyajeurs* or *courreurs de bois*." These "abominations attracted the 'growing attention' of strict sober-sides from the land of Jonathan Edwards, as he passed these dens of Apollyon, on his way to the place where prayer was wont to be made."[72]

From an Anglo-American perspective, then, Detroit's lack of racial borders seemed to have produced a community that mirrored the pagan manners of its least civilized inhabitants—the Indians. Instead of the French raising Indians to civilization, Indians had reduced the French to savagery. Consequently, New Englanders viewed Detroiters not simply as immoral or sinful, but as "heathen," a term often reserved for Indians and other seemingly subhuman groups. Further, Willcox suggests that what most concerned New Englanders were sexual promiscuity and miscegenation or interracial couplings. French women violated the Sabbath in particularly heinous ways, by dancing, flirting, and engaging in openly sexual behavior. Worse, the men with whom they carried on were *voyageurs,* individuals who lived like Indians and were often of mixed race.

CAPTIVITY NARRATIVES

Much to the horror of Michigan's elite, some Anglo-Americans seemed to be following the precedent established by their French predecessors. These concerns about the wildness of whites become evident in captivity narratives, which ran regularly in Michigan newspapers. The tales both documented the phenomenon of Indianization and sought to establish cultural boundaries that would curb it more effectively than did those created by the law. Michiganians did not invent these tales. They simply took a literary genre from the colonial era and used it to shore up racial barriers on the frontier. The stories often contained similar plots: Native warriors kidnapped white men or women and sought to transform them into Indians before the captives escaped and returned to Anglo-American settlements.[73]

Traversing borders played a central role in these stories. Depicting hybridization as an involuntary phenomenon that Indians imposed on whites, the stories began with Indians violating white boundaries, invading Anglo-American communities, and capturing innocent white settlers, usually children. Indians also trespassed on internal boundaries, seeking to turn captives into Indians. But whites also traversed racial boundaries, initially by becoming Indian and then by resuming their old white personas. The narratives thus revealed anxiety about the elasticity of identity and the ease with which individuals could cross the line separating civilization from savagery. They also allegorized the process of boundary crossing and revealed why some settlers may have found Indian ways alluring while others viewed them as repellent.

The Falcon: A Narrative of the Captivity and Adventures of John Tanner (1830) deals with both issues. Tanner's narrative, one of the few autobiographies from this region and period, apparently was not published in Michigan newspapers. But the book was known to Michigan readers. The *Detroit Gazette* announced in 1828 that the manuscript would probably be "published in New York or Philadelphia in the course of a few months."[74] The book described important differences between Indian and white culture, especially the ways in which each established boundaries to govern sexuality and gender. Tanner reported that gender roles seemed less confining in Indian than in white culture. Although some settlers found these ways liberating, they may have provided further evidence for others that Indians were depraved creatures who, like wild animals, lived without moral or spiritual boundaries.

Tanner's captivity began when a band of Michigan Indians, seeking to replace a dead child, captured the author as a boy near his family's home in Kentucky. His captors, according to H. R. Schoolcraft, were "Saginaw" Ojibwa, among whom he "learned the language, customs and superstitions of the Indians." They had "stolen" Tanner during one of the "marauding forays which they waged against the frontiers about 1777."[75]

Tanner remained with the Indians through a significant portion of his adult life, marrying and raising children with an Indian woman, even though he could have escaped and returned to the white settlements much earlier. Tanner's decision to remain with the Indians was complex. For one, his Indian captors deceived him into believing that they had killed his father and friends some time after kidnapping him. He believed as well that Indians were more compassionate to the destitute than were whites. "I recalled the laborious and confined manner in which I must live if I returned to live among the whites." Without friends or property, "I must, of necessity, be exposed to all the ills of extreme poverty," and Indians were kinder to the poor than were whites. "Among the Indians, I saw that those who were too young or too weak to hunt for themselves were sure to find some one to provide for them." At the time, Tanner also was becoming more closely integrated into Indian society, "rising in the estimation of Indians and becoming one of them."[76]

Several other reasons for remaining Indian are implied. As noted earlier, Tanner reported that men and women had greater freedom in Indian than in white society. Indians, for instance, seemed more tolerant of powerful women than did whites. One such woman, his second adoptive mother, Net-no-kwa, was the "principal chief of the Ottawwaws."[77] A commanding figure, she feared neither Indians nor white men. In one instance, she lent a canoe to French traders. When they refused to give it back, "the old woman took it from them without their consent," and the traders "dared not make any resistance."[78] On another occasion, Net-no-kwa single-handedly saved Tanner and his Indian brother during a very dangerous passage across a storm-tossed Lake Winnipeg.[79]

Tanner certainly might have been exaggerating the bravery and power of his adopted mother. But other observers also believed that Indians accepted powerful women more readily than did whites. While visiting Mackinac Island, Margaret Fuller reported that Indian women exercised great power. One source told her that "the Indian woman is subjected to many hardships . . . yet her position, compared with that of the man, is higher and freer than that of the white woman."[80] Similarly, Schoolcraft observed that women occupied important religious positions in indigenous cultures. Women, for example, could be prophets or Jossakeeds, important figures in Indian religion. Indeed, one female Jossakeed whom Schoolcraft knew exercised "much influence."[81]

Indian women could also wield considerable economic clout. Madame Madeline LaFramboise, for example, was a Métis who took over her husband's fur-trading business after he was killed by a drunken Indian. She spent winters in Michigan's interior and returned in the spring with "her furs" to her home on Mackinac Island, which she had left in the care of her servants, according to Elizabeth Thérèse Baird, one of her neighbors. The daughter of a powerful Ottawa chief, Madame LaFramboise was a "graceful and refined Person," who spoke French with a "diction that was as pure as that of a Parisian." During the early nineteenth century, "there was . . . no better fur trader than she."[82]

Indian men also seemed to possess greater freedom than white men did. One winter, a male homosexual named Ozaw-wen-dib, who was the son of a chief, came to stay at Tanner's lodge. Ozaw-wen-dib "was one of those who make themselves women." He "had lived with many husbands" and "was very expert in the various employments of women." Looking for a new mate, he eventually married an Indian man with two female wives. Their marriage "was attended with less uneasiness and quarreling" than if the new wife had been female. The Indians called these homosexual men A-go-kwa. A number of these individuals lived among "most, if not all . . . tribes." Tanner was not a berdache, but his tale suggests that he remained

Indian partly because he preferred to live in a culture in which men and women possessed greater freedom to experiment with their sexuality.[83]

Although no evidence indicates that other whites knew of these openly homosexual practices, it seems likely that at least a number of them did. If so, many would have regarded such practices as abhorrent, seeing the approval of sexual deviation not only as unmanning and feminizing Indian men, but also as further proof that Indians lived without even the most rudimentary boundaries needed to prohibit blasphemous behavior and maintain a civilized society. It also seems probable that many whites would have condemned the Indians' acceptance of strong-willed women exemplified by Tanner's adoptive mother; such behavior blurred the gender boundaries needed to distinguish men from women.

To discourage such conduct, fictional captivity narratives sought to strengthen boundaries that defined gender roles and separated Indians from whites. These tales, however, were not simple exercises in propaganda. Rather, they reveal a complex tension between the desire to become Indian and the wish to remain white. The stories begin by celebrating hybridization, portraying Indians, especially Native American mothers, in warm sympathetic terms. In doing so, however, they remapped boundaries, placing Indians in traditional Anglo-American gender roles and erasing some of indigenous culture's most distinctive features. By the story's end, moreover, the protagonists realized the impossibility of shedding their white identity and permanently erasing the boundary between civilization and savagery.

The stories also demonstrated that women also were tempted by boundary crossing. In one narrative, set in early New England, Indians captured Martha Walton shortly after her marriage to George Montague. He eventually rescued Martha, just before her Indian captor stabbed her. In this case, the tale presented Indianization as violating the boundaries that protected marriage, the family, and white womanhood. Martha's flirtation with her captor and savagery threatened to prevent the consummation of her relationship with George; the Indian's attempt to stab Martha represented the sexual undercurrents at work in these tales. Only by saving Martha from the Indian, who represented her darker, wilder impulses, could George preserve her purity and restore the border between savagery and civilization.[84]

Rescuing captives became more difficult when whites became Indian. No white hero appeared to save these individuals. Instead, they returned to the settlements because of a growing awareness of their true identity. Such decisions were difficult, because these tales often portrayed at least some Indians sympathetically. One such tale, set in the late eighteenth century, described how Indians abducted William Moore, a member of Rogers Rangers. He was saved from torture and certain death by an old woman, who adopted him. After living with her for six years and becoming Indian, he began to miss his friends. Realizing that he could not shed his white identity, he escaped to the Anglo-American settlements.[85]

A young Florida woman reached a similar conclusion in an 1839 narrative. After getting lost in the woods and being seized by Indians, she was "treated with much barbarity." But the chief's son "became enamored with her beauty and . . . on account of his influence she met with kindness and respect." Although she was "initiated into the manners and customs of the Indians," she hankered for "civilization" and "her friends." This yearning became more pronounced after she learned that she soon would be compelled to marry the chief's son, suggesting that sexual fears played an important role in her decision to escape. Although the heroine missed her friends, she decided to return to the settlements because of the threat posed by interracial marriage. Such a union symbolized the ultimate boundary violation, both racial and sexual, and highlighted the importance of family in preserving racial purity. On one hand, interracial marriage endangered the purity of white womanhood. On the other, the prospect of producing mixed-race children represented the erasure of racial identity.[86]

Notions of racial identity also framed the structure of *Edward Wilton, Or, Early Days in Michigan* (1851), a novel set on the eve of the War of 1812 that initially ran in serial form in the *Detroit Tribune*. Captured by the Potawatomi as a boy, the hero initially enjoyed a happy life with the Indians, gradually losing all "knowledge of his home and kindred." Aiding this process was the "unvarying kindness" of his captors, who helped Edward to acquire their "habits and manners."[87] But the Indians could not eradicate all of Edward's white traits. Unlike Indians, Edward displayed features linked to the culture of sensibility, demonstrating the ability to display emotion and feel compassion for others. Unlike his "dark-skinned" companions, Edward had been unable to "smother every demonstration of natural feeling," or to conceal "each thought of his mind with that deep cunning which seems innate in the heart of an Indian." He also possessed "an instinctive chivalry" and would aid his mother "in her more severe labors." Consequently, his relationship with her was "more like that between a white mother and her son, than the relation as it usually exists in the Indian Lodge."[88]

Edward's white attributes grew stronger after he met a Frenchman and a British officer, bent on inciting the Potawatomi to war against America. "The memory of whites had long faded." But after seeing a "pale face," he remembered his childhood home. Edward's growing awareness of his white roots was linked to national as well as racial borders. As if by magic, Edward realized that he was not simply white, but also American, and decided to leave his Indian captors after his adopted father, Sagito, decided

to take up arms against America in the War of 1812. In explaining his decision to Sagito, Edward combined notions of race and nationalism, stating
that he would not "lift the tomahawk" against members of his own "race."
Instead, he would return to his "white father and stand by the side of his
white brothers in battle." Remaining Indian would be treasonous, as well
as fratricidal; it would force Edward to destroy his "white brothers."[89]

Upon returning to the Anglo-American settlements, Edward found that
white ways meshed "far more with his own than the silence and reserve
of the Indian warrior."[90] After a sentimental reunion with his family, Edward resumed his Yankee identity. Like other captivity narratives, *Edward
Wilton* began by celebrating the hybridization but then undermined it by
demonstrating the need for boundaries between Indians and whites. By
contrasting white and Indian ways, the tales reinforced racial boundaries.
Even after being raised by Indians, captives discovered their true identity,
which was biologically determined and which no amount of socialization
could erase; Edward's Indian persona turns out to be a false face. Such
white traits as his "buoyancy and vivacity" could be only temporarily sup-
pressed, as if culture were powerless in the contest with biology. The tales
thus chronicle the triumph of the white race and its ability to overcome
even the most resistant Indian acculturation.

Scholars have observed that in colonial New England such tales often
served to demonstrate the triumph of Christianity over the dark forces
of Satan, with the white captives representing godliness, and the Indians
symbolizing the forces of the Antichrist. In antebellum Michigan, these al-
legories became secular, concerned more with the threat of hybridization
than with the decline of piety. Captivity stood for the possibility of settlers
on the frontier abandoning civilization and appropriating the ways of a
savage culture. To illustrate how tempting such a choice could be, authors
often portrayed the Indians sympathetically. But just as Christianity triumphed over paganism in colonial-era narratives, so civilization and the
white race usually triumphed over barbarism in these early-nineteenth-
century tales. Despite the attractiveness of Indian ways, captives eventually returned to civilization and reclaimed their white identities.[91]

Tanner's autobiography, however, suggests that disentangling Indian
and white identities was far more difficult than these fictional tales assumed. After his years in captivity, Tanner adopted a persona that was
neither totally Indian nor completely white, never feeling entirely at
home in either culture. He could not become fully Indian, because some
Indians refused to accept him as one of them. One warrior named Waw-
bebe-nais-sa accused Tanner of being an outsider, even after he had spent
many years living as an Indian. "'You are a stranger,' said he 'and have
no right among us.'"[92]

Tanner experienced similar problems when he tried to return to white society. Upon repatriation to Kentucky, he discovered that he was not "content" among his friends and went back to Indian country to work as an interpreter.[93] Unlike the heroes of fictive captivity narratives, Tanner was unable to reclaim his old white identity, because it had disappeared during his years as an Indian. In the end, Tanner was neither white nor Indian, but a combination of the two cultures; as an interpreter he embodied two languages and two cultures.

Several of Tanner's contemporaries viewed him in just this way. Schoolcraft, who knew Tanner when the former captive worked as an interpreter on Mackinac Island, believed that Tanner was a man caught between two worlds and at home in neither. Having "lost every virtue of the white man, and acquired every vice of the Indian," Tanner's "habits were . . . so inveterately savage that he could not tolerate civilization." Try as he might, Tanner could not adjust to white society. He was a "singular being—out of humor with the world, speaking ill of everybody, suspicious of every human action, a very savage in his feeling . . . and philosophy of life." Nor did Tanner express affection for or a desire to return to his Native captors, viewing indigenous culture as a "perfect hell" and Indians as "thieves and murderers."[94] Elizabeth Baird, who also knew Tanner during his residence on Mackinac Island, confirmed Schoolcraft's assessment, reporting that Tanner was "cruel" and lived the "life of a heathen." He was "worse than an Indian," because he combined the faults of . . . two races."[95]

Tanner thus serves as a symbol of Michigan's frontier culture. Like Tanner, Michigan settlers were unable to create boundaries that separated Indian and Anglo-American cultures. Rather than reestablishing the traditional Yankee borders, they developed new norms that were more traditional than those of the French, but more Indianized than those in the East.

Indeed, memoirs, newspapers, and fiction from the period provide evidence of these new hybridized, western boundaries. Michiganians, as Calvin J. Thorpe recalled, in "close and constant contact with the aborigine, easily and usually gravitated toward his peculiar ways, many of which were best adapted to frontier life." In his view, some of these adaptations were relatively minor. The Indians, for example, had "a simple, original method of curing meat." His father grew so fond of this process that it at times supplanted "the usual domestic mode of cookery."[96]

But in other cases, Indian influence was more pronounced and threatening, resulting in infidelity, idleness, and sin. The Reverend H. C. Baldwin, who worked as a Presbyterian missionary in Saginaw in 1846 and 1847, voiced alarm at the effects that boundary crossing was having on both Indians and whites. "The whites have depraved the Indians by intemperance," and the "Indians, by vile commerce, have depraved the Whites."

Consequently, many Anglo-Americans in Saginaw engaged in "profanity, Sabbath-breaking" and great "looseness of morals."[97]

But religion and morality were not the only elements of Yankee culture that hybridization influenced. Language—that great carrier of culture—was also altered when some settlers learned to speak the Indian's language. In Pokagon's *Queen of the Woods,* the narrator described running into an Indian boy and his Anglo-American companion. Pokagon discovered not only that the white boy had taught his Indian friend to speak English, but that the Indian child had taught his white companion to speak Algonquian. When asked to say whether the white boy had taught him to speak English, Nonnee responded, "'Me guess meby he be; and me learn him to talk like Injun.'"[98]

Similarly, a settler named Jane M. Kinney reported that her mother could speak Algonquian fluently. When Indians stopped into their home, Kinney's mother could "converse with them in their native tongue," because Kinney's grandfather had been a merchant who often did business with Indians. "Once when some Indians came to our home and my mother had a bed prepared for them in a chamber she amused them by telling them, in Indian language, that they might go up to heaven instead of bed."[99]

Evidence of whites absorbing or adopting Indian ways also appears in Caroline Kirkland's work. Kirkland, a New Yorker of refined manners who wrote about her experiences on the Michigan frontier, reflected the concern with which Michigan's elite viewed hybridization. In a sketch set in the 1840s about "Idle People," she described a group of settlers who eschewed hard work and lived more like Indians than white men. In part, Kirkland held the West responsible for this transformation. The fertility of the region was pictured in typically female terms as a temptress who could seduce men into indolence and savagery. Because the bounteous West presented a "thousand temptations to idleness,"[100] many men preferred to "snatch a precarious subsistence from the lap of Nature, instead of paying the price which she ever demands for a due and full enjoyment of her bounties."[101] Rather than farm, they fished, picked wild fruit and berries, or chased bees in search of honey and hunted for deer.

Living in this way transformed civilized men into savages. "To be content with what supplies the wants of the body for the present moment, is, after all, the characteristic rather of the brute than of the man." Kirkland concluded the sketch by contrasting the behavior of the more respectable members of the community with these idlers. Interestingly, the savage seemed unmanly when contrasted to more respectable white men, because he lacked two key masculine traits—industriousness and discipline. "Our better farmers, though they may see deer tracks in every direction round the scene of their daily rail-splitting, seldom hunt." They knew that it was "cheaper to buy venison of the Indians." But "now that the Indians are all gone, there are white Indians enough—white skins with Indian tastes and habits under them—to make hunting a business of questionable respectability." A new group of white savages thus had replaced the Indians and with them shattered the borders that separated the civilized from the savage. In taking on Indian traits, these white settlers threatened to undermine the order based on industry and discipline that Yankees sought to establish in the West.[102]

Nor did Indians escape from this syncretic regional culture. Indeed, Pokagon's *Queen of the Woods* traces the narrator Simon's futile attempt to recover an indigenous world unsullied by white ways. Like Tanner, Simon straddles the boundary between Anglo and Indian culture. An assimilated Indian, he was educated in white schools, but he longed to return to his ancestors' ways. That desire is expressed in his love for Lonidaw, the queen of the novel's title, whom he encountered on a hunting trip in Michigan's Indian country. More a mythical than a realistic figure, she symbolizes both the essence of Potawatomi culture and Pokagon's hope for its resurgence.[103]

Unlike Simon, Lonidaw is not influenced by Anglo-American culture. She speaks only Algonquian, has little or no contact with whites, and is contented living with her "mother" and her "people."[104] Born in the forest after her mother escaped from U.S. troops seeking to expel her people from Michigan, Lonidaw describes herself as a "wild child of the woods." Animals, especially birds, often symbols of transcendence, love the queen. "I have seen assemble at her alluring call," reports one Indian character, "flocks of me-zhe-say-wog (turkeys), pe-na-wog (partridges), she-shep-og (ducks), and all kinds of singing be-nesh-i (birds)." Additionally, Lonidaw was an expert with a bow and arrow and could make whatever she desired from "flags, rushes, sweetgrass, birch bark, and porcupine quills."[105]

Simon's marriage to Lonidaw represented his effort to shed his hybrid identity and recapture the purity of the past. Shortly after Simon and the queen wed, a sacred white deer, who jealously protected Lonidaw and the ancient ways that she symbolized, vanished. His disappearance foreshadowed the novel's conclusion—the alcohol-related deaths of Lonidaw and the two children that she and Simon produced. These deaths demonstrate that just as Tanner was unable to recover his old white persona, Simon was incapable of recapturing the pure Indian identity that he hoped to achieve by marrying Lonidaw. Instead, the opposite occurred: after marrying Simon, Lonidaw was contaminated by his hybrid identity, symbolized by alcohol, and the purity that she represented was destroyed. Even the novel's text, which combines English and Algonquian, suggests the hybrid nature of the narrator and of Michigan's frontier culture. Neither Yankees nor Indians thus succeeded in creating boundaries that prevented hybridization.

New Englanders began creating such borders after migrating to Michigan in the late 1810s and early 1820s. These restraints aimed to solve two problems: first, to end or at least reduce the violence, crime, and drunkenness associated with Indians; second, to protect the purity of Anglo culture by discouraging Yankee settlers from adopting Indians customs, values, and beliefs. Yankees were much more successful in solving the first problem than the second. After the War of 1812, settlers complained bitterly about Indian drinking, crime, violence, and indolence. Such behavior threatened to undermine Anglo efforts to create the orderly, stable, and godly communities that they had left in the East. Believing that much of the disorder associated with Indians stemmed from drunkenness, federal and local officials enacted a series of laws to prevent indigenous people from obtaining alcohol. The laws were largely ineffective, because it was nearly impossible to police the traders and backwoods men who sold alcohol to Indians. Strict enforcement of the laws also threatened to hurt the fur trade, which was an important element of Michigan's economy.

During this period, federal and local officials came up with a more effective method of taming Indian wildness. They negotiated a series of treaties in which Michigan tribes sold their land and agreed either to live on reservations or to move to new homes in Kansas. Settlers who favored the former policy argued that reservations established boundaries that protected Indians from the wildness and savagery of the forest and the corrupting influence of cities. In this protected environment, missionaries would find it easier to imbue Indians with Yankee values and beliefs. Critics of the program charged that Indian savagery was innate and insisted that no amount of education could erase it. They advocated removing Indians from Michigan. Eventually, Michigan adopted both strategies and succeeded in reducing Indian crime and violence.

These policies, however, failed to stop Anglo settlers from adopting Indian practices, values, and beliefs. Yankees began establishing cultural borders to solve this problem, periodically running captivity narratives in Michigan newspapers. On the surface, the narratives were simply adventure stories filled with melodrama, excitement, and suspense. On a deeper level, though, the stories served as parables that warned Anglo settlers about the dangers of boundary crossing and hybridization. They often began with protagonists becoming Indians before realizing the impossibility of shedding their white identity and returning to the Anglo settlements and resuming their white personas. Simon Pokagon's *Queen of the Woods* suggested that Native people also struggled to escape from the confusion of hybridization and to return to the purity and certainty of ancient ways.

Neither Indians nor whites succeeded in this endeavor. Evidence of this failure can be found in the captivity narratives, which allegorize the hybridization of identity that occurred on the frontier. The stories begin with Indians traversing Anglo boundaries, invading white communities, kidnapping young settlers, and symbolically injecting Indian ways into Yankee settlements. The Indians then perform a second act of hybridization when they bring Anglo settlers and Yankee culture into their own communities. Finally, the white captives traverse boundaries yet again, escaping from their Native families and bringing Indian ways back into the Anglo settlements. The stories thus reveal how Indians and Anglos continued to exchange customs, values, and beliefs, despite the best efforts of their leaders to prevent such cultural mixing. In the end, therefore, Yankee efforts to maintain the purity of their traditional culture were only partially successful. Michigan culture in the 1830s and 1840s contained fewer Indian elements than it had while under French rule. But Michigan seems to have been far more Indianized than New England.

Civilizing White Settlers

Antebellum Reform in

Early Michigan

In 1838, the *Detroit Daily Advertiser*, one of Detroit's main Whig newspapers, expressed great concern about the "progress of open licentiousness among us." Prostitution of late, the editors complained, had "fearfully increased" and "assumed so bold and unblushing a character as to cause the moralist to shudder." Detroit's "fair fame" had been "tarnished by nightly outbreaks of the most disorderly and riotous nature." Residents' "fears . . . were excited by the repeated discharge of pistols and guns and by other foul proceedings." The source of these riots had been "several females of abandoned character."[1]

Like the *Advertiser*, many settlers expressed alarm at what they viewed as the prevalence of prostitution, drinking, and other forms of vice in early Michigan. They loudly condemned the alleged barbarism of white settlers, many of whom seemed to behave almost as wildly as Indians did. Frontiersmen, Yankees complained, disobeyed the norms of genteel society, drinking heavily, refusing to attend church, violating the Sabbath, gambling, and engaging in rebellious, criminal, and sexually promiscuous conduct. This behavior, they believed, not only endangered the safety and norms that ensured a stable and peaceful society but also threatened to undermine efforts to establish a durable republic, which required a virtuous citizenry. To guarantee the existence of this polity, reformers initiated a campaign to tame Michigan's unruly white populace and clean up a society that was wallowing in vice.

This view of Michiganians as immoral and barbaric was not entirely accurate. Reformers undoubtedly exaggerated the sinfulness of Michiganians and painted a very dark portrait of the frontier to emphasize the need for change. Reformers also viewed early Michiganians exceptionally because of their eastern upbringing: natives of western New York and New England, they were deeply committed to evangelical Christianity and influenced by religious revivals and reform movements that swept across the nation in the second quarter of the nineteenth century. The latter stemmed from the changing nature of Christianity. Calvinists, who once had seen worshipers as powerless, now believed that individuals held the key to their own salvation. They could perfect not only themselves, but also the society in which they lived, thereby preparing the nation for the millennium and Christ's return. The faithful, therefore, had a duty to Christianize America, cleansing it of drunkenness and gambling, as well as other sins.[2]

To achieve these goals in Michigan, reformers employed two strategies: first, they enacted laws during the second quarter of the nineteenth century to make Michigan more righteous and God-fearing. These statutes sought to reduce or eradicate drinking, idleness, and other types of wickedness. Second, reformers relied on education and print culture to improve family governance. This effort to create more orderly households stemmed from their belief that vice stemmed from the inability of fathers to control their dependents: on one hand, they charged, drunkenness was undermining the ability of men to control their charges, transforming fathers into either abusive tyrants or ineffectual idlers who could barely earn a living and tend to their dependents. On the other hand, reformers asserted, men often became drunkards because their parents had been unable or unwilling to discipline them as children. Both abusive, tyrannical fathers as well as ineffectual, passive ones created a sinful society.

This problem was not confined to the frontier. But its effects, Yankee settlers believed, were more pronounced in the West, because the frontier lacked the legal and social restraints of more established Eastern communities. In both Michigan and the East, reformers, steeped in Yankee culture, battled what they saw as sin and immorality. But while vice in the East seems to have evoked class consciousness and conflict, it possessed more racial overtones on the frontier, becoming inextricably linked to Indians and other nonwhite races.[3] Whites who drank, gambled, and indulged in other forms of vice were condemned because, like Indians and blacks, they lacked a key masculine trait; they were unable to control their impulses.

HOW REFORMERS VIEWED THE FRONTIER

Reformers who criticized this behavior included shopkeepers and artisans as well as lawyers, ministers, and other members of the elite. But many of its early members, particularly its leadership, occupied the top rungs of society. Between 1829 and 1834, roughly 64 percent of temperance reformers in Washtenaw County, Michigan, a hotbed of reform, consisted of professionals. Many were deeply religious and belonged to one of Michigan's evangelical churches and to the Whig Party. Typical of these early Washtenaw County leaders was Samuel W. Dexter. A Boston native, Dexter was born in 1792 and graduated from Harvard University before moving to northern New York and then Michigan in 1824. In addition to creating the *Western Emigrant,* the territory's first Anti-Masonic newspaper, in Ann Arbor, Dexter was named the chief justice of the Washtenaw County Court in 1826 and ran unsuccessfully five years later to become Michigan's nonvoting delegate to Congress. A tireless worker for reform, Dexter not only organized temperance meetings, but also helped drunkards and their families.[4]

The rowdiness and rudeness of the frontier appalled Dexter and his fellow Yankees. Mary Clavers, who narrates Caroline Kirkland's *A New Home: Who'll Follow?* an autobiographical novel that is set in early Michigan, frequently complains about the boorishness of her fellow settlers. Mrs. Jennings, one of Clavers's neighbors, drank from the "spout of the tea-pot, saying 'it tasted better so.'" Jennings was "equally imperious in the matter of dipping with her own spoon or knife into every dish on the table." Even more distasteful was Jennings's habit of helping herself to ham. She would grasp the hock and cut off "mouthfuls with her knife, declining all aid from the carver, and saying coolly that she made out very well."[5]

Such behavior also shocked the editors of the *Detroit Gazette,* who periodically published advice columns on etiquette. One ironic article satirized the vulgarity of Michiganians' eating habits: the author recommended that readers place their "elbows on the table like a church warden in a Parish vestry" and urged them to "hang over" their plates with their bodies "so bent that half" of the "meat, gravy" and other items that they consumed "may return again to the plate" from which they had been eating. Nor should they take time to cut their "meat into small pieces," but instead "take good substantial mouthfuls" and make their "cheeks stick out like full-blown bladders."[6]

But rudeness was not the only problem that disturbed Yankees. A greater concern was the alleged rebelliousness and rowdiness of idle young people, who seemed to enjoy nothing better than congregating in Detroit's streets and making mischief. A *Detroit Gazette* correspondent complained in 1819, the year of cataclysmic depression, that "for some Sundays past" there had been "an unusual commotion and noise in different parts of the city." He blamed much of this tumult on "idle persons" who gathered "in groups" and spoke loudly. Often, they called "aloud to one another from different corners of the street, greatly to the annoyance of the neighborhood."[7] A

Journal correspondent echoed these sentiments in 1835, protesting the "frequent recurrence of noisy and riotous proceeding in our streets at night." Barely an evening passed in which the "peace and quiet of our citizens is not destroyed by a gang of noisy desperadoes."[8]

This defiance of adult authority also is evident in *Shoepac Recollections: A Way-Side Glimpse of American Life,* a novel situated in Detroit during the 1820s and 1830s, which makes clear that such behavior was often associated with the wildness of nonwhite races. Early in the novel, the narrator described how a mulatto led his fellow schoolboys in a revolt against their new teacher. Earlier, school authorities had been unable to control their young charges and appointed a strict new instructor, euphemistically named "Merciful Thrasher," to discipline the students: "His first step was to thrash the largest youth." Led by the mulatto, Dick, the boys plotted their revenge and sneaked into the school at night to get rid of the birches that Thrasher had used to flog them. When they discovered Mr. Thrasher waiting for them in the darkened schoolhouse, they did not defer to his authority; instead, they wrestled the master to the ground and made him promise never to flog them again. "Gentlemen," said the teacher, "I have taught school in many places. This is my first defeat." The next morning, he left town. The author employed legal tropes to describe the new schoolmaster: he was the "chancellor of the rod" who soon began to lay down the law. This suggested that "Merciful Thrasher" represented not just attempts to quiet mischievous schoolboys, but also efforts to establish a peaceful and stable polity.[9] The analogy further implied that these projects were frustrated by the nefarious influence of both nonwhite races and rowdy white settlers who came to be identified with them.

This rowdiness, however, paled in comparison to the threat that the profusion of crime posed to order and stability. In 1818, a *Detroit Gazette* correspondent observed that despite efforts to improve education, crimes were "multiplying and the vigilance of officers of justice are almost constantly defeated." Detroiters complained incessantly about counterfeiting: in 1818, to give one example, the *Detroit Gazette* reported that the city was "at times infested with a gang of fellows who deal, while the trade is good, in bad money." Persons "not otherwise employed" had "obtained a plate from Canada" and were using it to counterfeit "thousands of five and ten dollar notes."[10] A few months later, the same newspaper warned Detroiters to watch out for another "gang of villains" that was passing off "a considerable number of 50 cent bills in imitation of those issued by Rev. Gabriel Richard," a priest and one of Detroit's most prominent citizens. "With sorrow and displeasure," Richard noted, "many small notes" had been counterfeited, and "several of his neighbors had suffered by receiving them." He estimated that "more than 200 fifty cent bills have been within the past fortnight put in circulation in this city; and it has been intimated to me that many more" would soon appear.[11]

Robbers also victimized Detroiters, breaking into their homes and stealing cherished items. If criminals failed to earn enough as counterfeiters, wrote a *Gazette* correspondent in 1818, they had "recourse to the more desperate but no less honorable means of plundering the inhabitants during the silent watches of the night." Recently, they had committed their crimes "in such close succession and so daring a manner" that it would require the "most spirited efforts of civil authority to arrest the progress of this alarming evil."[12] In 1818, for instance, one Detroit family was "plundered of money" by a housebreaker who accomplished his goal by "tearing off a clapboard and making his way through" the plaster. Local officials warned "merchants, innkeepers and others . . . to keep a strict lookout for the villain."[13]

DRUNKENNESS, IMPIETY, AND SEXUAL PROMISCUITY

Reformers also expressed alarm about drunkenness, impiety, and sexual promiscuity. They attributed this conduct in part to the nature of Detroit's population. During the late 1810s and early 1820s, Detroit consisted mostly of young men. In 1819, men outnumbered women by 596 to 444 and constituted nearly 60 percent of Detroit's populace. These men were largely between sixteen and twenty-six years of age.[14] Not surprisingly, reformers often depicted drunkards, gamblers, and the impious as young men who, like Indians, were unable to control their boyish impulses. Women, on the other hand, usually were associated with prostitution and other sexual vices.

In 1836, Presbyterians condemned what they viewed as the sexual promiscuity of Michigan women. The committee that governed the area's churches urged ministers to "preach on this subject with a view to enforcing the obligations of the SEVENTH COMMANDMENT," which forbade adultery and other forms of sexual license. "Moral purity can never be maintained triumphantly among either sex, but through the instrumentality of VIRTUOUS AND CHRISTIAN FEMALES." Women had to "withdraw all countenance and society from men whose characters are liable even to reasonable suspicion." The committee urged Presbyterian churches to "adopt all suitable and efficient measures for the suppression of licentiousness" and parishioners to make this subject "one of earnest and frequent prayer."[15]

Sexual promiscuity, however, was not the only sin that Michigan women committed. Caroline Kirkland's autobiographical novel, *A New Home: Who'll Follow?* documents how Michigan women violated genteel codes of conduct. In the fictional village of Montacute, women smoked tobacco and consumed snuff. In one incident, Kirkland recalled that while speaking with the village schoolteacher, the "sallow damsel arose from her seat, took a short pipe from her bosom . . . filled it with tobacco, which she carried in her 'work-pocket.'" She then reseated herself, and began to "smoke with the greatest gusto, turning ever and anon to spit at the hearth." Such masculine behavior was common in the territory, Kirkland reported. "I can vouch for it, that a large proportion of the married women in the interior of Michigan use tobacco in some form, usually that of the odious pipe."[16]

Kirkland's fictional alter ego, Mary Clavers, discovered a similar defiance of genteel conventions when she looked for a maid. After asking one of her neighbors how she might find a domestic, the woman "smiled rather scornfully," explaining that not many girls in the village "wanted to live out a long time." Later, Kirkland discovered this for herself. She had "since that day seen many a wretched dwelling, with almost literally nothing in it but a bed, a chest, and a table; children ragged to the last degree and potatoes the only fare." No daughter in such homes, however, would work for long as a maid. She might take such work in an emergency, "but never as a regular calling, or with an acknowledgment of inferior station."[17]

In addition to such rebelliousness, reformers condemned impiety as a potential source of social disorder. Many settlers seemed to have to let their Christianity lapse after moving west. In 1890, Mrs. S. M. Williams recited a poem at the semicentennial anniversary of the Baptist Church in Portland, Michigan, that recalled the lack of piety in the frontier era. In her view, pioneers failed to observe the Sabbath and demonstrated little, if any, devotion to God.

> No church bell sounded out the hour,
> 'Of all the week the best,'
> And some amid the toils of life
> Forgot the day of rest.
>
> And did these sons of Christian sires,
> Like Israel's sons of old,
> Forget like them, their father's God
> Of whom they had been told?[18]

Similarly, Rev. Ira Mason Weed, a Vermont native who moved to Michigan in 1830, found that Michiganians had little interest in religion. While living in Ogdensburg, New York, Weed had relinquished his legal studies to become a minister, after being swept up in the fervor of the Second Great Awakening. In Ypsilanti, Michigan, where he ministered to the town's First Presbyterian Church, he discovered that the "number of professing Christians" was "small indeed," recalled Mrs. Mark Norris, one of his contemporaries. Some Ypsilanti residents even "rebelled against" Reverend Weed's authority, hoping to prevent the "light of the gospel" from shining on their heathen ways. Consequently, Weed sometimes preached as "stones were thrown . . . at the windows" of the school, in which the congregation then worshiped. Settlers, moreover, threatened Reverend Weed with "rough treatment" when he rode at night to an "outlying neighborhood."[19]

Baptist missionaries, too, were shocked by the irreverence of Michiganians. Several complained that Michigan inhabitants were unreceptive to their pleas. Deacon Squire Manro discovered "great moral darkness" in Michigan and a society "very much needing the labor of missionaries."[20] In St. Joseph, the Reverend Thomas Ward Merrill reported that "the first emigrants" in western Michigan were "devoted supremely to gain" and were "a disorganized and irreligious population."[21] Judge Caleb Eldred also encountered resistance as he struggled to establish religion on the frontier. Alarmed by "the moral waste" that pervaded early Kalamazoo, he insisted that the righteous would need to work hard "to combat" sin and "expose error."[22] Similarly, the Reverend William Bronson reported that his missionary efforts in Dexter were "met with much opposition from the enemies of the Cross."[23]

Caroline Kirkland also found that Michiganians lacked piety. Ministers from several denominations visited the fictional village of Montacute, the author reported. Though many of the townsfolk made a "point of being present," a "far greater proportion reserve the Sunday for fishing and gunning." To make matters worse, the village lacked a church, and services were held in a "little log school-house," which consisted of a "bare cold room" with "seats formed by laying rough boards on rougher blocks, and the whole covered thick with the week's dirt of the district school."[24]

Just as alarming as the absence of religion was the pervasiveness of drink in Michigan. Reformers were shocked not only by how many Michiganians drank, but also by the amount of liquor each of them consumed. One group of reformers relied on the imagery of a "raging" inferno to highlight the utter destructiveness of drink, observing that "intemperance" was sweeping through Michigan's towns and villages "like fires upon our prairies."[25] The territory's Indian agent, Henry R. Schoolcraft, agreed. In 1836, Schoolcraft reported that Detroit "abounds" in taverns. Describing these grog-shops as "misery-making, poverty-begetting establishments," he lamented that "our whole city is but one neighborhood of them."[26] Others shared Schoolcraft's outrage. "When I began my labors here, intemperance was a vice exceedingly common, and prevalent among all classes," recalled the Reverend Abel Bingham, a missionary from Sault St.

Marie, in 1852. The army doled out "a gill of whiskey a day to the enlisted men." Worse, soldiers could "purchase another gill" at a nearby "store, and few if any failed of taking their full allowance."[27]

In 1891, the Reverend R. C. Crawford recalled that before the days of temperance reform, "there had never been a building raised in the township of Troy, and I presume not in Oakland County, if there had in Michigan," where settlers did not drink "whiskey."[28] Jesse Turner, a settler from Kalamazoo, named the malady directly: Michigan settlers were a "wild set." At one party, the liquor "was tried pretty thoroughly" and "after an hour or two 'twas solemnly concluded the whiskey wasn't strong enough . . . so one of the boy's boots was pulled off and the whiskey cooked in that."[29] Another writer remembered that "the use of ardent spirits as a beverage was universal" in early Michigan.[30]

Alcoholism and other forms of immorality horrified reformers in part because they were closely identified in Michigan with the indolence and violence of Indians and other nonwhites. White men who drank and gambled not only fraternized with Indians and blacks but also seemed to take on their worst traits—in the case of Indians, drinking; and with blacks, gambling.

The association between blacks and gaming was articulated in an 1819 article that a *Detroit Gazette* correspondent euphemistically named "Hovering Spirit." He described a house in the city in which two white men sat "at a card table" with "two black men." Each of the four "had staked all of the money he was worth." The blacks supposedly played cards because they were too lazy to learn to read; the whites behaved just like them. Before long, their master interrupted them. "'You scoundrels,' said he, 'how dare you play cards? How much better if you were at night school.'" One of the blacks replied that it was "hard to read."[31]

Not surprisingly, Indians became a symbol of drunkenness. In Michigan, liquor had long been a key item of exchange in the fur trade, and local tribes were famous for consuming prodigious amounts of it. Images of Indians and drunkenness, therefore, merged inextricably. The drunken Indian became a metonym of the wildness that undermined Yankee reformers' notions of masculinity. On one hand, they condemned liquor for transforming Indians into idle, passive creatures who never sought to improve themselves but instead were content to live off the land like wild animals. On the other hand, they observed that alcohol could have the opposite effect, turning drinkers into violently aggressive savages who inflicted great harm on their neighbors.[32]

Reformers attributed such barbarism to the inchoate nature of frontier society, which lacked the order and stability of more settled communities. Wrote a *Pontiac Courier* journalist in 1836, Michigan was "in the embryo of its existence" and therefore lacked the laws and well-established social norms that checked wildness in older communities. "The influence of legislative authority and the restraints of social order can scarcely be said, as yet to be recognized among us," said one group of temperance crusaders. "Our soil is yet unsubdued; our habits unformed; and our manners unassimilated."[33]

The absence of virtue, civility, and stability threatened to undermine efforts to establish a republic. Without a virtuous citizenry, such polities would fail, many early Americans believed. Several Michigan leaders echoed these classical republican ideas: citizens in a republic had to be willing to sacrifice their own private interests to the common good when the two were in conflict.[34] Otherwise, demagogues could use money and other inducements to persuade the people to relinquish their liberty. "No republican government, however excellent in its form, can long exist without intelligence and virtue in the people," insisted A. G. Whitney in a July 4, 1818, address. "This position is warranted by the recorded experience of four thousand years." The people "must have virtue to resist corruption themselves, and to elect only those who are free from it to offices of trust—and to enable them to make those sacrifices for the good of their country, which patriotism may demand."[35]

That same year, "Juvenile," a correspondent for the *Detroit Gazette,* emphasized the importance of virtue in both republican officials and ordinary citizens. He noted that Michigan residents would soon gain self-rule. "Like citizens of the States, they will soon elect their own officers, and transact their own public business." Whom would they elect to such offices? They would not entrust such positions "to those young men who have spent their evenings in a Jockey Club or at a card table." Those who guarded a "republic must be virtuous and enlightened men"—that is, individuals "whose habits and private life may safely be imitated by every class of citizens, and as places of distinction are accessible by all ranks so every man should endeavor to qualify himself by virtuous habit and by a cultivated mind."[36]

To create virtuous individuals and prepare for statehood, reformers established local temperance and Bible societies as well as other benevolent associations. These organizations flourished in the 1830s, with reformers establishing nine temperance societies alone.[37] To root out drunkenness and sin, reformers focused on two boundary-setting institutions: the family and the law. Using the latter to reduce alcohol consumption and vice in Michigan was not new. Federal and local officials had enacted statutes in the late eighteenth and early nineteenth centuries to reduce Indian drinking (see chapter 4). Building on that precedent, reformers in the 1830s sought statutes to cut alcohol consumption in Michigan towns either by increasing the cost of licenses needed to sell alcohol or by getting rid of such licenses altogether. They also hoped to reduce alcohol consumption by prohibiting merchants from selling small amounts of liquor. In 1838, reformers even petitioned Michigan's legislature to ban the sale of liquor entirely in Michigan.[38]

But reformers did not rely solely on the law to combat vice. They also sought to strengthen the family, which, they believed, played an equally important role in maintaining order and stability. Critics charged that, in recent years, families had been failing to fulfill this vital function. In sermons, advice columns, and sentimental stories, they attacked men who were unable to govern their households and failed to establish the boundaries needed to control their dependents. Weak fathers, Michigan critics insisted, were responsible for several ills that plagued society: they failed to discipline their wives and children, refused to provide them with paternal support and care, and sometimes were violent and abusive. Whether these problems stemmed from character flaws or were due to alcohol and other vices, these disordered families produced adulterous wives as well as wild and unruly children. Many of these children, in turn, became addicted to vice and threatened the public peace and safety.

At the heart of the problem were men who, like weak and ineffectual kings, were incapable of governing their domains and disciplining their dependents. In 1817, the *Detroit Gazette* published a story about one such husband who was unable to control his cheating wife. In the tale, the adulterous woman "reluctantly" agreed to put the itinerant preacher Lorenzo Dow up for the night. The woman's husband was "absent and not expected that night." After eating and attending the "family worship," Lorenzo went to bed, but was unable to sleep. As he lay awake, he heard the lady's "paramour" enter the house. The lovers sat up a while, conversing together, and then retired to bed. Before long, the husband returned "unexpectedly." The wife hid her lover in "a large barrel" and tossed "some cotton locks . . . over him." After letting her drunken husband into the house, the woman informed him that "the famous Lorenzo Dow was asleep in the next room." The husband then challenged Lorenzo to "raise the Devil." Before Lorenzo complied, he asked the husband to open the door, so that the devil could "escape." He then "set the cotton on fire in the barrel" and "out came the devil amidst the flames and made a rapid retreat through the door."[39]

The flames that engulfed the wife's lover symbolized both sexual passion and the punishment meted out for breaking the Ten Commandments. The fire also represented the potential destructiveness of the wife's infidelity, which threatened to destroy not only the adulterous couple, but also the household. The tale implied, furthermore, that the husband's drunkenness impaired his ability to govern his household effectively and was partly to blame for his wife's adultery. His weakness was symbolized both by his absence from home and his seeming ignorance of his wife's affair. In challenging Dow's ability to raise the devil, the husband failed to realize not only that Satan was dwelling under his own roof, but also that the preacher had the power to cleanse his household of such demonic power. Only the preacher, a symbol of reform and godliness, was able to accomplish what the husband had failed to do, punish the adulterer, and restore patriarchal authority by helping the husband to see his failure.

Other authors satirized some men's inability to control their children, charging that they abdicated one of the main responsibilities of manhood. The *Pontiac Courier* published a sketch in 1836 criticizing a man who let his children run roughshod over him. When the father attempted to visit with a friend, "half-a-dozen boys and girls" disturbed them. The children "pushed into the room and with a boisterous sound of words and laughter confused, and almost drowned our conversation." The father told his children to be quiet, but they ignored him. "He might as well have been silent; for they had been too long acquainted with his irresolute and unsteady government to pay the least attention to what was said." Later, as the father began to tell a story, one of his sons interrupted him. "Father, you don't tell that story right," said the boy. Although the man replied that it was rude of the boy to interrupt him while he was talking, the boy ignored his father and continued speaking. "His father was silent and the son went on with his story" and "the man was tame as a whipped spaniel till it was finished." Finally, the father asked his children to fetch some wood, and when they refused, he wound up getting it himself. Unable to discipline his children, the father permitted them to humiliate and unman him. In this case, the father's weakness as a household head supposedly originated in character flaws. Because of his timidity, he could not stand up to his children. The pathos of the tale derived largely from an unnatural reversal of roles, in which the children assumed positions of authority and the father bowed meekly to their power.[40]

In granting children such power, these weak fathers failed to fulfill one of their main duties as parents, to help safeguard public order by disciplining their dependents. Typically, observers viewed boys as more of a threat to peace and safety than girls and chided parents who failed to establish boundaries to control their sons. The *Detroit Journal* reflected this attitude in 1835 when it castigated permissive parents who allowed their sons to go out at night and create mischief. Keeping the young off the streets at night was a "duty" that many parents seemed "almost entirely to overlook." These parents preferred "to get rid of the noise" their "boys" created so that they might "pursue their avocations in peace." Rather than asking where their children were, they ignored the problem. This neglect of their parental duty had dire consequences: permitting boys to congregate after dark led them to "vices" that "destroy both the body and soul." Not only did these boys use foul language, but they also engaged in "the evil practice of smoking tobacco."[41]

Observers also linked intemperance to this failure of parental authority, insisting that the unwillingness of parents to establish moral boundaries encouraged wildness and immorality in their children. In an address to the Oakland County Temperance Society in 1839, Reverend L. P. Bates testified that he had known "children that were not half so blamable for being drunkards as their parents. I have seen the mere child made a drunkard before he could reason or even knew the contents of the cup." If parents permitted a child to develop "intemperate habits," it was as unrealistic to "expect him to be a man" or a Christian as to "look for figs on the thorn and grapes on the thistle."[42]

Bates then explained how parents could prevent their children from succumbing to vice. Those who wished to "save their children from ruin" should monitor "their early habits." Once parents allowed their children "to set out the down hill course no barrier may stop them, until they arrive at perdition." Parents often failed to understand the danger of granting their children so much freedom, because they had an "exalted opinion of the good sense of their children" and "their ability to counteract any bad habit." This was like permitting "our dwelling to be set on fire, because we have power to extinguish the flames; or, turn some mighty current through our fields, because we have the power to dam its course." By invoking the images of fire and flood, Bates underscored the tremendous danger that children's untrammeled instincts posed to hearth and home. Both symbols likened such drives to forces of nature and their ability to consume that which man created. In addition, the metaphors of fire and flood evoked biblical references and in all likelihood reminded Bates's listeners of the power of God's wrath. Consequently, it was foolish for parents to think that they could permit their children's wickedness to grow unabated and then check it at some later date.[43]

Others reformers relied on the image of fire to symbolize the destructiveness of sexual and other types of passion. A *Detroit Gazette* correspondent in 1819 employed this imagery while criticizing parents for failing to teach their children self-control. "How does my heart grieve within me, when I see parents fanning the spark of passion in earliest youth and furnishing it with fuel to raise it to an unquenchable flame." These parents encouraged "a restless, turbulent disposition" by instilling "pride and ambition" in their children.[44]

Parents who refused to steer their children away from the wrong kind of friend were also targets of reformers' wrath. In 1837, a *Pontiac Courier* correspondent asked, "why it was that so many of our young men" spent so much time in the bowling alley, the barroom and the theater. It was the fault of parents who failed to employ "active and effectual measures to nip in the bud the first wanderings from the path of virtue—because they do not check the first rising inclination to unlawful and pernicious pleasures." Most parents knew that "bad habits" were "much more easily acquired than correct principles and evil companions much more numerous than the virtuous." They ought "to entreat, to demand of their children to associate only with those of irreproachable characters and to exercise the greatest care in forming their habits."[45]

Reformers, however, condemned fathers not only for failing to prevent their children from developing bad habits, but also for abandoning their role as household head. Michigan newspapers periodically condemned men who spent time in saloons and gaming rooms rather than at home caring for their dependents. In 1838, for example, a *Pontiac Courier* correspondent excoriated the man who made "his home but a boarding house, where he may eat and sleep." Rather than tending to his loved ones, he spent his time in "the billiard room" and "the whist party." All the while, he neglected his children, treating them "as necessary evils to be kept out of the way as much as possible." These household heads were usually addicted to alcohol, which could transform them into either violent, angry creatures or weak and passive ones.[46]

In *The Oak Openings, or, The Bee-Hunter,* a novel situated in Michigan on the eve of the War of 1812, James Fenimore Cooper used a character named Gershom Waring to ridicule the latter. Waring, a New England native, became a drunk after migrating to Michigan as a young man with his wife, Dolly, and his sister, Blossom. "With the commencement of his migratory life, Gershom began to 'dissipate' as it has got to be matter of convention to term drinking," spending most of his savings on liquor. "Several years, however, had been consumed by the way, the habits growing worse and the money vanishing, as the family went farther and farther toward the skirts of society." Cooper's use of the word "skirts" perhaps suggests that Gershom became both feminized and marginalized by drinking. Unable to support his family as men were supposed to do, he moved farther into the wilderness and closer to the Indians and other savage creatures.[47]

Indeed, Waring's drunkenness eventually incapacitates him and undermines his masculinity. It prevents him from passing that key nineteenth-century test of manhood—the ability to act decisively and, like any good household head, to protect his dependents in the face of danger. Shortly after the opening of the novel, Gershom had stopped drinking. But during a crisis, when the settlers were fleeing from Indians, the novel's hero, the bee-hunter, learns that Gershom had once again succumbed to alcohol. "The bee-hunter was greatly concerned at this unwelcome intelligence, feeling all its importance far more vividly than either of his companions." By drinking again, Boden realized that Waring became an "incumbrance instead of being an assistant."[48] Drunkenness disables Gershom, transforming him into a feminine figure who cannot protect his family.

Alcohol could also have the opposite effect, transforming men into violent savages who abused their dependents. This brutality was dramatized in stories that appeared in Michigan newspapers during the 1830s and 1840s, dramatizing the ways in which drunken fathers violated the boundaries established by the cult of domesticity: they not only neglected their dependents, but also abused them. Though their details varied, the main features of these melodramas were often the same. A wife and her children waited at home for the man of the family. Because the father had spent all of the family's money on liquor, his dependents were impoverished; their home contained little or no furniture, and the cupboards were bare. The father then returned in a drunken rage and abused his wife and children. These tales sacralized the hearth and demonized fathers. One such story likens the father's entry to an "evil spirit" that "had invaded this Eden of the heart," noting that the "very air was poisoned." The household, which "once was sacred to purity and repose," now was "desecrated," and "misery brooded o'er the scene." In effect, the home was defiled by the public symbol of the household, the father.[49]

Other tales worked variations on this theme, underscoring the neglect and abuse that drunken fathers visited on their loved ones and emphasizing that such conduct was unmanly. In 1830, Ann Arbor's anti-Masonic *Western Emigrant* published a story in which a drunken father refused to return to his home and support his dependents. As he passed by his family's house, his wife raised a window and did "in vain . . . entreat him to spend the night under the roof that had sheltered them many a happy hour." Ignoring her pleas, the drunkard demanded food and "refused to enter" the dwelling. The woman finally acquiesced, giving him bread. With "tears streaming from her eyes, she said take this! Cruel man! Tis all we have!"[50] That same year, the *Emigrant* published a tale that sounded a similar theme, describing a gambler who came home as his wife and children "lay moaning on the couch of sorrow." The father was described as a "monster in a human shape" whose "distorted features and horrid imprecations" would make "a demon tremble." His wife had once been as "dear" as his "own self." But now he treated her as a "menial slave— extorting shrieks and groans and cries from a mother half-starved and bewildered children." In each of these tales, alcohol transformed fathers into uncaring brutes who abandon their duties. Rather than protecting and providing for their dependents, they took food from their mouths. This neglect is especially clear in the second tale: the writer not only condemned the father for violating the precepts of companionate marriage but also compared his cruelty and injustice to that of a slave master.[51]

This critique of irresponsible fathers was part of a Victorian effort to civilize men and integrate them more fully into the feminine cult of domesticity. Reformers sought to convince men to become more actively involved in child rearing and to spend leisure time with their spouses instead of barroom friends. This effort to domesticate men began as early as the 1830s in Michigan, when reformers transformed drunkards into symbols of flawed fatherhood. Their addiction to drink and depravity symbolized the misery and ruin that weak and ineffectual or harsh and abusive fathers brought on their dependents.[52] Authors usually rendered this conduct in fairly explicit sexual imagery. The home was feminized, so the father's entry represented a union. But he was described in violent and shocking language as a sexual predator rather than a loving companion, thereby transforming love into rape. The father's drinking, rage, and spendthrift ways robbed the home of its harmony and defiled it.

To improve family governance and to reduce crime and immorality, reformers turned to education. As early as 1817, a *Detroit Gazette* writer insisted that if Michiganians were better educated, "lawyers, sheriffs and jails would not need to be so large and our lives and property would be more secure." Many of the social ills that "we have suffered we have drawn upon ourselves by neglecting the morals and the religion of the people." If settlers did not "actively and immediately" take steps to improve education, they would "but postpone the hour of destruction."[53]

To accomplish that goal, Michiganians established one of the most forward-looking public school systems in the nation. The roots of that system dated back to the Northwest Ordinance of 1785, which required that a portion of land in each of the region's townships be dedicated to schools. Education in the early nineteenth century, however, was mostly limited to private academies, despite efforts by Michigan's legislature to expand public education in the territory between 1827 and 1833.[54]

The most significant improvement in education occurred in 1835, when delegates to the constitutional convention included an article in the new Constitution that laid the foundation for Michigan's public school system.

Isaac Crary, a Democrat from Marshall, Michigan, was the main architect of that provision. After graduating from public schools in his native Connecticut, and from Trinity College in Hartford, Crary became an attorney before migrating to Michigan in 1833. He modeled Michigan schools on the Prussian system. At its head, a state superintendent of public instruction was responsible for the quality of the state's schools, which stretched from the elementary to the university level.[55]

But reformers did not simply leave teaching in the hands of public schools. They also devoted much of their effort to educating Michiganians, asserting that drunkenness, vice, and immorality were inextricably linked to ignorance and illiteracy. By conquering the latter, they could eradicate the former. They relied primarily on sacred texts as well as religious and vocational instruction to instill such Yankee values as sobriety, industriousness, and self-control in Michiganians.

Laura Haviland, for instance, established a vocational school in Lenawee during the 1830s to instill these Yankee values in poor children. Haviland, a Quaker, was born in Canada in 1808 and moved with her family to western New York seven years later; she immigrated to Michigan with her husband in 1829. After conquering the religious doubts that had plagued her as a child, Haviland became active in reform. Her school sought to inculcate sobriety, industriousness, and other Yankee values by teaching vocational skills to children from the county poorhouse. While Haviland "taught house-work, sewing and knitting," her husband and brother showed the boys how to do farm work. Later, Haviland opened a school to inculcate these norms in African American students.[56]

Similarly, Detroit's Sunday School Association saw instruction as a way not only to teach, but also to instill moral discipline. The school's "main object," wrote a reformer in 1820, was to provide the young "with an understanding of the holy scriptures and to teach them to draw from them those practical precepts which will guide their morals, and elevate their affection to love and fear the great author."[57]

Reformers also viewed charity as a way of educating and curbing the savagery of the poor, insisting that such aid could help them relinquish their addiction to vice. In 1818, members of Detroit's Moral and Humane Society insisted that poverty was a product of sin. They sought to alleviate it by educating and Christianizing the poor. That year, the society announced that many in the city "live in the most distressing poverty."[58] But simply giving money to the poor failed to address the roots of the problem. "The usual method of bestowing charities, without knowing the characters to whom they are given or the use to which they are applied," was often counterproductive. This type of aid "only increases the evil it is intended to remedy, by furnishing the means of intemperance." Because much of "the poverty that prevails is the offspring of immorality," the key to fighting poverty was to suppress "vice."[59]

Reformers relied heavily on print culture to achieve this goal. In newspapers, they published fiction, advice columns, and other vehicles to warn their readers about the dangers of violating genteel norms. Members of the Detroit Bible Society believed that books also could help establish boundaries to curb the immorality and vice of the frontier. In their view, the Bible was a much more effective civilizing agent than was money or other life necessities. By giving Bibles rather than cash to the poor, the society offered a present that was "not wasted in a day." Rather, it remained an "inexhaustible treasure, probably during the life of its possessor" and maybe as "an inheritance to the next generation." The Bible could not be abused, as were "so many other gifts" lavished on the needy. Donating money tempted the poor "to indulgence or vice," but the Bible redeemed its "possessor from those pernicious habits." More importantly, the Good Book helped improve family governance, teaching "parents to provide for their own household" and "children to obey their parents." Consequently, it provided "a relief to the poor and distressed which no bounty of the rich can afford."[60]

But accomplishing these goals initially proved difficult. Reformers complained at first about their lack of resources and the intransigence of settlers who resisted education. The Sunday School Association reported in 1820 that it had achieved only limited success in Detroit and that it was difficult to obtain books on the frontier. Although the association had purchased some texts, it had "been able to procure but few of such as we desired." Additionally, many parents clung to their irreverent ways, declining to send their children for religious instruction. As a result, the "attendance of the children" at the school had been so "irregular as materially to retard their progress . . . and at times to discourage, and almost overthrow the design of the teachers." A lack of qualified teachers also hampered progress. "The want of a competent number of punctual, faithful teachers" had been one of "the greatest impediments to the prosperity of the school."[61]

Detroit's Bible Society encountered similar obstacles, lamenting in 1817 that few if any Michiganians seemed interested in learning to read or in acquiring the Holy Scripture. Almost no "demand for the Bible" existed in the territory. In part, reformers attributed this disinterest to Michigan's low rate of literacy, observing that a "very considerable proportion" of Michigan's population was illiterate.[62] Three years later, they complained that the faithful were not doing enough to aid their cause. Although many Michigan residents said they believed that the "revealed truth" was the "greatest blessing that men enjoy," they bequeathed a "small portion of their income . . . to promote its influence." Too frequently, they squandered their money "for trivial purposes," instead of aiding a cause that "would produce the most important and lasting benefits to mankind!"[63]

Much work remained to be done in Michigan. "Our frontier settlements are known to be lamentably deficient" in religion, reported the Bible Society. Aside from Indians, they pointed to two groups that desperately

needed the word of God—sailors on the Great Lakes and "common laborers." The "sea-faring men who navigate the lakes" were a particularly wild
lot. "Cut off from the ordinary advantages of civil and religious society,
and religious institutions, they require above all others the spiritual treasure." Working men made up an even "more numerous class" requiring
salvation. "There are multitudes of them in this place and the vicinity who
have no means of improving their minds, of directing their morals, or of
seeking their eternal salvation." Reading counteracted the wickedness and
licentiousness of the frontier. In the East, "civil and religious institutions"
dispensed such discipline; but, on the frontier, such guardians of order
and stability were few and far between. Consequently, it was difficult to
suppress the wildness of settlers. Reformers had to rely on education, and
especially on books, to establish boundaries and discipline the poor—a
difficult goal in a setting with low literacy rates.[64]

Despite these obstacles, reformers claimed that efforts to educate Michiganians began paying dividends in the 1820s and 1830s, as growing numbers of settlers turned away from drinking and vice. Although problems
persisted, the Detroit Sunday School reported in 1820 "a visible improvement in the morals and manners as well as intellectual knowledge of the
scholars." Students who once had been "idle profaners of the Sabbath"
now observed the sacred day and had become "diligent seekers of religious
knowledge."[65]

Similarly, temperance reformers reported progress, insisting not only
that drinking in Michigan had declined, but also that family governance
had improved as a result. In 1837, a temperance crusader noted that "the
inebriate" was no longer "seen tottering thro' our streets."[66] Other reformers bragged that they had rescued families from the scourge of drunkenness. Because of temperance reform, alcohol had been "extensively driven
from the family circle, where it was once so kindly entertained." Reformers
had domesticated fathers, curbing their drunken rapacity and transforming the home into a place of harmony and contentment. Liquor, "that
enemy of personal character and domestic happiness," now rarely placed
"his ruthless foot" inside the home. Instead, intemperance was compelled
to live "abroad from the purity and affection of the fireside."[67] Wives no
longer wept "with tears of bitter grief." Husbands and fathers were "restored to the endearing ties of their hitherto deserted homes. Misery, discontent and sorrow have given place to the smile of affection, of joy, and
undying love."[68]

Michigan newspapers also published fiction that demonstrated how
the temperance crusade had domesticated men, transforming them from
violent and unpredictable creatures into loving fathers. Typically, this
occurred the morning after the father committed his drunken outrages.

He wakened, recalled his misdeeds, and vowed to change. He took the Washingtonian Pledge, promising never to drink again. The pledge took on a sacred significance, a ritual that cleansed men of alcohol and rapacity. On a symbolic level, it also marked their passage from an older, punitive form of fatherhood and rapacity to one that was benevolent and more suited to the Victorian home. The new father respected household boundaries: he was kinder, gentler, and more docile than his predecessors had been.

While celebrating this success, reformers also expressed concern that education had produced unintended consequences. Though schooling had helped to tame wildness in men, it seems to have had the opposite effect on women, making some of them unruly and rebellious individuals who subverted efforts to improve family governance. Evidence of this rowdiness is far from definitive; much of it is based on fiction that ran in local newspapers. Yet it does suggest some concern about education subverting gender boundaries. During the 1820s and 1830s, for instance, many authors complained that education had transformed women into creatures who shunned housework. They also worried about the effects of popular literature, especially the novel, on its largely female audience, insisting that such works were turning women into critics who had become more and more dissatisfied with their lot in life and their subservient role in the family. The *Pontiac Courier* observed in 1837 that the Scottish moral philosopher Dr. Thomas Chalmers warned "against the indulgence of novel reading," adding that he "would tremble for the friend greedily addicted to the perusal" of such works. "They are, without doubt, dangerous to anyone." This was because they depicted "life as it is not and never should be." But novels were especially dangerous for women. They bred discontent and unhappiness, causing the daughter to turn against her parents and eventually her husband and children.[69]

Although they disliked novels, reformers were even more critical of literature that Fanny Wright and other women's rights advocates produced. A utopian British reformer and free-love advocate, Wright sparked controversy when she visited the United States in 1818 and 1824.[70] The *Pontiac Courier* insisted in 1838 that the influence of free thinkers like "Fanny Wright and others of the same school" was "positively pernicious." The literature that Wright and her allies produced represented a threat to both "young and old," whose minds were "safer in total ignorance, than when storing such monstrous doctrines." These radicals "would, without remorse, snatch from us all that renders life tolerable or death welcome." The term "monstrous" leaps out of this passage and suggests why these critics found ideas about the "free love" that Wright championed so threatening. In challenging traditional boundaries that defined the family and relations between men and women, these notions seemed both wild and unnatural. They posed a grave threat to patriarchy and traditional ideas of family governance.[71]

But these radicals were not the only targets of criticism. Many critics saved their harshest attacks for the schools and academies that women attended. The *Detroit Gazette* in 1818 published an article by a British author who criticized female educators for devoting so much of their energy to training women in the arts. These pedagogues believed that the "object" of educating women was to turn them into "artists" and "to give them an excellence in drawing, music, painting and dancing." There was nothing wrong with giving females artistic training. Rather, the "error" was to "make these things the grand and universal object."[72]

Because of this misstep, educators had unwittingly destabilized family governance by inducing women to turn their backs on housework. The *Pontiac Courier* emphasized this point, complaining in 1838 that "too many ladies consider themselves made far more for ornament than usefulness." These women were "taught to look on all sober duties and realities of life as utterly at variance with that feminine delicacy which is the true characteristic of woman." Such young women were completely self-absorbed, living "only for themselves." Scarcely "a thought, feeling, pleasure or desire" went through their minds "of which self was not the ultimate object. Their actions begin in self, and issue in self, their own gratification, adornment, or success, have been exclusively pursued."[73] In stories and poems, observers frequently ridiculed the educated woman, who put on intellectual airs but was useless in the home. In one such tale, an uncle criticized his niece for playing the piano and then informed her that her grandmother used "to play on a much better instrument." Eventually, he revealed that this instrument was "a spinning wheel."[74] Educated women thus were abhorrent, because, like drunken husbands, they violated gender boundaries and neglected their role as housewives: they shunned productive labor and refused to be self-sacrificing, both of which were seen as essential to the maintenance of stable family governance.

In another tale, the narrator and his friends visit Alonzo and Maria, his well-educated wife. The author satirizes not only Maria's inability to take care of her husband, but also the culture of sympathy, which placed such a premium on the feminine sensibilities. The tale also pokes fun at Alonzo's inability to control his wife, suggesting his ineptitude both as a family governor and as a man. As the story opens, several guests are accompanying Alonzo to his home for dinner, and they meet a friend named Dagget. Shortly thereafter, Alonzo informs his companions that his wife, Maria, is far superior to Dagget's spouse. The latter has "not the heart of a woman, which ought to be all sensibility." Although Dagget is "a fellow of mind and of genius," he had married someone below him, who cannot "appreciate him" and is "a complete nobody."[75] But the guests are soon shocked to discover the untidiness of Alonzo's home: "I glanced at the stair-case and saw that a broom had not passed over it lately." Later, the narrator "stumble[s] over a broom and a band-box, which lay in elegant negligence in the middle of the floor" and then makes his "way to a chair thickly covered with dust." After greeting their guests, Maria goes to the kitchen to prepare dinner. A half an hour later she returns; "but instead of bearing in her hands a smoking platter or table, her arms [are] loaded with books and pictures." Rather than scolding Maria, Alonzo expresses pride in having "an intellectual wife."[76]

After more delays, Maria finally does make a meal. But as "she [comes] in with a platter of meat," it falls "from her grasp." The plate breaks "into fragments and the meat roll[s] upon the carpet." Finally, the guests go to Dagget's house and are quickly fed by his wife. "She asked us if we had supped and when we told her we had not . . . she moved out of the room as noiseless as a spirit and as quick as lightning." In "five minutes," she has placed a "snowy cloth" on the table, and covering it with "viands of a most delicious flavor."[77]

The story contrasts the households of Alonzo and Dagget, demonstrating the falseness of Alonzo's claim, early in the tale, that his learned wife, Maria, is far superior to Dagget's uneducated spouse. Maria is unable to fulfill a wife's most basic duties, while Dagget's spouse epitomizes traditional conceptions of the good wife. Unlike Maria, Dagget's spouse remains nameless, speechless, meek, faceless, and compliant. "When her husband spoke, she was all attention, and before he had finished, the thing wanted was produced—the half expressed command was executed."[78] Maria, on the other hand, finds the most basic household duties challenging. Her home is dirty, and her intellectual interests so distract her that she was unable to serve Alonzo and his friends a meal. This portrait castigates Maria's intellectual achievements, presenting them as a grotesque distortion of womanhood that prevents her from accomplishing her wifely obligations. Education unsexes women and subverts orderly households by preventing them from fulfilling their main role—to serve their husbands.

In some cases, schooling had even more dire consequences. It produced gossips, excessively independent individuals who spoke too freely and dared to criticize patriarchal households. Michigan newspapers contained a number of stories that condemned these figures, typically portrayed as women. These tales often reflected fears about the subversive power of women's speech, with one editor characterizing gossips as "pests to a well ordered community" and urging that they "be driven out of it with as little ceremony as we would kill a mad dog."[79]

A story entitled "The Tea Table" demonstrates why gossips may have seemed so threatening. It depicts Polly Gaw, a town gossip who promoted women's independence and women's speech, as threatening the stability of marriage and family governance. As the story begins, Polly is visiting Julia Pellew and overhears Julia telling her husband that she could "take care" of herself. The remainder of the tale centers on the conflicting interpretations that Polly and Julia's husband, Mr. Pellew, gave to Julia's remarks, with Polly insisting that Julia's comments meant she planned to end her subservience to her husband and Mr. Pellew viewing them as the kind words of a deferential helpmate. In examining this battle, the author sought to demonstrate that Polly's radical reading of Julia's comments was incorrect and represented a serious threat to domestic stability.[80]

Polly, the villain of the piece, operates as Julia's alter ego, expressing sentiments that Julia represses. She offers a subversive reading of Julia's statement, interpreting it as a declaration of independence, a refusal to bow to patriarchal authority, and an indication that the Pellews are about to separate. Her reading undermines traditional notions of marriage, in which women are supposedly weak and dependent creatures. After hearing Julia's remark, Polly commiserates with her neighbor and launches into a critique of men, noting "the savage unsociability of husbands and insisting that they were as restless and unhappy in the marriage noose as caged up tigers." The language suggests that Polly views men in much the same way as did the authors of tales about drunken and abusive husbands. Like ferocious, wild animals, men represent a threat to life and limb and can never be domesticated. They cannot adapt to the sociability required in the domestic sphere and are by nature ill suited to marriage, because the institution "cages" their wild masculine impulses. Once freed of their wives, "how gay and young and spruce they immediately became." Were Julia to die, "Mr. Pellew would, in ten days, be the most gallant and agreeable man in the village."[81]

Polly's skepticism about men, however, is not the only reason she assumes that Julia plans to escape her husband's dominance. This view also is buttressed by the Pellews' financial situation. Julia is much richer than her husband and possesses enough wealth to live independently of him. Mr. Pellew is dependent on Julia and several years earlier had relied on her fortune to start his business. Although Julia does not "control" the estate, her wealth permitted Pellew "to gain the credit necessary in his business, and he had done so." This wealth suggests that Julia, a symbol of Victorian women, is more powerful than she seems. Her riches inverted traditional roles and transformed her husband into one of his wife's dependents. Consequently, Polly's decision to make public what she sees as Julia's unhappiness and quest for autonomy also threatens to undermine Mr. Pellew's business and his financial prospects.[82]

This threat surfaces after Polly mobilizes the community to action. A growing number of Mr. Pellew's creditors and neighbors begin consoling Julia and ostracizing her husband for mistreating his wife. Initially, Julia and her husband are unaware of the gossip that Polly is spreading and are puzzled by the way their friends, family, and acquaintances treat them. Julia, on one side, realizes that "her visitors, who began to be much more numerous than before, put on long faces and in a condoling strain lectured on the trials of the marriage state" and the need to be patient. Mr. Pellew, on the other side, begins to encounter hostility. His wife's relatives treat him coolly, female acquaintances "scolded at him and what was worse . . . his customers began to neglect him." Pellew also discovers that "his creditors began to push." He grows "alarmed" and decides to find the cause of this strange behavior. He soon discovers that his neighbors believe that he and Julia are about to separate, and he eventually traces this rumor to Polly Gaw.[83]

In the concluding scene, Mr. Pellew calls the community to his house and restores patriarchal authority by countering Polly's interpretation of Julia's remarks. At her husband's urging, Julia explains that she had been helping her husband to a "pair of fine quails," when he insisted that she take some herself. Julia then uttered "the offensive words, 'Well, I can take care of myself.'" Julia's confession quashes Polly's subversive interpretation of her comments, demonstrating that the gossip had wrenched them out of context. Rather than rebelling against her husband, Julia had been acting as a deferential helpmate—cooking and serving her husband dinner. Julia's story also demonstrates the kindness and generosity of her spouse: he insisted on sharing the quails instead of eating all of them himself. Julia acted selflessly, refusing her husband's offer and defusing an apparent crisis in family governance. Her words were supposedly not intended to challenge male dominance; she remained a self-sacrificing housewife who put her husband's needs before her own.[84]

The story reveals concerns about woman's speech, which could undermine male authority and transform relations between men and women. The author defused the danger implicit in Julia's insistence on self-sufficiency by demonizing Polly, an independent, unmarried woman who dared to challenge patriarchy. Early in the story, the narrator characterizes Polly as an unwelcome and intrusive figure who threatens domestic peace and harmony. Polly "entered the room on one of her flying afternoon visits," and Julia "could not avoid coloring up a little at this sudden intrusion." Like the drunken fathers who abused their families, Polly's "visits were always intrusive," because she challenged the way families were governed. Polly violated boundaries that protected family governance from the eyes of the public. The author castigated her for publicizing such private matters, revealing events that previously had remained hidden behind bedroom doors and keeping the community informed about "the progress of courtships," "domestic squabbles," and the "scandals of the week." Although Mr. Pellew rescues his marriage, his victory may not be complete, because it is not clear that he was able to silence Polly.[85]

Others sources also provide evidence that educated women rebelled against traditional female roles. Elizabeth Chandler was a writer who moved to Michigan from Philadelphia with her brother and her aunt in 1830. After settling in the southeastern part of the territory, Chandler began preparing to teach school. At a time when only men taught math, she wrote to her relatives in the East, asking them to send her books on arithmetic, because she was preparing to teach the subject. Such violations of woman's role in the classroom seldom if ever occurred in the East.[86]

Caroline Kirkland's autobiographical novel, *A New Home: Who'll Follow?* meanwhile depicts grudging male acceptance of learned women in Michigan. Shortly after Kirkland's village established a Lyceum, its members organized a "novel" and "striking" debate, examining the "comparative mental capacity of the sexes." The dispute was "interesting to absolute breathlessness . . . and was gallantly decided in favor of the fair by a youthful member who occupied the barrel as president for the evening." In his view, women would be roughly "equal" to men, "if the natural and social disadvantages" under which they "labored . . . could be removed."[87]

CONCLUSION

Such unorthodox views suggest that efforts by reformers to tame the savagery of Michiganians secured only mixed results. Alarmed by the rudeness, drunkenness, crime, rebelliousness, impiety, and sexual promiscuity of their neighbors, reformers expressed concern that such behavior posed a threat to a social stability and republican governance. To survive, republics required a virtuous citizenry willing to sacrifice its interests for the common good. Additionally, rowdiness and drunkenness were dangerous because reformers associated such conduct with the disorder, instability, and wildness of non-European races. Settlers who indulged in these vices behaved like drunken Indians; they were rebellious and indolent and lacked the initiative to improve Michigan.

Reformers relied on law, education, and suasion to improve the morals and manners of Michiganians. They not only pressured legislators to enact statutes aimed at reducing drinking, prostitution, and other forms of vice but also launched campaigns to educate Michiganians and improve family governance. During the 1820s and 1830s, reformers argued that families were in a state of crisis and failing to fulfill one of their most vital functions—to discipline the young, thereby creating a stable social order. In much of their literature, reformers blamed this problem on household heads who failed to discipline their dependents adequately. In some instances, they castigated weak and ineffectual fathers who failed to prevent their wives from committing adultery or their children from acting rudely and disobediently. In others, they condemned drunken fathers whose indolence, violence, and addiction had destroyed the families that they were supposed to support.

To remedy these ills, reformers launched an ambitious educational program to strengthen the patriarchal family by rescuing weak and ineffectual fathers as well as those addicted to alcohol and other vices. They also relied on print culture and education to do what these incompetent household heads had failed to accomplish—to discipline wayward women and children and transform them into virtuous members of the community. They hoped that schools, newspapers, books, and other forms of print culture would do what household heads once had done: instill the moral and religious boundaries needed to create a righteous community and stable society.

After initial setbacks, this program seems to have scored important victories. By the 1830s, reformers announced that Michiganians had become godlier as a result of their efforts. Drunkards had taken the Washingtonian Pledge and became sober and industrious; fathers ruled their households more effectively than they had in the past. But efforts to civilize Michigan also had unintended consequences that helped to undermine patriarchy and traditional notions of family governance. Under the instruction of evangelicals, men became more tranquil and less rebellious. Education, however, seems to have had a very different effect on women, inducing some to become increasingly outspoken and critical of male authority. In response, a growing chorus of critics in the press castigated learned women. Typically, this literature attacked the wife who was unable to cook or to perform routine household chores.

Education thus was erasing or at least blurring gender boundaries and seemingly transforming women into hermaphrodites who were neither female nor male and could no longer serve their husbands properly. Schooling also helped to create gossips, women who urged their sex to interject disruptive voices into the household. Such women threatened to undermine family governance by challenging male authority and criticizing the wife's role as a deferential helpmate. Education thus proved to be a double-edged sword. It tamed the wildness of men and turned them into fathers who could discipline their dependents more effectively than they had in the past. But reformers believed that it had the opposite effect on women, transforming them into wild creatures whose critique of male authority threatened to destabilize family governance.

Cholera and the Conflict

over Cultural Boundaries

in Early Michigan

As the summer of 1834 drew to a close, Detroit residents looked back on one of the most difficult periods in their history. "We have passed through a melancholy and trying season," and the people have sunk into "a gloom which cannot easily be dispelled," noted the *Detroit Courier,* one of the city's three newspapers. What was most "appalling" was to watch people "falling around us," the *Courier* continued. One day "our friends and neighbors" appeared to be healthy, ensconced in "the comforts of life, while on the brow was seated the promise of length of days—the next a lifeless corpse—deposited by the side of kindred mortality to moulder beneath the green grassy sod of the churchyard."[1]

The source of these woes was that great scourge of the nineteenth century—cholera. The malady struck Europe, the United States, and Canada in 1832 and 1834, taking countless lives and severely disrupting communities on both sides of the Atlantic. Examining how these crises affected one western community offers a unique glimpse into the workings of boundary setting on the early-nineteenth-century frontier. Although people sicken and die in every culture, epidemics strike down large segments of the population, illustrate how communities cope with pain and suffering, and expose social tensions hidden in healthier times.

In Michigan, cholera revealed mounting discord between urban and rural settlers not evident during more tranquil periods. For rural Michiganians, the disease became a metonym for the anarchy and chaos characteristic of cities, a means by which urban dwellers might spread such disorder to the countryside. Exacerbating the crises in Michigan was the absence of amenities that eased the problems that epidemics created in more settled areas.

Michigan, moreover, was one of the few places in the nation where violence erupted in response to the disease. It grew out of a lively debate in the 1830s between Detroiters and rural residents over how cholera spread. While newspapers in Detroit insisted that the disease was not transmitted through human contact, those outside the city asserted that it did. These differences over the etiology of cholera produced conflicting strategies for battling the disease. Prompted by their noncontagionist views, Detroit officials opposed establishing quarantines, arguing that they were counterproductive. Artificial borders would simply spread panic, leaving the local populace more vulnerable to cholera, and hamper efforts to care for the sick and dying.

Settlers in rural Oakland and Washtenaw counties saw things differently. They not only established quarantines but also destroyed bridges and threatened Detroiters seeking to enter their communities. Violence ensued. Regional conflict over cholera in turn produced a partisan political battle, with Whigs and Democrats debating how far local officials could go in defending borders designed to protect their communities from urban contagion.

CHOLERA'S EFFECTS ON MICHIGAN

The debate over cholera resulted from the mysterious nature of the ailment. Cholera is caused by bacteria invading the digestive tract, precipitating severe vomiting and diarrhea. It often killed 50 percent of those it infected, frequently within a matter of hours, because of precipitous loss of vital minerals and bodily fluids.[2]

Prior to the 1830s, cholera was unknown in either Europe or the Americas. In 1817, the malady migrated from southern Asia to other parts of the world in concert with increased trade and Britain's increased economic influence on the subcontinent. After the transportation revolution of the early nineteenth century, the disease traveled along rail and steamship lines, leaving death and destruction in its wake. Cholera initially devastated East Asia, Africa, and the Caucasus, and then attacked Europe before crossing the Atlantic in 1832, arriving in Canada and spreading throughout North America.[3]

Cholera reached Michigan in July 1832, on board the *Henry Clay,* a ship transporting troops from Buffalo to Chicago to fight in the Blackhawk War. The first outbreak occurred after the *Henry Clay* entered the Detroit River; when the vessel docked in Detroit, two passengers were sick. Detroit authorities ordered the ship to leave town, but by then two Detroiters who had contact with people on the ship became infected.[4]

Soon the illness spread. The *Detroit Free Press* estimated that cholera infected fifty-eight of the city's five thousand residents, killing twenty-eight Detroiters between July 4 and July 18. After establishing quarantine on their port, Detroit's Board of Health ordered Detroiters to maintain the "strictest cleanliness . . . in persons and dwellings" and directed the city to "clean all Streets, Alleys and Houses." Detroit's "impure atmosphere" was to be "rendered harmless" through the "use of Chloride of Lime."[5]

Cholera returned to the United States in 1834, striking Detroit in August of that year. The *Detroit Courier* reported that the disease, "which made such fearful ravages two years since, seems by the accounts from all parts of the country to have revisited its old haunts." The 1834 epidemic was even more deadly than its predecessor. Hon. George C. Bates recalled years later that in 1834 cholera entered the city "with a ferocity and slaughter that it had never exhibited elsewhere," creeping "up and down the river," climbing the "decks and shrouds of our vessels." People "fell as if struck by lightning." A long line of carts passed through the city most mornings taking "festering corpses" to the cemetery.[6]

A shortage of doctors and hospitals worsened the city's plight. Although Detroit had a board of health in the 1830s, it possessed few of the resources found in more developed regions. Because Michigan possessed few physicians, the sick usually were treated with home remedies.[7] When cholera struck Michigan in the 1830s, therefore, local officials had few resources to combat the crisis.

In 1832, Father Gabriel Richard created a makeshift hospital in Detroit's capitol building to combat the epidemic. Richard was a Catholic priest and one of Michigan's most prominent citizens. After fleeing the French Revolution and working as a missionary in Illinois, he moved to Detroit in 1798, where he played an active role in education, served briefly as Michigan's nonvoting representative in Congress, and published a short-lived newspaper. He recruited young women in the 1832 cholera outbreak to help him care for the sick, before falling victim to the disease himself and dying in September 1832. Conditions had not improved two years later when, George C. Bates recalled, Detroit possessed "no hospitals, no asylums, no place of refuge or safety for the sick and dying."[8]

Estimates of the death toll from the 1834 epidemic varied. The *Free Press* reported in August that cholera killed about 150 people during an eighteen-day period. George Bates estimated that cholera "swept away" 10 percent of Detroit in 1834, while historian Silas Farmer in 1889 calculated that some 7 percent of the populace died. The rising death toll even forced the city to abridge the length of burial rites. No details exist on how cholera entered Michigan, but the *Detroit Journal* stated that it came "in from abroad," because of contact with passengers on "an infected vessel."[9]

THE VICTIMS OF CHOLERA

Like other Americans, Michiganians believed that cholera preyed primarily on drunkards, the poor, and others who were lazy and lacked self-control.[10] Michigan's Whig and Democratic newspapers both echoed such views. The *Free Press*, a Jacksonian paper, reported that the "greatest number of deaths have occurred among the intemperate drinkers of ardent spirits; next to these, those who were destitute of the comforts of life, uncleanly, and irregular in their habits have suffered the most." Likewise, the *Detroit Journal*, a Whig imprint, reported in 1832 that "deaths from cholera . . . have been, with few exceptions, confined to those who have been intemperate in the use of ardent spirits."[11]

Victorians linked cholera to immorality because they had no way of knowing what caused disease.[12] In Michigan, such views reinforced the message of evangelical reformers who believed the frontier, and Detroit in particular, was filled with sinners. After the completion of the Erie Canal in 1825, and the upsurge of Yankee immigrants from New England and western New York, the size of Michigan's temperance movement increased dramatically (see chapter 5).

Such groups viewed the epidemic as a divine effort to tame the wildness of Michigan's frontier. Whig newspapers published jeremiads describing cholera as God's punishment for infidelity, drinking, gambling, and other sinful behavior. One exhortation attributed the 1832 epidemic to religious decline, noting that America had formerly been a godly nation. "Showers of righteousness," said the "Observer of Providence," descended on America, and nearly one hundred thousand sinners were converted. Lately, these revivals had all but disappeared, and "desolations, darkness, and mortal death" reigned.[13]

Two years later, the *Courier* published a similar message, describing cholera as the "sword of the Almighty" sent to destroy the "infidelity of the world and of the church!" Only a fraction of those who claimed to be Christians actually practiced the faith, and many who feigned piety were more concerned with "self love, love of ease," and "love of the world" than the love of God. To thwart this wickedness, "the insulted majesty of heaven" rose "to vindicate his injured honor" and conquer the "bold, heaven-daring attacks made on the kingdom of Christ by the infidels and skeptics of the present day!"[14]

Several Whig commentators hoped that cholera would help eradicate sinfulness, convincing the depraved to curb their immoral ways to remain healthy. The *Detroit Courier* reported in July 1832 that "some good at least" had "resulted from the unwelcome visit of this scourge of nations." Detroiters were "willing to be made clean, and many have become temperate."[15]

Others, however, lamented cholera's failure to discipline Detroit's unruly population. The *Detroit Journal* observed in 1834 that though Detroiters knew that cholera preyed on those "intemperate in diet or drink," drunkenness seemed to have increased during the epidemic. The display of "inebriety" had "since the disease made its appearance been more frequent than usual." It was common not only "to see men lying in the street drunk," but also to witness "such spectacles" on the Sabbath. Nor was there an hour of the day "during this awful period . . . when God's judgments" were "abroad . . . that the sounds of drunken revelry and blasphemy are not borne upon the air infecting the moral atmosphere even more fatally than the disease."[16]

Such immorality was alarming because of uncertainty about how cholera spread, and the possibility that sinners might infect respectable citizens. If cholera was not contagious, then temperate churchgoers need not worry, because it was a "scourge not of mankind but of the sinner." Although many Michiganians shared this view, others disagreed. As one Detroiter explained in 1832, "all accounts of the progress of cholera, state that its first victims are the drunkards." After enough of them "have fallen . . . then it assails the more temperate and useful citizens and thus spreads its influences through the community."[17]

THE DEBATE OVER HOW CHOLERA SPREAD

Confusion about how cholera spread stemmed from its contradictory features. Because cholera moved along well-known thoroughfares, it looked like a contagious disease. Yet the malady often infected some parts of town and left others unscathed, suggesting that it did not spread through human contact. Scientists now can explain this discrepancy. Though cholera is contagious, victims contract it by eating or drinking infected food or water, or touching their mouths with infected hands. Thus, strangers who live in different towns but eat or drink from the same tainted source might become ill, while members of their family remain healthy.[18] But in the early nineteenth century, medical knowledge was limited, and questions persisted about how cholera spread.

Educated opinion soon split into warring camps, as contagionists battled noncontagionists over cholera's etiology. Contagionists embraced a theory that dated back to the classical world, while their opponents espoused a nineteenth-century idea that emphasized the environment's role in causing disease. They attributed cholera and other ailments to miasmas or poisonous vapors that arose from garbage and other rotting substances. Preventing disease involved sanitizing the environment. Because both sides could marshal compelling data to support their claims, conflict over how cholera spread persisted during the malady's initial appearance.[19]

In Michigan's countryside, officials embraced contagionism. Those in Detroit espoused noncontagionism. Noncontagionist views were first aired in response to the panic that sent Detroiters fleeing during the 1832 epidemic. "The aspect of things in this city is truly mournful," observed the *Detroit Courier*. Many residents had "given up their businesses" and gone to the country, reported the paper's editors. In a letter to his father that summer, Theodore Williams was more precise, calculating that roughly one-third of Detroiters had deserted the city. Those who stayed wore "the most intense anxiety on their brow."[20]

To stop such flight, Detroit newspapers insisted that cholera did not spread through human contact. The *Journal* claimed in July 1832 that fleeing was useless, because cholera did not "occupy any particular spot." Rather, it pervaded "every country and place." Running was more dangerous than staying put, because a change in diet and the stimulation that occurred during travel made people more vulnerable to the disease. That same month the *Courier* insisted that if the epidemic in Detroit were like the one that visited Canada, "strong proof" indicated that it was not contagious, and that it was "as likely to prevail in one place as in another."[21]

Similarly, the *Free Press* printed a letter in July 1832 from J. R. Rhinelander, a medical expert, who insisted that cholera was not contagious. Although many physicians believed that cholera spread through human contact, Rhinelander had been unable to discover any data to back this theory. Rather, evidence from earlier outbreaks indicated that the malady was not contagious. In Canada, the disease afflicted those living twenty miles from the epidemic "who had not even heard of it." Contagion had "never extended its power" this far. The appearance of cholera in Montreal before navigation opened also demonstrated that cholera was not contagious. Instead, easterly winds had blown continuously for over a month, carrying cholera to North America.[22]

Not everyone agreed with these views. The *Michigan Sentinel,* a Democratic newspaper from Monroe, reprinted a *Worcester Spy* article insisting that cholera was contagious because it followed the same route in 1834 that it had traveled two years earlier, spreading west, and "showing itself at most of the principal places on the great line of inland water communication." Though "physicians may quarrel" about how cholera spread, the *Sentinel* was certain that it was contagious. Mortality was higher among those who had been exposed to the sick than among those who had "kept aloof" from them. Cholera might not be as contagious as "the measles or small pox," but the "experience of years" had "proved it to be amazingly contagious, and . . . Doctors, the most dogmatical of all men," were "becoming of one opinion regarding this point."[23]

Likewise, Ann Arbor's anti-Masonic *Emigrant* found this argument compelling. In 1832, it summarized an authoritative English article that concluded "unequivocally" that cholera was contagious. "Like man," it traveled "along the high roads from town to town," attacking the "most populous and commercial cities first." When going to an "uninfected country," cholera picked the "principal port or frontier town, and from thence" took the "most frequented thoroughfares to reach the largest cities." Where transportation was "rapid, the progress of the disease" was as well. Cholera did move in perplexing ways that seemed to undermine the contagionist position, the author admitted, sometimes attacking one town along a route yet leaving others untouched. This unpredictability stemmed from the paths that the infected traveled, heading "in one direction rather than another, or staying "not at the nearest, but possibly journeying on to a distant village."[24]

The *Free Press* in August 1832 sought to counter these contagionist views, pointing to a "Russian village," in which angry peasants "seized upon two doctors . . . stationed there by the government." They tied them to the corpses of two cholera victims, and threw them into a mass grave filled with others who had died during the epidemic. The doctors were rescued two days later "from their horrid prison" and remained healthy, despite prolonged exposure to the disease. Nor did cholera attack the "multitudes of people in Detroit" who had been exposed. Instead, it had infected some "who were much less exposed or not at all exposed."[25]

These conflicting interpretations of cholera led Detroit officials and those in the countryside to choose different strategies to combat the epidemic. Detroit authorities opposed quarantines, seeing them as counterproductive. The *Courier* insisted in June 1832 that "quarantine regulations and restrictions as to intercourse with the sick . . . are as useless as in the influenza last winter." They failed to prevent the spread of cholera and worsened the epidemic by "increasing the fear and depriving the patients" of proper care.[26]

Detroiters opposed quarantines for several reasons. At the start of the epidemic, their quarantine had failed to protect the city. By taking an anticontagionist stance, they also hoped to prevent panic and to ensure that the sick received adequate care. Detroit officials may also have had economic motives for avoiding quarantines, because such restrictions hampered not only travel, but also trade and commerce.[27]

The geography of Detroit may also have made quarantines impractical. In the 1830s, the city lacked boundaries that later segregated residents by class. Instead, rich and poor were often neighbors. On one street, for instance, middle-class professionals lived near artisans and workers. Given the mixed nature of Detroit neighborhoods, quarantines could have done little to protect Detroit's better sort from the cholera.[28]

Instead of establishing quarantines, Detroit organized campaigns to police and sanitize the poor. The *Courier* urged that Detroit's "streets be kept clean" and counseled local officials to inspect "those parts of the city where numerous collections of poor families reside," and to remove "all filth and rubbish." The paper proudly announced that Detroit officials had begun to follow its advice, setting up a hospital to care for the ill, and "tak[ing] active measures for cleansing the city and removing . . . nuisances." Two years later, the *Courier* reported that authorities had inspected "every house" in the city and "every spot where filth could be supposed to collect." The *Courier* also published a report that year by the Philadelphia Medical Society that reiterated the need to keep urban working-class districts clean. The report insisted that the "dwellings of the poor, particularly in damp, crowded and confined situations, should be cleansed and whitewashed at public expense and care taken to secure the constant maintenance . . . of perfect cleanliness."[29]

While not ignoring cleanup campaigns, rural officials relied primarily on quarantines to strengthen boundaries separating their communities from Detroit, an urban environment starkly contrasting with their locales. Detroit was growing rapidly and increasingly resembled cities in the East. Like them, it was plagued by growing poverty and disorder. The completion of the Erie Canal in 1825 and the surge of population into Michigan had transformed Detroit from a quiet western outpost into a crowded city. Between 1828 and 1834, Detroit's population more than tripled, jumping to 4,973 residents in 1834 from a meager 2,222 just six earlier. Rising population, in turn, brought increased crime and other urban problems.[30]

The quarantines established in Oakland and Washtenaw counties also divided Michigan's new Yankee settlers from their French predecessors located in Detroit and other old settlements. Before the 1830s, Michigan's mostly French population shaped its culture. French settlers not only borrowed Indian customs and values but also coupled with indigenous people, producing a sizable mixed-blood, or Métis, populace (see chapter 4). New Englanders, who began streaming into the territory in the 1820s, condemned this social and racial mixing, which, they believed, reduced Europeans to the savagery of Indians.[31]

This Yankee abhorrence of the Métis, who lived in Detroit and other older Michigan communities, may help explain why the countryside responded to cholera by singling out Detroiters as carriers of the disease. The *Journal* reported in 1832 that fear of cholera had caused many in towns to end contact with Detroit. "We understand that the panic is so great in the country, that at several places, all communication with Detroit is suspended by force." Townspeople had destroyed bridges and constructed barriers "across roads leading to this city," stationing guards "to prevent the introduction of the disease into the interior." That same month, the *Free Press* reported that the appearance of cholera in Detroit had produced a "fear . . . among the people in adjacent counties" that "manifested itself in an extraordinary manner, and . . . led to measures not only ridiculous, but censurable."[32]

Rochester residents, the *Free Press* stated, forced Detroiters to leave "public houses" and threw "their baggage . . . after them." They also destroyed bridges to prevent Detroiters from getting into the town. Similar incidents occurred elsewhere in 1832. Pontiac, another neighboring village, the *Free Press* observed, established an armed guard on its highways "with directions to stop all persons from Detroit." After interrogating the *Free Press* editor, the guards refused to let him "pass through" Pontiac until enough time had passed "to prove himself free of the contagion."[33]

The *Free Press* editor then proceeded to Auburn, where he received a much warmer reception, finding "the inhabitants free from the panic which had seized" others. "The public houses as well as the dwellings of citizens were open" to those "excluded from neighboring towns." Soon a meeting was organized, with most attendees agreeing that cholera was not contagious and concluding that citizens should seek "to calm the public alarm, and to extend to the unfortunate sick all the assistance in their power." Attendees also adopted a resolution condemning Rochester and Pontiac for overreacting to the crisis, declaring that their actions had produced "much inconvenience to citizens who were obliged to travel" and prevented "many from obtaining medical and other assistance in case of sickness."[34]

Despite such resolutions, violence erupted after two mail stages violated Ypsilanti's quarantine in July 1832. When the stages attempted to enter the village without first undergoing a medical examination, local officials opened fire, killing one horse and wounding another. In response, Michigan governor George Porter dismissed several Ypsilanti officials involved in the incident, which in turn sparked a war of words between Detroiters and Washtenaw County residents. Democrats generally sided with Governor Porter, while Whigs backed Ypsilanti officials who claimed that they had been defending their community from cholera. In late 1832, Washtenaw County residents organized a convention to protest Governor Porter's actions and issued a report criticizing the governor for unjustly firing the local officials.

The dispute, which one newspaper dubbed "the quarantine war," stirred the passion of both Whigs and Democrats during the summer and fall of 1832, with each side indicting the lawless savagery, in their eyes, of their opponents.[35] At issue was how far officials could go in protecting their borders, to contain anarchy and danger, and whether such conduct violated individual rights. As cholera approached Detroit in the summer of 1832, Michigan had enacted a statute permitting local officials to establish quarantines to protect the health of their communities. The two sides disagreed on whether the statute empowered Ypsilanti officials to shoot at the stages and whether these individuals had acted recklessly. Both sides agreed that, under normal circumstances, firing on unarmed citizens for minor offenses would be unwarranted and perhaps illegal.

Ypsilanti's defenders, however, insisted that the times had not been normal and that, given the crisis created by the cholera epidemic of 1832, local officials justifiably resorted to violence to defend their town's borders and protect its citizens from what they considered an urban pestilence. They also insisted that those enforcing the quarantine resorted to violence only after being provoked. According to the report issued by the Washtenaw County Convention, local officials "called repeatedly to the driver to stop; instead of doing which he urged his horses to a more rapid gate [*sic*]," and only then did Captain Burton of the local militia order "his men to fire." Because the driver refused to stop, officials had the "right and duty to compel him" to do so, concluded the *Emigrant*. Had the guards "neglected the necessary means to stop him," they would have been neglecting their duty, "as the constable who suffers a prisoner to escape."[36]

Whig newspapers in Detroit agreed. The *Detroit Journal* criticized Governor Porter for dismissing Ypsilanti officials who had defended the "sanitary regulations adopted" by the citizens of their town. These officials were acting under the authority of a new law that granted public officers broad power to protect towns from infection: they had the right, therefore, to take measures needed to preserve public health. "It was the very object and intention of the law to release our citizens from all legal restraints inconsistent with the great and paramount right of self protection."[37]

Those defending the governor viewed the incident differently, portraying Ypsilanti residents as a bloodthirsty "mob" bent on destruction. A *Free Press* correspondent calling himself "A.B.," insisted the governor had "removed" Abel Millington, Salmon Champion, and Joseph H. Peck "from office not for sanctioning quarantine law," as some Whigs charged, but for joining a "mob" that sought "unlawfully to stop the United States Mail by force and arms." Democrats charged the officials with firing on the "driver of the mail stage," in addition to shooting the horses.[38]

In firing on the stages, Ypsilanti officials had acted illegally, Democrats charged. "We deny that the provisions of the law can be so distorted as to justify" their actions, averred the *Free Press*. Violators of quarantines or other measures to protect public health were "guilty of a misdemeanor." Yet in shooting at the coaches, Ypsilanti officials greatly exceeded the punishment meted out for minor infractions. They seem to have "imagined" that law granted them the authority "to kill and wound the stage horses and fire upon the driver."[39]

Nor was the attack on the stages the only instance of such precipitate conduct. The previously noted *Free Press* correspondent "A.B." reported that the mob also had warned a local resident returning from Detroit that if he refused to stop, "they would shoot his horse," and then him. These "outrages," and "others too numerous to mention" violated "our civil liberties, and ought to be punished not only by removal from office, but by fine and imprisonment in the county gaol." How, moreover, did these actions combat cholera? Where did Ypsilanti officials expect to find the disease? It had not infected the "horses, stage, or driver," because they all "had been changed two or three times between Detroit and Ypsilanti." If Ypsilanti residents feared that the passengers were infected, why had town officials refused to examine them and permitted them to "pass through the village unmolested"?[40]

Some Whig commentators expressed disappointment that cholera failed to unite the community and end partisan bickering. In August 1832, the *Courier* editor noted that he had hoped that "cholera, in its rapid strides to universal dominion, would have put an end for a short time, at least, to the petty warfare of individuals, and that the most inveterate politicians . . . would have tacitly consented to throw aside their favorite weapons and take up" those needed to subdue the "common enemy." Rather than "dying away," however, the "flame seems to have shot up broader and brighter and still continues to burn."[41]

Cholera also failed to end political warfare in 1834. Rather than debating the usefulness of quarantines, Democrats and Whigs disagreed on whether Detroit officials were doing enough to clean the city. In August, the *Free Press* criticized the city's common council for failure to clean the streets. Heavy rain fell earlier in the week, and little had been done to remove the standing water. "Physicians assure us, that the action of the hot sun upon the water standing in every part of the city increases the number of cases." Detroiters planned a "public meeting to express" their discontent with the "course pursued by the Council."[42]

Whigs charged critics with behaving irresponsibly, with the *Detroit Journal* chiding them for being "ungenerous and cruel." In a crisis, the paper observed, some had a "tendency to throw the blame of inevitable evils somewhere." The *Free Press* took "a malicious pleasure" in attacking the city for "things, which they could by no exertion within their power either prevent or control." The council had done more to remove "nuisances" from Detroit "since their election in April," the *Journal* insisted, than that body had done in the last two years, spending more to clean the city in four months than its predecessor had done in the "previous two years or in 1832." The council also had taken steps to improve garbage removal; this project, however, was impeded by the difficulty in finding those willing to undertake such work "when panic and disease had become general." Earlier, the council had proposed getting rid of "one of the greatest nuisances in the city, the old sewer system, and it is highly probable that those who were instrumental in defeating the measure are now the loudest in attributing apathy and negligence to the council."[43]

The *Free Press* wondered why, if Detroit officials had worked so hard to sanitize Detroit, the city remained so filthy. "Will the honorable member of the Common Council," who made such claims, the correspondent asked, "point out the places where the attention has been bestowed? It certainly cannot be found in the improvement of streets, or in the abatement of nuisances in any part of the city." If Whig officials spent more than their predecessors, it simply proved "their incapacity and want of judgment in the disbursement of public" funds, since "little or nothing" had "been done where it was most needed," to improve the health of the city.[44]

Most citizens agreed, the *Free Press* continued, that Detroit had never been so "filthy." Visitors, too, reported finding "no place of its size, where so little attention" had been "paid to public cleanliness." Not all of the blame, however, could be placed on city government. It was "incumbent on every householder to look carefully to his own premises." Detroit, nonetheless, had the "most disgraceful appearance." Jefferson Avenue, one of the city's major thoroughfares, had been in "shocking condition" for the last two or three months. Yet the common council could claim only "to have scattered a few bushels of lime about several of the principle [*sic*] streets—the result of unceasing importunity on the part of these citizens."[45]

The question of how to combat cholera thus revealed regional and political boundaries that divided Michiganians into separate, and sometimes warring, camps. These differences were not apparent when cholera reached Michigan in 1832. Initially, Michiganians saw the malady in much the same way as did those elsewhere. They viewed cholera in moral and religious terms, believing that immoral or unhealthy lifestyles predisposed some to contract the malady. Similarly, many Michiganians echoed the view of easterners who believed cholera was sent by God to punish sinners.

In important respects, however, the effects of the epidemics that struck Michigan in the 1830s differ from the consequences of those that swept through the East. In frontier communities such as Michigan, the shortage of doctors and medical care not only increased the suffering of those afflicted with the malady but also created a crisis that was more difficult for public officials to resolve. The doctrine of predisposing causes, moreover, strengthened ideas preached by Yankee reformers who railed against the moral degeneracy of the Michigan frontier. Evangelicals viewed Michigan's epidemics as God's punishment for the drunkenness, lewdness, and infidelity of its uncivilized populace. Rather than causing sinners to change their ways, cholera seemed to be making Michiganians rowdier than usual.

This behavior was particularly alarming, because of concerns that cholera could spread from sinners to their more respectable neighbors. Although some Michiganians dismissed these fears, others insisted that they were well founded. Subsequently, a furious debate raged in the territory's newspapers over this question, with imprints in the countryside insisting that the disease was contagious and those in Detroit contending that it was not. These differences produced different strategies for combating cholera.

Two years later, Michigan conflict over quarantines largely disappeared. Rather than debating the importance of borders, political parties battled over the effectiveness of efforts to clean Detroit. There are no easy explanations for this change, but evolving perceptions of the frontier and cholera may have had an impact. After the 1832 epidemic, a growing body of European opinion came to embrace noncontagionist views, and Michigan may have followed suit. Then, too, as more and more New Englanders and New Yorkers moved to Michigan, Yankee settlers may have become convinced that the boundaries separating urban from rural space, as well as Anglo from Métis culture, became more secure and no longer required the presence of armed guards.[46]

In 1832, however, cholera generated considerable social conflict in a small corner of the frontier, setting in sharp relief the vital role assigned by those living in the West to defending cultural and regional boundaries. Westerners surely were interested in and responsive to scientific discourse, but tensions along cultural boundaries may have played a more important role in frontier communities than has hitherto been appreciated. Although historians recently have produced a growing body of work on national and cultural borders, less clearly defined boundaries, such as those separating cities from the countryside have remained understudied. Examining such barriers, particularly in western locations, can offer new and more nuanced insights into how borders functioned.

Conclusion

When settlers from New England and western New York began migrating to Michigan in the 1820s, they discovered a frightening world, one that was shaped by values and customs of Native peoples and French settlers. Yankees soon launched crusades to replace these alien and, in their view, savage ways with New England culture, emphasizing the importance of evangelical Christianity, education, sobriety, industriousness, and thriftiness. To inculcate these values in their fellow settlers, Yankees created a variety of boundaries. Boundary setting, they hoped, would enable them to reestablish New England norms and to distinguish acceptable practices from those that they deemed taboo. More specifically, these restraints were designed not only to tame what they viewed as the wildness of Native peoples and many white settlers, but also to protect Michiganians from the alleged immorality and greed of power-hungry territorial officials, bankers, and Ohioans.

To accomplish these tasks, leaders established two types of boundaries. First were the formal boundaries enacted by legislatures and administered by law courts and other official institutions; second, the informal boundaries created by families, newspapers, public opinion, and churches. Such informal, customary barriers helped establish the stable and orderly base on which formal, legal restraints rested.

Establishing these formal boundaries played an important role in helping Michiganians achieve their long and difficult quest for self-rule. Tracing the development of such restraints demonstrates that the state's antebellum political development involved more than the rise and fall of the second party system and indicates that boundary setting preceded and established the foundation on which the party system rested. Michiganians believed that creating these restraints would establish the rule of law and curb the despotism of territorial officials, neighboring states, and cultural outsiders. The Northwest Ordinance played an important role in several of these battles, because settlers believed that this boundary-setting document possessed constitutional qualities that protected their rights.

After the War of 1812, Michiganians expressed growing concern that the territory's officials, who they believed were despotic and lawless, endangered those rights. They complained that these men regularly violated the Northwest Ordinance and lacked any interest in the needs or concerns of Michiganians. Their rights, Michiganians insisted, were always at risk in a regime that lacked clear and stable constitutional boundaries. In addition, they asserted that they could not create a safe and stable community, because lawmakers violated the legal and constitutional boundaries they were supposed to uphold. This official wrongdoing created increasing skepticism about the legitimacy of Michigan's government, which, in turn, produced growing anarchy and disrespect for the law. These fears were eased in 1823 when Congress granted Michigan the right to an elected assembly after territorial residents mounted a vigorous campaign urging federal lawmakers to grant them some measure of self-rule.

The obsession with lawlessness and despotism also shaped two other disputes central to Michigan's political development—its battle with Ohio over Toledo and the debate over voting rights in the state's new constitution. In their dispute with Ohio, Michigan officials sought to persuade Washington to curb the aggression and rapacity of the Buckeye State, which refused to abide by the boundaries established in the Northwest Ordinance and instead seemed bent on conquering its weaker neighbors. Such conduct proved that Ohio was already too large and that unstable borders encouraged wildness and aggression. Not only had the Buckeye State attempted to take the territory's land without congressional approval, it also had stirred up anarchy and rebelliousness in southeastern Michigan. Giving Ohio the Toledo Strip, Michiganians predicted, would make it even larger and encourage more lawlessness and savagery. These dire forecasts did not impress Congress, which eventually awarded Toledo to Ohio.

But in making these predictions, Michigan officials emphasized the importance of maintaining a rough equality between states, warning that if some states got too large, they could threaten their smaller neighbors. Borders thus were important, because they determined how wealth and power were divided among the states. If Congress made some states too large, they might become drunk with power, threatening their neighbors and possibly the whole federation. To prevent such aggressive behavior, it was important to maintain a balance of power in the region, respect the boundaries laid out in the ordinance, and keep states approximately the same size.

The threat of violence and lawlessness also was at the heart of the debate over suffrage during the drafting of Michigan's new constitution in 1835. Whigs and Democrats disagreed about whether blacks or immigrants posed a graver threat to peace and stability. Whigs and some dissident Democrats opposed a Democratic proposal to enfranchise aliens in Michigan's new constitution, insisting that aliens' savagery and lack of independence endangered the polity. Having been socialized in monarchies, most aliens lacked an essential quality of manliness—independence. Demagogues or foreign despots could easily manipulate these voters and use them to destroy the republic. Some Whig newspapers also relied on nativist propaganda to evoke images of immigrants as barbaric hordes whose poverty, filth, and unruliness could destabilize society. Democrats who opposed black suffrage employed racist rhetoric to create a similar portrait of blacks. Enfranchising African Americans would breed anarchy and disorder by attracting growing numbers of violent and unruly blacks to Michigan. These arguments eventually enabled Democrats to pass a constitutional provision that denied the vote to African Americans but permitted many aliens to vote.

Disenfranchising blacks was not the only step Michiganians took to tame wildness. They believed, too, that economic development was vitally important in civilizing Michigan's frontier. A growing economy established new borders that transformed a wild and unruly land into one that contained cities, towns, counties, and private property. At the same time, it transformed forests and meadows from wasteland into productive farms, diminished the importance of the fur trade, and dramatically reduced the importance of Native peoples in Michigan's economy. After prices collapsed in 1837, however, their views of economic growth began to change. Both parties expressed increasing concern about the plummeting value of Michigan's currency and an economy that seemed to have gone haywire.

To explain the source of these woes, Michiganians engaged in a long and sometimes rancorous discussion about the kinds of legal and customary boundaries needed to control the wild speculation and acquisitiveness that prosperity unleashed. Though the two parties largely agreed on the kind of customary boundaries required to rein in the greed and recklessness of individuals, they differed on the type of legal restraints required to curb the power of banks and control the amount of currency in circulation. On the national level, Michigan's Democrats and Whigs differed on the merits of a central bank: Whigs asserted that such a bank was vital to economic growth and stability because it was the only institution capable of setting boundaries that restrained the wild speculation of state banks. Democrats, however, insisted that the national bank was a tyrant and that its unlimited, moneyed power represented a grave threat to republican values and institutions. On the state level, the two parties debated the wisdom of a new law that enabled entrepreneurs to establish banks without first getting legislative approval. Democrats defended the measure as a way to remove the artificial boundaries created by monopolies and enabling many more Michiganians to enter the banking business. Whigs criticized the bill for erasing barriers needed to protect Michigan bill holders from greedy charlatans who did not possess the specie needed to redeem their currency.

Despite these differences, the two parties agreed on the need to strengthen the customary boundaries that checked the greed and rapacity unleashed by rampant commercialization. During the Panic, Democratic and Whig newspapers both denounced the acquisitiveness and "speculative mania" that had spread through the state during the boom of the 1830s and eroded the boundaries that the moral economy established, emphasizing the importance of industry, thrift, and sobriety. To reestablish those boundaries, newspapers published fiction, editorials, and advice columns that condemned men who gambled recklessly in land and other investments. They also chastised women who ruined their husbands by spending wildly. The Panic, they insisted, represented the just deserts of those who engaged in such conduct.

Michiganians established these legal, ethical, and social boundaries to re-create the Yankee culture they had known in the East. Did they succeed? The evidence suggests that Yankees were relatively successful in establishing traditional legal boundaries in politics, economics, and law. Their efforts to curb the power of bankers, speculators, and Michigan officials during the territorial period, for example, enabled them to construct legal and constitutional restraints that resembled those in the East. Yet even in these areas, some notable differences distinguished Michigan's polity from those of eastern states. Like other western states, Michigan's constitution featured a provision on alien voting rights that was far more liberal than those of its eastern counterparts. This may have been because the control of seemingly savage Native, black, and Métis populations made differences based on race seem much more important than those tied to ethnicity.[1]

Such racial fears were also reflected in the reform crusades that Yankees launched in early Michigan. These campaigns to tame the supposed savagery of the frontier shared important characteristics with reform crusades in the East, but they also differed from those movements in important ways.

In both regions, evangelical Christians enthusiastically embraced the effort to create a more moral and religious nation. Eastern reformers, however, often focused on towns and cities as hotbeds of immorality and wildness. These urban areas, after all, were seen as teeming with criminals, drunkards, prostitutes, gamblers, and immigrants. More than one study suggests, furthermore, that the rising bourgeoisie in the East used reform to create a new ethos that enabled them to control unruly employees. Though employers may not have done so consciously, they employed evangelicalism as a tool to defeat rebellious workers and create a more pliant workforce.[2]

Michigan reformers shared many of these concerns and adhered to the same bourgeois ethos as did their eastern counterparts. Michiganians nonetheless viewed wildness much more broadly than did easterners, equating it not only with urban dwellers, but also with Native peoples, the French, and many of their white neighbors. Rather than seeking explicitly to manipulate workers who resisted labor discipline or to civilize urban dwellers, they sought to tame the perceived or incipient savagery and wildness of settlers throughout Michigan. While vice in the East seems to have evoked the fear of cities, as well as class consciousness and conflict, it seems to have taken on greater racial overtones on the frontier, becoming inextricably linked to Indians and other nonwhite races. Whites who drank, gambled, and indulged in other forms of vice were condemned, because, like Indians and blacks, they lacked a key masculine trait: they were unable to control their impulses.

To help Michiganians gain greater self-control, reformers launched campaigns to tame the alleged wildness of drunken Indians and whites who adopted their savage ways. Yankees mistakenly believed that Native peoples were primarily hunters who represented a primitive stage in human evolution and lived without the spiritual and ethical restraints that were so vital to European civilization. Natives were like wild animals, Yankees alleged, motivated by bloodlust and other savage impulses. Additionally, Yankees depicted Natives as drunks who engaged in crime and violence. The French, meanwhile, were nearly as bad as Native peoples. Instead of taming Natives, the French had permitted the reverse to occur: abandoning civilization, they had adopted the barbaric ways of local tribes, a fate that Yankees feared might befall them as well. Anglo settlers also worried that the alleged wildness of Native peoples might destabilize society and hamper economic growth by frightening easterners and slowing migration to Michigan.

To combat these problems, Michigan's elites established legal and cultural borders to control alleged Indian barbarism. They created laws to stop Indians from drinking and negotiated treaties that either confined Natives to reservations or exiled them from Michigan to new homes west of the Mississippi. To stop whites from adopting Native ways, Michigan editors published captivity narratives that allegorized concerns about hybridization and sought to strengthen cultural boundaries between Indians and whites. These stories, which portrayed Indians capturing whites and converting them to alien ways, often began by depicting Native peoples in a warm and sympathetic light. Eventually, however, they demonstrated the incompatibility of Natives and whites and the need to prevent Indian contamination of Yankee culture.

Reformers also condemned the behavior of white settlers who gambled, drank heavily, visited prostitutes, violated the Sabbath, and failed to attend church. Echoing the fears of their revolutionary ancestors, Michigan leaders expressed concern that a republic could not survive without a virtuous populace. In addition, drunkenness and other vices connected to it were closely associated with the barbarism of Indians and, in some cases, African Americans. To subdue such behavior, reformers enacted laws to reduce drinking and other forms of wickedness. They also asserted that the wildness of Michiganians was due in part to poor family governance. Too many Michigan families, reformers claimed, were ruled by weak, ineffective fathers who could not control their dependents. To remedy the problem, they established schools and relied on print culture, especially newspapers, to teach men how to be better fathers and to discipline women and children more effectively.

But these efforts to transport the patriarchal family to Michigan were largely unsuccessful. Rather than rescuing patriarchy, efforts to reform sinners and their dependents led to the creation of new companionate families. In this respect, Michigan evidence resembles what Mary P. Ryan found in her pioneering study of western New York. Many of the values associated with the cult of domesticity—such as the decline of patriarchal authority and the growing importance of mothers in rearing children—grew out of the voluntary associations organized to carry out the work of reform. These groups served as laboratories in which members could develop new forms of sociability, undermining the patriarchal family by emphasizing strong bonds of affection between equals instead of "stern reverence to elders." Temperance reformers "eschewed father figures and banded together as brothers." In this process, reformers, especially female reformers, developed what Ryan describes as new "family practices." Such sentimental notions as the "pure, loving mother" arose in benevolent societies, but eventually migrated back to the home and transformed families.[3]

In Michigan, the rise of domesticity was accompanied by conflict over traditional gender roles. Although education helped to tame the drunkenness and viciousness of men, it seems to have had the opposite effect on some women, enabling them to become more outspoken and critical of male authority. Education thus blurred the boundaries that defined femininity, producing women who did not fit neatly into traditional categories of masculinity or femininity and no longer could assume their proper role in the family. Efforts to tame the savagery of the West thus may have inadvertently helped to create women who were more outspoken and difficult to govern than their eastern counterparts.

Efforts to prevent Native practices from contaminating Yankee culture encountered similar problems. These difficulties were reflected in the captivity narratives, which attempted to strengthen racial barriers and to stop the Indianization. To make these boundaries more impermeable and demonstrate the incompatibility of Indians and whites, authors often concluded fictional tales by depicting captives returning to their families and reassuming their white identities.

John Tanner's autobiography, however, demonstrates that separating white from Indian identity was probably tougher than these fictional tales suggested. After decades in captivity, Tanner left Indian country and returned to his white family in Kentucky. But unlike fictive protagonists, he was unable to become white again, finding that his old personality had vanished during his years of captivity. Nor was Tanner able to resume his Indian identity. Instead, he experienced a phenomenon that anthropologist Renato Rosaldo argues is common in borderlands. Describing the heroine of a Hispanic novel, Rosaldo observes that she inhabits a "border zone crisscrossed by a plurality of languages and cultures. Multiple subjectivities intersect in her own person, where they coexist . . . each with its own gravity and density." Much the same could be said of Tanner. At the end of his long travail, he discovered that he was neither Indian nor white, but a complex combination of the two cultures. Tanner might serve, therefore, as a representation of Michigan's borderland culture and the inability of Michigan officials to create a totally impermeable border that could prevent Native influence from entering New England culture.[4]

Yankee efforts to transplant New England ways to Michigan thus met with mixed success. The formal legal boundaries that they established in Michigan closely resembled those that they had left behind in the East. Transferring informal cultural norms, however, proved to be a much more daunting task. Both Michigan Yankees and their counterparts in the East launched campaigns to tame drunkenness and immorality. Easterners, however, viewed wildness differently than did those in Michigan. The former saw savagery as a largely urban and class phenomenon and created restraints that aimed to control urban dwellers, workers, immigrants, and other groups who threatened their genteel ways. Michigan reformers defined wildness much more expansively, linking it to the allegedly savage ways of Native peoples, the French and other Anglo settlers. Their efforts to eradicate Native culture and tame the savagery of their white neighbors

were only partially successful. Michigan leaders succeeded in confining local tribes to reservations or expelling them from the state. But they could
not prevent Native ways from infiltrating Yankee culture. Similarly, Anglo settlers managed to reduce drinking and other forms of immorality in
Michigan. But in doing so, they seem to have produced a group of educated women who violated traditional gender norms.

These developments shed new light on an old debate about the frontier.
Since the days of Frederick Jackson Turner Jackson in the late nineteenth
and early twentieth century, historians have debated whether pioneers created a new culture in the West or simply transplanted their traditional Eastern ways to that region. Neither of these models adequately describes the
experience of Michiganians in the first third of the nineteenth century.

Initially, settlers from New England and western New York hoped to
reestablish Yankee ways in Michigan by transferring both the formal legal
and informal customary boundaries of the East to the Michigan frontier.
Such restraints, they believed, would tame a society that to their eyes
seemed savage and uncivilized. The borders that private property created
would tame forests and fields, transforming Michigan's wild landscape
into productive farms and villages, which would form the backbone of
the new republic Yankees hoped to create in the West. Legal restraints,
they believed, would establish the rule of law and tame the wildness of
Michigan officials, bankers, and Ohioans. Yankees insisted, moreover, that
schools and print culture, especially newspapers, would enable them to
recreate Eastern norms in Michigan and to discipline the alleged savagery
and barbarism of Native Peoples, the French and early Anglo settlers.

Setting boundaries, however, turned out to be far more complicated
than Michigan elites expected. For one thing, Yankees often disagreed not
only about the type of boundaries that were needed to tame this seemingly savage land, but also about whether boundaries were needed at all.
For another, they discovered that ordinary Michiganians could reconfigure
boundaries in ways that the elite hadn't imagined. Rather than simply
transferring Eastern ways to West, Michiganians wound up doing something far more complex: they inadvertently created a regional culture that
was predominantly Eastern, but that also contained Native and French
and western elements.

Studying early Michigan thus reveals the importance of boundary setting in understanding the rise of regional cultures. Mary Douglas and other anthropologists have demonstrated that such rules and restraints help
groups to define identity, to understand the world, and to divide power
and wealth. In Michigan, Yankees found that imposing these boundaries
on what they imagined to be an empty land was simply impossible. They
discovered, instead, that ordinary settlers and Native Peoples tweaked
and changed these rules when possible to meet their own needs.[5]

Notes

INTRODUCTION

1. *Detroit Courier,* Sept. 27, 1832.

2. Ronald Takaki, *A Different Mirror: A History of Multicultural America* (Boston: Little, Brown, 1993), 26–27, 31.

3. *Detroit Courier,* Sept. 27, 1832.

4. Christopher L. Tomlins, "The Many Legalities of Colonization: A Manifesto of Destiny for Early American Legal History," in Christopher L. Tomlins and Bruce H. Mann, eds., *The Many Legalities of Early America* (Chapel Hill: University of North Carolina Press, 2001), 1; and Kathleen Neils Conzen, "Pi-ing the Type: Jane Grey Swisshelm and the Contest of Midwest Regionality," in Andrew R. L. Cayton and Susan E. Gray, eds., *The American Midwest: Essays on Regional History* (Bloomington: Indiana University Press, 2001), 103.

5. There is a large literature on Yankee culture. One of the classic works is Richard L. Bushman, *From Puritan to Yankee: Character and the Social Order in Connecticut, 1690–1765* (Cambridge: Harvard University Press, 1967).

6. U.S. Bureau of the Census, *Historical Statistics of the United States from Colonial Times to 1970,* vol. 1 (Washington, DC: Government Printing Office, 1975), 8; and Stephan Thernstrom, ed., *Harvard Encyclopedia of American Ethnic Groups* (Cambridge: Harvard University Press, 1980), 410, 528.

7. The number of works on U.S. economic and political development in the nineteenth century is large and growing. Some of the most influential interpretations include Daniel Walker Howe, *What Hath God Wrought: The Transformation of America, 1815–1848* (New York: Oxford University Press, 2007); Charles Sellers, *The Market Revolution: Jacksonian America, 1815–1846* (New York: Oxford University Press, 1991); Sean Wilentz, *The Rise of American Democracy: Jefferson to Lincoln* (New York: W. W. Norton, 2005); Daniel Feller, *The Jacksonian Promise: America, 1815–1840* (Baltimore: Johns Hopkins University Press, 1995); and George Rogers Taylor, *The Transportation Revolution, 1815–1860* (New York: Rinehart, 1951; rept. Armonk, NY: M. E. Sharpe, 1989).

8. The literature on settling the West is enormous. Some of the most influential works include Alan Taylor, *The Divided Ground: Indians, Settlers and the Northern Borderland of the American Revolution* (New York: Vintage Books, 2006); Stephen Aron; *American Confluence: The Missouri Frontier from Borderland to Border State* (Bloomington: Indiana University Press, 2006); Jeremy Adelman and Stephen Aron,

"From Borderlands to Borders: Empires, Nation-States, and the Peoples in Between in North American History," *American Historical Review* 104 (June 1999): 814–41; Bethel Saler, "Negotiating the Treaty Polity: Gender, Race and the Transformation of Wisconsin from Indian Country into an American State, 1776–1854" (PhD diss., University of Wisconsin, 1999); Richard White, *The Middle Ground: Indians, Empires and Republics in the Great Lakes Region, 1650–1815* (New York: Cambridge University Press, 1991); Patricia Nelson Limerick, *The Legacy of Conquest: The Unbroken Past of the American West* (New York: W. W. Norton, 1987); Gregory H. Nobles, *American Frontier: Cultural Encounters and Continental Conquest* (New York: Hill and Wang, 1997); David J. Weber, "Turner, the Boltonians, and the Borderlands," *American Historical Review* 91 (Feb. 1986): 66–81; Patricia Nelson Limerick, Clyde A. Milner II, and Charles E. Rankin, eds., *Trails: Toward a New Western History* (Lawrence: University Press of Kansas, 1991); William Cronon, George Miles, and Jay Gitlin, eds., *Under an Open Sky: Rethinking America's Western Past* (New York: W. W. Norton, 1992); and William Cronon, *Changes in the Land: Indians, Colonists and the Ecology of New England* (New York: Hill and Wang, 1983).

9. William Gronan, George Miles, and Jay Gitlin, "Becoming West," in Gronan, Miles, and Gitlin, *Under the Open Sky*, 10–18; and Limenck, *Legacy of Conquest*, 27.

10. David Shields, "The Emergence of Civic Culture in the Colonies to about 1770," in Jack P. Greene and J. R. Pole, eds., *A Companion to the American Revolution* (Malden, MA: Blackwell Publishing, 2000), 82.

11. See, for instance, Gloria Anzaldúa, *Borderlands / La Frontera: The New Mestiza* (San Francisco: Aunt Lute Books, 1987); Jeremy Adelman and Stephen Aron, "From Borderlands to Borders: Empires, Nation-States, and the Peoples in Between in North American History," *American Historical Review* 104 (June 1999): 814–41; and William Cronon, George Miles, and Jay Gitlin, "Becoming West: Toward a New Meaning for Western History," in *Under an Open Sky: Rethinking America's Western Past*, ed. William Cronon, George Miles, and Jay Gitlin (New York: W. W. Norton, 1992); and Patricia Nelson Limerick, *The Legacy of Conquest: The Unbroken Past of the American West* (New York: W. W. Norton), 1987.

12. Peter S. Onuf, *Statehood and Union: A History of the Northwest Ordinance* (Bloomington: Indiana University Press, 1987), 88–108.

13. Many works have been published on Western culture. Two of the most important are Earl Pomeroy, *Territories and the United States, 1861–1890: Studies in Colonial Administration* (Seattle: University of Washington Press, reprt. 1969); and Frederick Jackson Turner, *The Frontier in American History* (New York: H. Holt, 1920; rept. Holt, Rinehart and Winston, 1962). The former argues that pioneers primarily transported their old ways to the frontier, while the latter contends that settlers created a new culture in the West, one that was distinctly American and democratic.

1—THE RISE OF MICHIGAN'S NEW CONSTITUTIONAL ORDER

1. Alec R. Gilpin, *The Territory of Michigan, 1805–1837* (East Lansing: Michigan State University Press, 1970), 72–74.

2. Frank B. Woodford, *Mr. Jefferson's Disciple: A Life of Justice Woodward* (East Lansing: Michigan State College Press, 1953), 4.

3. Woodford, *Mr. Jefferson's Disciple*, 47, 36, 45, 56–59, 60–62.

4. Ibid., 12.

5. Ibid., 17–35, 62.

6. Ibid., 59–62.

7. Ibid., 59–64; Silas Farmer, *History of Detroit and Wayne County and Early Michigan: A Chronological Cyclopedia of the Past and Present* (Detroit: Silas Farmer, 1890; 3rd ed., 1969), 96; and Woodford, *Mr. Jefferson's Disciple*, 47–50.

8. Willis F. Dunbar and George S. May, *Michigan: A History of the Wolverine State*, 3rd rev. ed. (Grand Rapids, MI: Eerdmans, 1995), 183–84.

9. R. Douglas Hurt, *The Ohio Frontier: Crucible of the Old Northwest, 1720–1830* (Bloomington: Indiana University Press, 1996), 275.

10. *Detroit Gazette*, Aug. 11, 1820.

11. Ibid., Aug. 11, 1820.

12. Ibid., Sept. 8, 1820.

13. Ibid., Sept. 29, 1820.

14. Ibid., March 15, 1822.

15. Woodford, *Mr. Jefferson's Disciple*, 66–67.

16. Ibid., 67.

17. *Detroit Gazette*, Nov. 8, 1822.

18. Ibid., May 29, 1818.

19. Ibid., Nov. 27, 1818.

20. Ibid., Nov. 28, 1817.

21. Ibid., Dec. 19, 1817.

22. Ibid., Dec. 12, 1817.

23. William Wirt Blume, ed., *Transactions of the Supreme Court of Michigan*, vol. 3, case number 564 (Ann Arbor: University of Michigan Press, 1938).

24. *Detroit Gazette*, Oct. 10, 1817.

25. Ibid., Aug. 3, 1826.

26. Ibid., Aug. 11, 1820.

27. Ibid., Jan. 24, 1823.

28. Ibid., March 14, 1823.

29. Ibid., Nov. 28, 1817.

30. Ibid., Dec. 5, 1817.

31. Ibid., March 14, 1823.

32. Ibid., Nov. 28, 1817.

33. In recent years, scholars have produced a growing literature on manhood. A few of the seminal works include E. Anthony Rotundo, *American Manhood: Transformations in Masculinity from the Revolution to the Modern Era* (New York: Basic Books, 1993); Michael Kimmel, *Manhood in America: A Cultural History* (New York: Free Press, 1996); and Mark C. Carnes and Clyde Griffen, eds., *Meanings for Manhood: Constructions of Masculinity in Victorian America* (Chicago: University of Chicago Press, 1990).

34. *Detroit Gazette*, Oct. 25, 1822.

35. Ibid., Nov. 29, 1822.

36. Ibid., Jan. 24, 1823.

37. Ibid., Nov. 28, 1817.

38. Ibid., Oct. 25, 1822.

39. Ibid., Dec. 5, 1817.

40. Ibid., Dec. 26, 1817.

41. Ibid., Aug. 15, 1822.

42. Ibid., March 22, 1822.

43. Dunbar and May, *Michigan*, 183–84.

44. Ronald P. Formisano, *The Birth of Mass Political Parties: Michigan, 1827–1861* (Princeton: Princeton University Press, 1971), 80–84.

45. *Detroit Journal and Michigan Advertiser,* Jan. 14, 1835.

46. Harold Dorr, ed., *The Michigan Constitutional Conventions of 1835–1836* (Ann Arbor: University of Michigan Press, 1940), 14.

47. Daniel Walker Howe, *What Hath God Wrought: The Transformation of America, 1815–1848* (New York; Oxford University Press, 2007), 489–91; Jerrold G. Rusk, *A Statistical History of the American Electorate* (Washington, DC: CQ Press, 2001), 16–18, 32.

48. Ibid., 176–77.

49. Ibid., 222.

50. Ibid., 227–28.

51. Ibid., 228–29.

52. *Detroit Journal,* April 8, 1835.

53. Ibid., April 8, 1835.

54. Ibid.

55. Dorr, *Michigan Constitutional Conventions,* 232.

56. Ibid., 243.

57. Ibid., 251.

58. Ibid., 257.

59. Ibid., 203–4.

60. Ibid., 205.

61. Ibid., 208–9.

62. Ibid., 155; and Ronald Formisano, "The Edge of Caste," *Michigan History,* 22.

63. Dorr, *Michigan Constitutional Conventions,* 157.

64. Ibid., 159.

65. Ibid., 162–63.

66. Ibid., 163.

67. Ibid., 163–64.

68. Ibid., 157.

69. Ibid., 157–58.

70. Ibid., 246.

71. Ibid., 247.

72. Constitution of Michigan of 1835, http://www.legislature.mi.gov/documents/historical/miconstitution1835.htm.

73. Ibid., 30; and *Michigan Sentinel,* June 6, 1835.

2—OHIO AND THE BATTLE FOR MICHIGAN'S SOUTHERN BORDER

1. *Michigan Sentinel,* Aug. 1, 1835.

2. The idea of a nation or, in this case, a state as an imagined political com-munity is derived from Benedict Anderson, *Imagined Communities,* rev. ed. (New York: Verso, 1991), 6.

3. Peter S. Onuf, *Statehood and Union: A History of the Northwest Ordinance* (Bloomington: Indiana University Press, 1987), has greatly influenced my discus-sion of the Toledo conflict and concerns about maintaining a balance of power between states.

4. Willis F. Dunbar and George S. May, *Michigan: A History of the Wolver-ine State* (Grand Rapids, MI: Eerdmans Publishing Company, 1995, 3rd rev. ed.), 159–62 and 204.

5. Peter S. Onuf, *Origins of the Federal Republic: Jurisdictional Controversies in the United States, 1775–1787* (Philadelphia: University of Pennsylvania Press, 1983), 49–57, 127–45.

6. Onuf, *Statehood and Union,* 88–89; Dunbar and May, *Michigan,* 95.

7. Dunbar and May, *Michigan,* 211–13; and Onuf, *Statehood and Union,* 95.

8. Dunbar and May, *Michigan,* 213.

9. *Detroit Free Press,* Jan. 22, 1834.

10. Ibid., April 23, 1834.

11. Lawton T. Hemans, *Life and Times of Stevens Thomson Mason: The Boy Gov-ernor of Michigan* (Lansing: Michigan Historical Commission, 1920), 11–14, 17–19, 22, 28–29, 32–33, 36, 53–55, 119.

12. Frank E. Robson, "The Michigan and Ohio Boundary Line," *Michigan Historical Collections,* vol. 11 (Lansing, MI: Thorp and Godfrey, 1888), 222–23; Law-ton T. Hemans, *Life and Times of Stevens Thomson Mason* (Lansing: Michigan State University Press, 1920), 137, 138–39; and Alec Gilpin, *The Territory of Michigan, 1805–1837* (Lansing: Michigan State University Press, 1970), 173–82.

13. Gilpin, *Territory of Michigan,* 173–82; and Hemans, *Life and Times of Ste-vens Thomson Mason,* 139.

14. Hemans, *Life and Times of Stevens Thomson Mason,* 143–46; and John A. Mousty, "The Trammels of Territory: The Toledo Border War and Michigan's Admis-sion Struggle," master's thesis, Wayne State University, 1994, 26–28.

15. *Michigan Sentinel,* March 17, 1835.

16. Ibid., May 2, 1835.

17. *Democratic Free Press,* April 15, 1835.

18. Michigan governor Stevens T. Mason to Ohio governor Robert Lucas, 2 April 1835, Papers of Stevens T. Mason, 1827–1842, Michigan Historical Collection, Bentley Historical Library, University of Michigan.

19. Robson, "The Michigan and Ohio Boundary," *Michigan Historical Collec-tions,* 223–24.

20. *Michigan Sentinel,* March 17, 1835; and Roger L. Rosentreter, "Michigan's Quest for State," in Richard J. Hathaway, ed., *Michigan: Visions of Our Past* (East Lansing: Michigan State University Press, 1989), 82.

21. J. Wilkie Moore, "Mr. Moore's Personal Recollections of the Contest with Ohio Fifty Years Ago," *Michigan Historical Collections,* vol. 7 (Lansing, MI: Thorp and Godfrey, 1886), 69–70.

22. *Democratic Free Press,* April 29, 1835.

23. *Michigan Sentinel,* May 2, 1835; and Hemans, *Life and Times of Stevens Thomson Mason,* 146–47.

24. *Michigan Sentinel,* April 11, 1835.

25. *Free Press,* July 22, 1835.

26. Dunbar and May, *Michigan,* 215.

27. *Free Press,* July 22, 1835.

28. Ibid.

29. Michigan governor Stevens T. Mason to U.S. secretary of state John Forsyth, July 17, 1835, Papers of Stevens T. Mason, 1827–1842, Michigan Historical Collection, Bentley Historical Library, University of Michigan.

30. *Michigan Sentinel,* Aug. 1, 1835.

31. Henry M. Utley and Byron M. Cutcheon, *Michigan as a Province, Territory and State* (New York: Publishing Society of Michigan, 1906), 35.

32. *Detroit Free Press,* Dec. 24, 1834.

33. Ibid., June 18, 1834.

34. *Michigan Sentinel,* July 11, 1835.

35. *Detroit Free Press,* Feb. 18, 1835.

36. *Michigan Sentinel,* March 7, 1835.

37. Onuf, *Statehood and Union,* 97–98.

38. *Michigan Sentinel,* March 7, 1835.

39. Ibid., Feb. 28, 1835.

40. Onuf, *Statehood and Union,* 89–90; and Peter S. Onuf, *Origins of the Federal Republic: Jurisdictional Controversies in the United States, 1775–1787* (Philadelphia: University of Pennsylvania Press, 1983), 194–96.

41. *Detroit Free Press,* June 18, 1834.

42. *Michigan Sentinel,* Sept. 27, 1834.

43. *Detroit Free Press,* June 18, 1834.

44. Onuf, *Statehood and Union,* 89–90.

45. Bernard Bailyn, *The Ideological Origins of the American Revolution* (Cambridge: Belknap Press of Harvard University Press, 1967), 56, 59–60.

46. *Detroit Journal,* April 12, 1836.

47. Ibid., Nov. 1, 1836.

48. *Michigan Sentinel,* July 11, 1835.

49. Ibid., Aug. 1, 1835.

50. Ibid., June 18, 1834.

51. George N. Fuller, ed., *Messages of the Governors of Michigan* (Lansing: Michigan Historical Commission, 1925), vol. 1, 125–26.

52. *Detroit Free Press,* July 9, 1834.

53. *Detroit Journal,* Nov. 7, 1835.

54. Ibid., March 4, 1835.

55. Ibid.

56. Ibid., March 5, 1835.

57. Fuller, *Messages of the Governors of Michigan,* 122; and Michigan governor Stevens T. Mason, Address to Michigan's Legislative Council, Nov. 19, 1834, Papers of Stevens T. Mason, 1827–1842, Michigan Historical Collection, Bentley Historical Library, University of Michigan.

58. Dunbar and May, *Michigan,* 216; and *Free Press,* March 16, 1836.

59. *Detroit Free Press,* March 23, 1836.

60. Quotations come from the following issues of the *Free Press,* March 16, 1836; March 23, 1836; and April 13, 1836; from *Register of Debates in Congress,* 1010; and from Hemans, *Life and Times of Stevens Thompson Mason,* 199.

61. Fuller, *Messages of the Governors of Michigan,* 180; and *Detroit Journal,* March 19, 1836.

62. *Detroit Free Press,* Aug. 3, 1836, Aug. 10, 1836, and Aug. 24, 1836.

63. Ibid., Aug. 10, 1836, and Aug. 24, 1836.

64. Ibid., Aug. 10, 1836.

65. Ibid., Aug. 24, 1836, Aug. 31, 1826, and Aug. 17, 1835.

66. *Detroit Journal,* March 19, 1836.

67. *Michigan Sentinel,* May 14, 1836. For other examples of this language, see the following issues of the *Michigan Sentinel,* April 23, 1836, April 30, 1836, May 21, 1836, and May 28, 1836.

68. Ibid., April 9, 1836.

69. Ibid.

70. *Detroit Journal,* Sept. 6, 1836.

71. Ibid., Aug. 30, 1836.

72. *Michigan Sentinel,* June 25, 1836; and *Detroit Journal,* Aug. 23, 1836.

73. *Detroit Free Press,* Sept. 21, 1836.

74. Gilpin, *The Territory of Michigan,* 191; Harold Dorr, ed., *The Michigan Constitutional Conventions of 1835–36* (Ann Arbor: University of Michigan Press, 1940), 543–44; and Dunbar and May, *Michigan,* 218.

75. *Detroit Free Press,* Sept. 28, 1836; and Dorr, *Michigan Constitutional Conventions,* 569.

76. *Detroit Free Press,* Nov. 2, 1836.

77. Ibid., Dec. 17, 1836, and Nov. 9, 1836.

78. Dorr, *Michigan Constitutional Conventions,* 568–69, 570–71.

79. Gilpin, *Territory of Michigan,* 192.

3—ECONOMIC DEVELOPMENT AND THE PANIC OF 1837

1. Daniel Walker Howe, *What Hath God Wrought: The Transformation of America, 1815–1848* (New York: Oxford University Press, 2007), 116–20, 562–69; Charles Sellers, *The Market Revolution: Jacksonian America, 1815–1846* (New York: Oxford University Press, 1991), 40–45, 391–92.

2. Sean Wilentz, "Society, Politics and the Market Revolution, 1815–1848,"

72, in Eric Foner, ed., *The New American History,* rev. and expanded ed. (Philadelphia: Temple University Press, 1997). The literature on the Market Revolution has recently grown dramatically. For two seminal works, see Charles Sellers, *The Market Revolution: Jacksonian America, 1815–1846* (Oxford, NY: Oxford University Press, 1991); and Harry L. Watson, *Liberty and Power: The Politics of Jacksonian America* (New York: Hill and Wang, 1990). For a more critical view, see Howe, *What Hath God Wrought,* and Daniel Feller, *The Jacksonian Promise: America, 1815–1840* (Baltimore: Johns Hopkins University Press, 1995).

3. Hon. Byron M. Cutcheon, "Fifty Years of Growth in Michigan," an address delivered in 1892 before the Michigan State Congregational Assoc., *Michigan Historical Collections,* vol. 22 (Lansing, MI: Robert Smith, 1894), 483.

4. Willis Dunbar and George S. May, *Michigan: A History of the Wolverine State,* 3rd rev. ed. (Grand Rapids, MI: Eerdmans, 1995), 163, 165.

5. Caroline Kirkland, *A New Home: Who'll Follow? or, Glimpses of Western Life* (New York: C. S. Francis, 1839; repr. New York: Garrett Press, 1969), iii, 42.

6. Dunbar and May, *Michigan,* 164.

7. Cutcheon, "Fifty Years of Growth in Michigan," *Michigan Historical Collections,* vol. 22, 479.

8. *Detroit Journal and Michigan Advertiser,* Aug. 13, 1834.

9. *Western Emigrant,* Nov. 18, 1829.

10. *Pontiac Courier,* Feb. 2, 1838.

11. Several historians have shown that this view of Indians was incorrect. Although their economies differed from those of whites, they did engage in agriculture and commerce. See, e.g., William Cronon, *Changes in the Land: Indians, Colonists and the Ecology of New England* (New York: Hill and Wang, 1983).

12. *Detroit Journal,* March 19, 1834.

13. *Detroit Free Press,* May 3, 1832.

14. Ibid., Nov. 3, 1831.

15. Ibid., Nov. 16, 1836.

16. Reginald Charles McGrane, *The Panic of 1837: Some Financial Problems of the Jacksonian Era* (Chicago: Chicago University Press, 1924), 91–93; Peter Temin, *The Jacksonian Economy* (New York: W. W. Norton, 1969), 174; and Dunbar and May, *Michigan,* 230.

17. *Detroit Journal,* May 9, 1837.

18. Ibid., Feb. 27, 1838.

19. Ibid., Sept. 11, 1838.

20. *Michigan Whig* (Adrian, MI), Aug. 22, 1838.

21. Ibid.

22. *Pontiac Courier,* June 8, 1838.

23. *Detroit Journal,* April 10, 1838.

24. Ibid.

25. *Detroit Free Press,* May 9, 1838; and *Detroit Morning Post,* May 9, 1838.

26. William G. Shade, "Banks and Politics in Michigan, 1835–1845: A Reconsideration," *Michigan History,* 57, 1 (1973).

27. Martin Hershock, *The Paradox of Progress: Economic Change, Individual Enterprise and Political Culture in Michigan, 1837–1878* (Athens: University of Ohio Press, 2003), 31–33.

28. *Detroit Journal,* May 16, 1837.

29. Ibid., July 11, 1837.

30. *Pontiac Courier,* Aug. 14, 1837.

31. *Detroit Daily Advertiser,* June 1, 1837.

32. *Detroit Free Press,* July 12, 1837.

33. Ibid., Jan. 25, 1837.

34. Ibid., July 12, 1837.

35. Ibid., Aug. 1, 1838.

36. Ibid.

37. Ibid., July 5, 1837.

38. Ibid., Aug. 16, 1837.

39. Ibid..

40. Ibid., Aug. 2, 1837.

41. *Detroit Journal,* June 26, 1838; Aug. 6, 1839.

42. William Shade, "The Background of the Michigan Free Banking Law," *Michigan History* 52, no. 3 (1968): 228, 241.

43. *Detroit Daily Advertiser,* Nov. 28, 1837.

44. Ibid., March 15, 1838.

45. Utley and Cutcheon, *Michigan as a Province, Territory and State,* vol. 3, 98.

46. *Detroit Journal,* Jan. 31, 1838.

47. Ibid., Feb. 20, 1838.

48. Ibid., March 27, 1838.

49. Kirkland, *New Home,* 212–13.

50. *Detroit Free Press,* Aug. 2, 1837.

51. Ibid., March 24, 1837.

52. *Detroit Morning Post,* Feb. 9, 1838.

53. *Detroit Free Press,* Feb. 14, 1838.

54. Ibid., March 28, 1838.

55. Alpheus Felch, "Early Banks and Banking in Michigan," *Michigan Historical Collections,* vol. 2 (Detroit, MI: Wm. Grahm's Presses, 1880), 121–22.

56. Ibid., 121–22; Kirkland, *New Home,* 212.

57. *Detroit Journal,* June 26, 1838.

58. Friend Palmer, "The Old Banks of Michigan," *Michigan Historical Collections,* vol. 30 (Lansing, MI: Wynkoop Hallenbeck Crawford, 1906), 422.

59. *Detroit Journal,* Aug. 6, 1839.

60. *Detroit Daily Advertiser,* June 10, 1839.

61. Ibid., May 20, 1839.

62. *Detroit Journal,* Oct. 30, 1838.

63. Dunbar and May, *Michigan,* 237.

64. The term "moral economy" was coined by E. P. Thompson to describe resistance to industrialization in eighteenth-century England. See E. P. Thompson,

The Making of the English Working Class (New York: Vintage, 1963), 63.

65. Karen Halttunen's *Confidence Men and Painted Women: A Study of Middle-Class Culture in America* (New Haven: Yale University Press, 1982) has influenced my interpretation of the literature on the moral economy.

66. *Detroit Journal,* Feb. 27, 1838.

67. *Detroit Free Press,* April 26, 1837.

68. Ibid., May 10, 1837.

69. George N. Fuller, ed., *Messages of the Governors of Michigan* (Lansing: Michigan Historical Commission, 1925), 208.

70. *Detroit Journal,* March 5, 1839.

71. *Detroit Morning Post,* May 2, 1838.

72. Ibid., Aug. 23, 1837.

73. Gordon S. Wood, *The Creation of the American Republic, 1776–1787* (New York: W.W. Norton, 1972), 52.

74. *Detroit Morning Post,* Aug. 28, 1837. The literature on luxury is large and growing. Some of the more notable works include Gordon S. Wood, *The Radicalism of the American Revolution;* J.G.A. Pocock, *The Machiavellian Moment: Florentine Political Thought and the Atlantic Republican Tradition* (Princeton: Princeton University Press, 1975); and John Crowley, *This Sheba, Self: The Conceptualization of Economic Life in Eighteenth-Century America* (Baltimore: Johns Hopkins University Press, 1974).

75. *Detroit Daily Advertiser,* March 28, 1837.

76. *Detroit Journal,* May 31, 1836.

77. Kirkland, *New Home,* 140–42.

78. Halttunen, *Confidence Men and Painted Women,* xv.

79. *Pontiac Courier,* Dec. 5, 1836.

80. Ibid., Dec. 5, 1836.

81. See the *Western Statesman,* Nov. 5, 1840; and the *Pontiac Courier,* June 26, 1837.

82. *Pontiac Courier,* June 26, 1837.

83. Ibid.

84. Ibid., June 26, 1837, and March 15, 1838.

85. Halttunen, *Confidence Men and Painted Women,* xv.

86. *Western Statesman,* April 23, 1840.

87. Halttunen, *Confidence Men and Painted Women,* 50.

88. *Pontiac Courier,* Feb. 23, 1838.

89. Ibid.

90. Ibid.

91. *Detroit Gazette,* Nov. 10, 1820.

92. *Pontiac Courier,* June 19, 1837.

93. Ibid.

94. Ibid.

95. See, for example, Wilentz, "Society, Politics and the Market Revolution,"

74–81; Watson, *Liberty and Power*, 195–97; and Sean Wilentz, *The Rise of American Democracy: Jefferson to Lincoln* (New York: W. W. Norton, 2005), 511–18.

96. Wood, *Radicalism of the American Revolution*, 315.

97. Halttunen, *Confidence Men and Painted Women*, xiv–xv.

4—TAMING THE "SAVAGERY" OF MICHIGAN INDIANS

1. Lewis Cass, "Policy and Practice of the United States and Great Britain in Their Treatment of the Indians," *North American Review*, April 1827, 372, 391–392, 404–5.

2. Willard Carl Klunder, *Lewis Cass and the Politics of Moderation* (Kent, OH: Kent State University Press, 1996), xiii, 1, 5, 15, 49.

3. My discussion of Yankee views on the differences between civilization and savagery is indebted to Richard G. Bremer, *Indian Agent and Wilderness Scholar: The Life of Henry Rowe Schoolcraft* (Mount Pleasant, MI: Clarke Historical Library, Central Michigan University, 1987), 234–35.

4. Ronald Takaki, *A Different Mirror: A History of Multicultural America* (Boston: Little, Brown, 1993), 26–31.

5. Willis F. Dunbar and George S. May, *Michigan: A History of the Wolverine State*, 3rd rev. ed. (Grand Rapids: Eerdmans, 1995), 141, 152, 165; Charles Cleland, *Rites of Conquest: The History and Culture of Michigan's Native Americans* (Ann Arbor: University of Michigan Press, 1992), 24, 46–49.

6. Though the Blackhawk War was bloody, most of the action took place outside of Michigan. Dunbar and May, *Michigan*, 79–84, 121–37, 178.

7. Peter C. Mancall, *Deadly Medicine: Indians and Alcohol in Early America* (Ithaca: Cornell University Press, 1995), 42–43.

8. Cleland, *Rites of Conquest*, 165.

9. Simon Pokagon, *Queen of the Woods* (Hartford, MI: C. H. Engle, Publisher, 1899), 105. Controversy surrounds the authorship of the novel. At least one critic believes that a ghostwriter helped Pokagon write the novel, while others insist that he did. For a discussion, see Tracey Sue Jordan, "Braving New Worlds: Breed Fictions, Mixedblood Identities," PhD diss., Columbia University, 1999, 24–28.

10. *Detroit Gazette*, Feb. 18, 1822.

11. Ibid., Dec. 22, 1820.

12. Jesse Turner, "Reminiscences of Kalamazoo," *Michigan Historical Collections*, vol. 18 (Lansing, MI: Robert Smith, 1892), 572.

13. Mrs. E.M.S. Stewart, "Childhood Recollections of Detroit," *Michigan Historical Collections*, vol. 18 (Lansing, MI: Robert Smith, 1892), 463.

14. Turner, "Reminiscences of Kalamazoo," 575.

15. *Detroit Gazette*, May 28, 1819.

16. Ibid., July 23, 1829.

17. Ibid., Oct. 19, 1821.

18. Ibid., Feb. 21, 1826.

19. Richard G. Bremer, *Indian Agent and Wilderness Scholar: The Life of Henry*

Rowe Schoolcraft (Mount Pleasant, MI: Clarke Historical Library, Central Michigan University, 1987), vii, 12–15, 54.

20. H. R. Schoolcraft, *Personal Memoirs of a Residence of Thirty Years with the Indian Tribes on the American Frontier: With Brief Notices of Passing Events, Facts and Opinions, A.D. 1812 to A.D. 1842* (Philadelphia: Lippincott, Grambo, 1851), 75. Schoolcraft may have greatly exaggerated or even fabricated the violence in these incidents to highlight what he viewed as the savagery of Native peoples. Richard Bremer, Schoolcraft's biographer, found that significant portions of the Indian agent's memoirs are inaccurate. Bremer, *Indian Agent and Wilderness Scholar*, 303–4, 336.

21. Schoolcraft, *Personal Memoirs*, 199.

22. Bremer, *Indian Agent and Wilderness Scholar*, 29.

23. *Detroit Gazette*, Dec. 22, 1820.

24. Ibid., Jan. 18, 1822.

25. Ibid.

26. Ibid.

27. Slavcheff, "Temperate Republic," 23–24.

28. Ibid., 33–34, 24–37.

29. *Detroit Gazette*, Nov. 9, 1821.

30. Christine Bolt, *American Indian Policy and American Reform* (London: Allen and Unwin, 1987), 43–70; Francis Paul Prucha, *The Indians in American Society* (Berkeley: University of California Press, 1985), 12–15; Daniel Walker Howe, *What Hath God Wrought: The Transformation of America, 1815–1848* (New York: Oxford University Press, 2007), 255–56, 342–57, 414–23.

31. Dunbar and May, *Michigan*, 146–52; and Cleland, *Rites of Conquest*, 205–30.

32. Bremer, *Indian Agent and Wilderness Scholar*, 233–35.

33. *Detroit Gazette*, Feb. 18, 1822.

34. Ibid., Feb. 18, 1822.

35. Ibid.

36. Ibid., Dec. 5, 1823.

37. Ibid.

38. Ibid., Aug. 6, 1829.

39. Ibid., Sept. 22, 1820.

40. Rev. Abel Bingham, "The Early Mission at Sault Ste. Marie," *Michigan Historical Collections*, vol. 28 (Lansing, MI: Robert Smith, 1900), 521–22.

41. Cleland, *Rites of Conquest*, 199–203. For broader discussions of these issues, see Ronald Takaki, *A Different Mirror: A History of Multicultural America* (Boston: Little, Brown, 1993), 144. Takaki argues that English settlers initially saw the savagery of the Irish as a product of culture, but that they came to believe that the wildness of Indians might be a product of race.

42. *Detroit Gazette*, July 28, 1820.

43. Ibid., Nov. 21, 1823.

44. Ibid., July 28, 1820.

45. Bremer, *Indian Agent and Wilderness Scholar*, 183.

46. Although Judge Leib wrote his report on Indian education on November 20, 1824, the *Detroit Gazette* did not publish it until Sept. 26, 1826.

47. Ibid., Sept. 26, 1826.

48. Ibid.

49. Edward W. Barber, "Recollections and Lessons of a Pioneer Boyhood," *Michigan Historical Collections*, vol. 31 (Lansing, MI: Wynkoop Hallenbeck Crawford, 1902), 193.

50. Melvin D. Osband, "The Michigan Indians," *Michigan Historical Collections*, vol. 29 (Lansing, MI: Wynkoop Hallenbeck Crawford, 1901), 708.

51. Bremer, *Indian Agent and Wilderness Scholar*, 185.

52. Ibid., 187–88.

53. Klunder, *Lewis Cass and the Politics of Moderation*, 50–51.

54. Lewis Cass, "Policy and Practice," 391.

55. Wilma Wood Henrickson, ed., *Detroit Perspectives: Crossroads and Turning Points* (Detroit: Wayne State University Press, 1991), 51, 53.

56. Bremer, *Indian Agent and Wilderness Scholar*, 32–33, 189–90. Klunder, *Lewis Cass and the Politics of Moderation*, 39, 50–51.

57. Cleland, *Rites of Conquest*, 222–23.

58. Edward Barber, *Michigan Historical Collections*, vol. 29, 348.

59. Pokagon, *Queen of the Woods*, 81–82, 100.

60. Cleland, *Rites of Conquest*, 222.

61. As quoted by Michigan governor Lewis Cass, "Policy and Practice," 368.

62. Stewart, "Childhood's Recollections of Detroit," 463.

63. Floyd Russell Dain, *Every House a Frontier: Detroit's Economic Progress, 1815–1825* (Detroit: Wayne State University Press, 1956), 4–6. Like other secondary works of the period, Dain's study uncritically repeats the views of New England settlers. Melvin G. Holli describes French Detroit as "precommercial," asserting that it was "immobilized by an archaic social system" in "French Detroit: The Clash of Feudal and Yankee Values," in *The Ethnic Frontier: Essays in the History of Group Survival in Chicago and the Midwest*, ed. Melvin G. Holli and Peter A. Jones (Grand Rapids: Eerdmans, 1977), 75.

64. Turner, "Reminiscences of Kalamazoo," vol. 18, 575.

65. Thomas J. Drake as cited in Dain, *Every House a Frontier*, 6.

66. Byron M. Cutcheon, "Fifty Years of Growth in Michigan," *Michigan Historical Collections*, vol. 22 (Lansing, MI: Robert Smith, 1894), 482.

67. Cass, "Policy and Practice," 368.

68. The background on Walter March was found in Wallace Genser, "'Habitants,' 'Half-Breeds,' and Homeless Children: Transformations in Métis and Yankee-Yorker Relations in Early Michigan," *Michigan Historical Review* 24, no. 1 (Spring 1998), 40.

69. Orlando B. Willcox [pseud. Walter March], *Shoepac Recollections: A Wayside Glimpse of American Life* (New York: Bunce and Brother, 1856), 59.

70. Ibid., vi.

71. Ibid., 10–11.

72. Ibid., 17–18.

73. Historians and literary scholars have produced a huge and growing literature on captivity narratives. A few of the most important works include Christopher Castiglia, *Bound and Determined: Captivity, Culture-Crossing, and White Womanhood from Mary Rowlandson to Patty Hearst* (Chicago: University of Chicago Press, 1996); Roy Harvey Pearce, "The Significance of the Captivity Narrative," *American Literature* 19 (1947): 1–20; Richard Slotkin, *The Fatal Environment: The Myth of the Frontier in the Age of Industrialization, 1800–1890* (Norman: Oklahoma University Press, 1985); John Demos, *The Unredeemed Captive: A Family Story from Early America* (New York: Vintage Books, 1994); Richard VanDerBeets, "The Indian Captivity Narrative as Ritual," *American Literature* 43 (1972): 548–62.

74. *Detroit Gazette*, July 31, 1828.

75. Schoolcraft, *Personal Memoirs*, 315.

76. John Tanner, *The Falcon: A Narrative of the Captivity and Adventures of John Tanner during Thirty Years Residence among the Indians in the Interior of North America* (G. & C. & H. Carvill, 1830; rept., New York: Penguin, 1994), 26.

77. Ibid., 15.

78. Ibid., 26–27.

79. Ibid., 28.

80. Margaret Fuller, *Summer on the Lakes, in 1843,* in *The Portable Margaret Fuller,* ed. Mary Kelley (New York: Penguin Books, 1994), 176.

81. Schoolcraft, *Personal Memoirs,* 105.

82. Elizabeth Thérèse Baird, *Reminiscences of Early Days on Mackinac Island,* Collections of the State Historical Society of Wisconsin, vol. 14 (Madison: Ruben Gold Thwaites, 1899), 30–33.

83. Tanner, *The Falcon,* 89–91 Scholars recently have disagreed over the degree of freedom Native People had in choosing gender and sexuality. Some insist that Natives chose freely to become berdaches, while others contend that elders forced them into that role. For information on the two sides in this debate, see Will Roscoe, *Changing Ones: Third and Fourth Genders in Native North America* (New York: St. Martin's Press, 1998); and Richard C. Trexler, "Making the American Berdache: Choice or Constraint?" *Journal of Social History* 35 (Spring 2002): 613–36.

84. *Emigrant,* Feb. 1, 1832.

85. *Detroit Gazette,* April 23, 1824.

86. *Michigan Whig,* March 20, 1839.

87. Fanny Woodville, *Edward Wilton, Or, Early Days in Michigan* (Detroit: F. B. Way, 1851) 5, 15.

88. Ibid., 23.

89. Ibid., 30–31.

90. Ibid., 76.

91. Richard Slotkin, *Regeneration through Violence: The Mythology of the American Frontier, 1600–1860* (Middletown, CT: Wesleyan University Press, 1973), 94–95.

92. Tanner, *The Falcon,* 226.

93. Ibid., 258.

94. Schoolcraft, *Personal Memoirs,* 315–16.

95. Baird, *Reminiscences of Early Days on Mackinac Island,* 51.

96. Calvin J. Thorpe, "Pioneer and Aborigine," *Michigan Historical Collections,* vol. 28 (Lansing, MI: Robert Smith, 1900), 471.

97. Maurice F. Cole, ed., *Voices from the Wilderness* (Ann Arbor, MI: Edwards Brothers, 1961), 15.

98. Pokagon, *Queen of the Woods,* 112–14.

99. Jane M. Kinney, "Pioneers of St. Clair County," *Michigan Historical Collections,* vol. 29 (Lansing, MI: Wynkoop Hallenbeck Crawford, 1901), 172.

100. Caroline S. Kirkland, *Western Clearings* (New York: Garrett Press, 1969), 88.

101. Ibid., 91.

102. Ibid., 93.

103. Pokagon, *Queen of the Woods,* 49, 52, 109, 111–12, 119–22, 151.

104. Ibid., 120.

105. Ibid., 93–94.

5—CIVILIZING WHITE SETTLERS

1. *Detroit Daily Advertiser,* June 16, 1838.

2. John W. Quist, *Restless Visionaries: The Social Roots of Antebellum Reform in Alabama and Michigan* (Baton Rouge: Louisiana State University Press, 1998), 1–2; Daniel Walker Howe, *What Hath God Wrought: The Transformation of America, 1815–1848* (New York: Oxford University Press, 2007), 168–95, 285–89.

3. Paul E. Johnson, *A Shopkeeper's Millennium: Society and Revivals in Rochester, New York, 1815–1837* (New York: Hill and Wang, 1978); and Anthony F. C. Wallace, *Rockdale: The Growth of an American Village in the Early Industrial Revolution* (New York: Alfred A. Knopf, 1978).

4. John W. Quist, *Restless Visionaries: The Social Roots of Antebellum Reform in Michigan and Alabama* (Baton Rouge: Louisiana State University Press, 1998) 284, 290–92, and 294; and *History of Washtenaw County* (Chicago: Chas C. Chapman, 1881), 267–68.

5. Caroline Kirkland, *A New Home: Who'll Follow? or, Glimpses of Western Life* (New York: C. S. Francis, 1839; repr., New York: Garrett Press, 1969), 87.

6. *Detroit Gazette,* Aug. 24, 1821.

7. Ibid., Aug. 13, 1819.

8. *Detroit Journal and Michigan Advertiser,* Jan. 7, 1835.

9. Orlando Bolivar Willcox [pseud. Walter March], *Shoepac Recollections: A Way-Side Glimpse of American Life* (New York: Bunce and Brother, 1856), 91–103.

10. *Detroit Gazette,* Oct. 16, 1818.

11. Ibid., April 23, 1819.

12. Ibid., May 29, 1818.

13. Ibid., May 1, 1818.

14. Ibid., Jan. 29, 1819.

15. *Detroit Journal,* Feb. 20, 1836.

16. Kirkland, *New Home,* 95–96.

17. Ibid., 67–68.

18. Mrs. S. M. Williams, poem read at the Semi-Centennial Anniversary of the Baptist Church at Portland, Michigan, *Michigan Historical Collections,* vol. 18 (Lansing, MI: Robert Smith, 1892), 482.

19. Mrs. Mark Norris, "Rev. I. M. Weed," *History of Washtenaw County* (Chicago: Chas C. Chapman, 1881), 273–75.

20. M.E.D. Trowbridge, *History of Baptists in Michigan* (n.p.: Michigan State Baptist Convention, 1909), 32.

21. Ibid., 36.

22. Ibid., 37.

23. Ibid., 39.

24. Kirkland, *New Home,* 215–16.

25. *Pontiac Courier,* Jan. 9, 1837.

26. *Detroit Daily Advertiser,* Dec. 31, 1836.

27. Rev. Abel Bingham, "The Early Mission at Sault Ste. Marie," *Michigan Historical Collections,* vol. 28 (Lansing, MI: Robert Smith, 1892), 523.

28. "Annual Meeting of the Michigan Pioneer and Historical Society," *Michigan Historical Collections,* vol. 18 (Lansing, MI: Robert Smith, 1892), 2.

29. Jesse Turner, "Reminiscences of Kalamazoo," *Michigan Historical Collections,* vol. 18 (Lansing, MI: Robert Smith, 1892), 574.

30. D. C. Walker, "The Evolution of Religion, Morals, and Legislation in This Country during the Past Century," *Michigan Historical Collections,* vol. 28 (Lansing, MI: Robert Smith, 1892), 455.

31. *Detroit Gazette,* Dec. 17, 1819.

32. See chapter 4 on Indians.

33. *Pontiac Courier,* Jan. 9, 1837.

34. Gordon S. Wood, *The Creation of the American Republic* (New York: Norton, 1972), 65–70; and Sean Wilentz, "Society, Politics and the Market Revolution," in *The New American History,* ed. Eric Foner, rev. and expanded ed. (Philadelphia: Temple University Press, 1997), 71.

35. *Detroit Gazette,* July 23, 1818.

36. Ibid., Jan. 30, 1818.

37. John W. Quist, "An Occasionally Dry State Surrounded by Water," in *The History of Michigan Law,* ed. Paul Finkelman and Martin J. Hershock (Athens: Ohio University Press, 2006), 62–63.

38. Ibid., 63, 65.

39. *Detroit Gazette,* Sept. 12, 1817.

40. *Pontiac Courier,* April 4, 1836.

41. *Detroit Journal,* April 1, 1835.

42. *Pontiac Courier,* March 15, 1839.

43. Ibid.

44. *Detroit Gazette,* Aug. 28, 1818.

45. *Pontiac Courier,* April 10, 1837.

46. Ibid., Feb. 9, 1838.

47. James Fenimore Cooper, *The Oak Openings, or, The Bee-Hunter* (New York: Burgess, Stringer, 1848). Cooper satirized reformers, but like many of those in Michigan, he came from western New York and embraced many of the same masculine ideals they did.

48. Ibid., 102.

49. *Western Statesman,* Dec. 2, 1841.

50. *Western Emigrant* (Ann Arbor), Jan. 27, 1830.

51. Ibid.

52. Margaret Marsh, "Suburban Men and Masculine Domesticity, 1870–1915," in *Meanings for Manhood: Constructions of Masculinity in Victorian America,* ed. Mark C. Carnes and Clyde Griffen (Chicago: University of Chicago Press, 1990), 112.

53. *Detroit Gazette,* Aug. 11, 1817.

54. Willis F. Dunbar and George S. May, *Michigan: A History of the Wolverine State,* 3rd rev. ed. (Grand Rapids, MI: Eerdmans, 1995), 93, 190, 279.

55. Ibid., 279–80.

56. Laura Haviland, *A Woman's Life Work: Including Thirty Years Service on the Underground Railroad and in the War,* 5th ed. (Grand Rapids, MI: S. B. Shaw, 1881), 9, 12, 28–35.

57. *Detroit Gazette,* Dec. 22, 1820.

58. Ibid., Jan. 19, 1818.

59. Ibid.

60. Ibid., Nov. 7, 1818.

61. Ibid., Dec. 22, 1820.

62. Ibid., Nov. 21, 1817.

63. Ibid., Feb. 25, 1820.

64. Ibid., Nov. 7, 1818.

65. Ibid., Jan. 14, 1821.

66. *Pontiac Courier,* Jan. 1, 1837.

67. Ibid., March 27, 1837.

68. Ibid., Jan. 1, 1838.

69. Ibid., Nov. 17, 1837.

70. Sandra VanBurkleo, *"Belonging to the World": Women's Rights and American Constitutional Culture* (New York: Oxford University Press, 2001), 95.

71. *Pontiac Courier,* April 13, 1838.

72. *Detroit Gazette,* Jan. 21, 1818.

73. *Pontiac Courier,* Feb. 6, 1837.

74. Ibid., Jan. 9, 1837.

75. Ibid., Aug. 14, 1837.

76. Ibid.

77. Ibid.

78. Ibid.

79. *Detroit Gazette,* April 30, 1824.

80. Ibid.

81. Ibid.

82. Ibid.

83. Ibid.

84. Ibid.

85. Ibid.

86. Marcia J. Heringa Mason, ed., *Remember the Distance That Divides Us: The Family Letters of Philadelphia Quaker Abolitionist and Michigan Pioneer Elizabeth Margaret Chandler, 1830–1842* (East Lansing: Michigan State University Press, 2004), xxiv, 114–15.

87. Kirkland, *New Home,* 175–77.

6—CHOLERA AND THE CONFLICT OVER CULTURAL BOUNDARIES IN EARLY MICHIGAN

1. *Detroit Courier,* Sept. 3, 1834.

2. Charles Rosenberg, *The Cholera Years: The United States in 1832, 1849, and 1866* (Chicago: University of Chicago Press, 1962), 1–4.

3. Richard J. Evans, "Cholera in Nineteenth Century Europe," in *Epidemics and Ideas,* ed. Terence Ranger and Paul Slack (Cambridge: Cambridge University Press, 1992), 150–51.

4. *Detroit Courier,* July 12, 1832.

5. *Detroit Free Press,* June 28, 1832.

6. *Detroit Courier,* August 13, 1832; Hon. George C. Bates, "Bygones of Detroit," *Michigan Historical Collections,* vol. 22 (Lansing, MI: Robert Smith, 1894), 336.

7. Irving F. Burton, "The Cholera Epidemic in Detroit 1832 and 1834," *Michigan Medicine* 68 (Oct. 1969), 1017; Howard Markel, "Medicine at Michigan," *Journal of the American Medical Association* 283 (Feb. 16, 2000), 915.

8. Burton, "Cholera Epidemic," 1017; Bates, "Bygones of Detroit," 430.

9. *Detroit Free Press,* August 20, 1834; Bates, "Bygones of Detroit," 430; Silas Farmer, *The History of Detroit and Michigan; or, The Metropolis Illustrated,* 2nd ed. (Detroit: Silas Farmer, 1889), 49–50; *Detroit Journal and Michigan Advertiser,* Aug. 13, 1834.

10. Rosenberg, *Cholera Years,* 72–74.

11. *Detroit Free Press,* July 12, 1832; *Detroit Journal and Michigan Advertiser,* July 18, 1832.

12. Rosenberg, *Cholera Years,* 72–74.

13. *Detroit Courier,* Aug. 2, 1832.

14. Ibid., July 19, 1834.

15. Ibid., July 26, 1832.

16. *Detroit Journal,* Aug. 13, 1834.

17. Rosenberg, *Cholera Years,* 40; *Detroit Courier,* Aug. 2, 1832.

18. Catherine Kudlick, *Cholera in Post-Revolutionary Paris: A Cultural History* (Berkley: University of California Press, 1996), 14.

19. Ibid., 13–14, 77; Laura Otis, *Membranes: Metaphors of Invasion in Nineteenth-Century Literature, Science, and Politics* (Baltimore: Johns Hopkins University Press, 1999), 10.

20. *Detroit Courier,* July 12, 1832; Theodore Williams, Detroit, Michigan, to General John R. Williams, Ypsilanti, Michigan, July 12, 1832, Williams Papers, Burton Historical Collection, Detroit Public Library.

21. *Detroit Journal,* July 11, 1832; *Detroit Courier,* July 12, 1832.

22. *Detroit Free Press,* July 19, 1832.

23. *Michigan Sentinel,* Sept. 20, 1834.

24. *Emigrant,* May 9, 1832.

25. *Detroit Free Press,* Aug. 2, 1832.

26. *Detroit Courier,* June 28, 1832.

27. Kudlick, *Cholera in Post-Revolutionary Paris,* 73.

28. John Schneider, *Detroit and the Problem of Order, 1830–1880* (Lincoln: University of Nebraska Press, 1980), 10–11.

29. *Detroit Courier,* June 28, 1832, Sept. 10, 1834, and July 19, 1834.

30. Willis F. Dunbar and George S. May, *Michigan: A History of the Wolverine State,* 3rd rev. ed. (Grand Rapids, MI: Eerdmans, 1995), 176–77.

31. Ibid., 63; Wallace Genser, "'Habitants,' 'Half-Breeds,' and Homeless Children: Transformations in Métis and Yankee-Yorker Relations in Early Michigan," *Michigan Historical Review* 24 (Spring 1998): 24, 27, 34. On the settlement of Oakland and Washtenaw counties, see George Newman Fuller, *Economic and Social Beginnings of Michigan* (Lansing, MI: Wynkoop, Hallenbeck, Crawford, 1916), 186–243; and John W. Quist, *Restless Visionaries: The Social Roots of Antebellum Reform in Alabama and Michigan* (Baton Rouge: Louisiana State University Press, 1998), 12.

32. *Detroit Journal,* July 16, 1832; *Detroit Free Press,* July 19, 1832.

33. *Detroit Free Press,* July 19, 1832.

34. Ibid., July 19, 1832.

35. Ibid., Nov. 8, 1832.

36. *Detroit Free Press,* Sept. 20, 1832; and *Emigrant,* Aug. 29, 1832.

37. *Detroit Journal,* Aug. 8, 1832.

38. *Detroit Free Press,* Sept. 6, 1832, and Aug. 23, 1832.

39. Ibid., Aug. 23, 1832.

40. Ibid., Sept. 6, 1832.

41. *Detroit Courier,* Aug. 16, 1832.

42. *Free Press,* Aug. 20, 1834.

43. *Detroit Journal,* Aug. 27, 1834.

44. *Free Press,* Aug. 27, 1834.

45. Ibid.

46. Kudlick, *Cholera in Post-Revolutionary Paris,* 14.

CONCLUSION

1. Jerrold G. Rusk, *A Statistical History of the American Electorate* (Washington, DC: CQ Press, 2001), 16–18, 32; Daniel Walker Howe, *What Hath God Wrought: The Transformation of America, 1815–1848* (New York: Oxford University Press, 2007), 490.

2. Paul E. Johnson, *A Shopkeeper's Millennium: Society and Revivals in Rochester, New York, 1815–1837* (New York: Hill and Wang, 1978); and Anthony F. C. Wallace, *Rockdale: The Growth of an American Village in the Early Industrial Revolution* (New York: Alfred A. Knopf, 1978); Howe, *What Hath God Wrought*, 188, 527–30.

3. Mary P. Ryan, *Cradle of the Middle Class: The Family in Oneida County, New York, 1790–1865* (New York: Cambridge University Press, 1981), 230–42.

4. Renato Rosaldo, *Culture & Truth: The Remaking of Social Analysis* (Boston: Beacon Press, 1989), 163.

5. Mary Douglas, *Parity and Danger: An Analysis of the Concepts of Pollution and Taboo* (New York: Praeger Publisher, 1966), 1–57

Bibliography

PRIMARY SOURCES

Manuscript Collections

Bentley Historical Library
  Papers of the Bingham Family
  Papers of Lewis Cass
  Papers of Stevens T. Mason
Burton Historical Collection, Detroit Public Library
  Papers of the Williams Family
Wisconsin Historical Collections
  Henry and Elizabeth Baird Papers

Newspapers and Periodicals

Detroit Courier, 1832–1834
Detroit Daily Advertiser, 1836–1849
Detroit [Democratic] Free Press, 1831–1842
Detroit Gazette, 1817–1830
Detroit Morning Post, 1837–1838
Detroit Journal and Michigan Advertiser, 1830–1839
Marshall Western Statesman, 1839–1842
Michigan Sentinel (Monroe), 1825–1836
Michigan Whig, 1835
North American Review, 1827
Northwestern Journal, 1829–1830
Pontiac Courier, 1836–1839
Western Emigrant (Ann Arbor), 1829–1836

Published Works

Blume, William Wirt, ed. *Transactions of the Supreme Court of Michigan*, vol. 3, case no. 564. Ann Arbor: University of Michigan Press, 1938.
Chas. C. Chapman & Co. *History of Washtenaw County*. Chicago: Chas C. Chapman, 1881.
Cooper, James Fenimore. *The Oak Openings, or, The Bee-Hunter*. 2 vols. New York: Burgess, Stringer, 1848.

Dorr, Harold M., ed. *The Michigan Constitutional Conventions of 1835–36: Debates and Proceedings.* Ann Arbor: University of Michigan Press, 1940.

Fuller, George N. *Messages of the Governors of Michigan,* vol. 1. Lansing: Michigan Historical Commission, 1925.

Fuller, Margaret. *The Portable Margaret Fuller.* Edited by Mary Kelley. New York: Penguin, 1994.

Haviland, Laura. *A Woman's Life-Work: Including Thirty Years Service on the Underground Railroad and in the War.* 5th ed. Grand Rapids, MI: S. B. Shaw, 1881.

Kirkland, Caroline. *A New Home: Who'll Follow? or, Glimpses of Western Life.* New York: Garrett Press, 1969. Reprint, New York: C. S. Francis, 1839.

———. *Western Clearings.* New York: Garrett Press, 1969. Reprint, New York: Wiley and Putnam, 1845.

Mason, Marcia J. Heringa., ed. *Remember the Distance That Divides Us: The Family Letters of Philadelphia Quaker Abolitionist and Michigan Pioneer Elizabeth Margaret Chandler, 1830–1842.* East Lansing: Michigan State University Press, 2004.

Michigan Historical Collections. Lansing MI: Wynkoop Hallenbeck Crawford Company, 1894.

Michigan Historical Collection. Lansing, MI: Robert Smith Printing Co., State Printers and Binders, 1900, 2nd ed.

Pokagon, Simon. *Queen of the Woods.* Hartford, MI: C. H. Engle, 1899.

Register of Debates in Congress.

Schoolcraft, H. R. *Personal Memoirs of a Residence of Thirty Years with the Indian Tribes on the American Frontiers: With Brief Notices of Passing Events, Facts and Opinions, A.D. 1812 to A.D. 1842.* Philadelphia: Lippincott, Grambo, 1851.

Tanner, John. *The Falcon: A Narrative of the Captivity and Adventures of John Tanner during Thirty Years of Residence among the Indians in the Interior of North America.* New York: Penguin, 1994. Reprint of *A Narrative of the Captivity and Adventures of John Tanner,* New York: G. & C. & H. Carvill, 1830.

Willcox, Orlando Bolivar [Walter March, pseud.]. *Shoepac Recollections: A Way-side Glimpse of American Life.* New York: Bunce and Brothers, 1856.

Woodville, Fanny. *Edward Wilton, Or, Early Days in Michigan.* Detroit: F. B. Way, 1851.

SECONDARY SOURCES

Adelman, Jeremy, and Stephen Aron. "From Borderlands to Borders: Empires, Nation-States, and the Peoples in Between in North American History." *American Historical Review* 104, no. 3 (June 1999): 814–41.

Anderson, Benedict. *Imagined Communities.* Rev. ed. New York: Verso, 1991.

Anzaldúa, Gloria. *Borderlands/La Frontera: The New Mestiza.* San Francisco: Aunt Lute Books, 1987.

Aron, Stephen. *American Confluence: The Missouri Frontier from Borderland to Border State.* Bloomington: Indiana University Press, 2006.

Bailyn, Bernard. *The Ideological Origins of the American Revolution.* Cambridge: Belknap Press of Harvard University Press, 1967.

"What was all of that about?" Parker asked.

"Oh, nothing. Nothing to worry about. Do you want get Luke for me?"

"Sure, but do you think he'll want to see you before the wedding?"

"I'm sure he'll want to check out his handy work."

"Okay," Parker said as she left the room.

I admired myself in the mirror as Luke came into the bedroom. He had changed into a white linen suit. The bright blue shirt under the jacket made his gray eyes seem blue.

"Wow, babe, even better than I imagined. You look breathtaking."

I blushed. "Thank you," I said.

"It's missing something though. I'll be right back."

I couldn't imagine what he had in mind, but I didn't have long to wait. He came back into the bedroom with Karla, who was carrying a tackle box.

Placing it on the chest of drawers, she opened the latches. "Sit," she said.

I obliged, a sinking feeling in my stomach.

"Luke?" I said.

He said nothing and I looked back over at Karla. She was applying alcohol to a large q-tip. When she touched it to my nipple, I yelped.

"Wait," I said. "Could you leave us for a minute, Karla?"

"That won't be necessary," Luke said. "Are you arguing with me, Jane?"

"Well, no but—"

"But?"

"Nothing," I said. I gripped the sides of the chair and held my breath.

She finished cleaning the right nipple of the gold lotion and took out another swab.

"Oh no, not both!" I blurted out.

"Jane?" he said. He walked over to the door and opened

it, catapulting me back to the first time we'd met. I had the choice then to walk away before all of this started and now he stood there offering me that choice once more. Standing in the hallway, Parker saw my tears.

"Jane, do you want—"

"I'm fine," I said. I looked away and watched Karla clean my left nipple. She took out a spray bottle and aimed the nozzle. I felt extreme discomfort and then nothing but icy cold.

"It's better if you don't watch," Karla said to me.

Luke took my clamped right hand off of the arm of the chair and held it in his.

"On three. One, two ...." Karla never said three. The excruciating pain shot through my nipple and coursed throughout my body.

"Fuck shit, fuck shit, fuck," I said, screaming inside.

She inserted the horseshoe shaped ring with diamonds facing out of the tips.

"Excellent," Luke said.

Luke came around to the other side of me and held onto my left hand.

Karla didn't even bother with her counting trick for the second side. She sprayed the nipple quickly and pierced me again.

"Motherfucker, UGH!" I said. I groaned and felt nauseous. "I think I need to lie down."

"One more minute, love. She's just going to put the ring in."

Karla quickly inserted the gold and diamond piece.

Luke helped me over to the bed. He opened the door and said, "Parker, could you please get Jane some OJ? Thanks."

Karla came over to me and touched up the gold lotion. A wave of nausea passed through me each time she touched my nipple. She dried my eyes and reapplied the gold sheen and eye makeup.

"Are you okay?" Parker asked, walking over to my side of the bed. She offered me the juice but Luke took it.

Luke lifted my upper body and helped me drink.

"I forgot to eat," I said as if that explained everything.

At first, when she noticed my piercings, Parker didn't say anything but it was written all over her face. She took Luke's place and whispered, "What the fuck are you doing? This isn't you. I could buy all the rest of it but this has gone too far and I'm honestly worried for your safety. There are no limits, are there? I'll be here and support you but don't think I support this."

I knew my piercings would bother my mother even more than my nudity.

"Please leave," Luke said to Parker and Karla.

Once they were out of the room and the door closed behind them Luke said, "Do you think you can stand?"

"I don't know," I said.

He took my hand and helped me out of the bed. He fed me more juice and led me to the mirror.

I didn't recognize myself.

"You are so beautiful, my Janey. I am so happy to be making you my wife."

His words warmed me, but I continued to stare at the stranger in the mirror. I no longer recognized her. I felt a tug of war going on inside me. I knew Jane lived in there somewhere. The person in the mirror was babe, love, Janey. If asked at that moment who I wanted to be, I would have had no answer. I looked like a sex goddess. I looked beautiful, but there could be no denying my purpose. The person in the mirror existed solely for pleasure. There could be no mistaking it. Luke wanted everyone to know who I'd become.

Up till now, the process of crossing over to the new me had seemed ongoing, and yet I recognized that *this* threshold, *this* hurdle was the most significant, heralding the end of my ability to cross back.

At the end of the aisle lay the point of no return.

CHAPTER TWENTY

I could hear the clamor and clattering and hustle and bustle of people in the house. The time drew near.

Luke and I walked out into the living room facing the back of the house. Between the bushes I could see people seated in the chairs. My stomach churned and I felt queasy.

Luke turned me to face him and said, "I know you're scared, Janey. Hey, look at me."

I tilted my head up trying to remember to breathe.

"You're doing this for me, doing this for us. I couldn't be any more proud of you. I need to go out there now. Wait about five minutes and join me on the beach."

He kissed me lightly on the lips and then left through the French doors.

I watched him walk around the pool, between the tables, and down the stairs. My heart pounded so hard that I began to hyperventilate. I knew I needed to start walking in another minute or two. I didn't know how I'd make myself put one foot in front of the other. I most dreaded walking past Sandy and my mother. I wondered how I could do it in front of so many people I'd never met. Such a deviation from the wedding I had spent so many hours rehearsing in my head. Mourning for a moment that it had to be this way, I breathed deeply.

A caterer came over and asked if I was all right. Aware that I was shaking and in full panic mode, she offered me water. I drank half the glass and settled down.

"Thank you," I said. "It's now or never, I guess."

"I could never do it myself but you do look amazing. They're waiting for you."

I picked up the bouquet of gold roses that had been left for me by the couch. I imagined myself to be very small and that the flowers I held hid my body from the crowd. I passed through the open French doors and snaked my way around the tables. When I got to the steps that led down to the beach I stopped. I could see all the people. Luke was waiting for me just inside the gazebo next to the Justice of the Peace and Parker.

Luke turned and saw me. The radiant smile on his face, the love shining in his eyes took all my fears away. He loved me. I wouldn't spend the rest of my life alone. I'd have a place where I belonged. Parker's words, a distant memory.

I walked slowly down the steps and everyone seated stood and turned to face me. I kept my eyes locked on Luke the entire time. No one else existed for me but Luke. Just Luke and his love calling me like a beacon in a foggy night. I moved with ease toward the life I had chosen. No one would understand. Not even I understood, but at that moment, I wanted it.

I knew my friends and mother were worried about me, worried what would become of me. Just before I reached Luke on the sand, I thought once again about my father and what he had always told me about choices. I couldn't be sure if this would be a good choice or a dreadful one, but I slipped my hand into Luke's and gave myself over to everything he had in store for me.

Following is an excerpt from

MY BODY-HIS (MARCELLO)

The next book in the *My Body* series

By Blakely Bennett

Coming in March 2013

"I can't wait until later," he said to me after our dance ended.

"Later?" I said. "I don't think so." I pulled myself free of his grip and furrowed my brow.

"You might want to watch how you speak to me," Marcello said. He looked directly into my eyes as if he could will my obedience.

"I think you've mistaken who you're speaking to," I said and stalked off to find Luke.

I pulled him away from a conversation with his friend Jim and said, "What does Marcello think is going to happen later? He's an extremely rude man and very disrespectful of you, I might add."

Luke laughed. "Of me? I don't think so."

"He kept rubbing his cock against me the whole time we danced and then he tried to talk to me as if he were you. That is disrespect, if you ask me."

"Well Marcello certainly has his ways and it might serve you well to be nicer to him."

"Nicer to him? You must be joking."

"I'm not."

I stood there with my mouth open. I couldn't believe what I was hearing. "What about protecting me? Wasn't that part of our vows?"

"When you require my protection, you will have it. Until then, be reverential of my friends and acquaintances."

"I'm going for a walk," I said, taking a step toward the beach.

Luke clutched my hand and pulled me back toward him. "Jane, you still need to throw the bouquet."

I stomped off toward Parker's table to retrieve my flowers as Luke summoned all the single women. I hoped Sandy would catch the bouquet. It would make her happy, and perhaps she could leave my wedding with one positive memory. As the women gathered behind me, I glanced over my shoulder to see where Sandy stood. At the same time I noticed Marcello off to the side, staring me down.

Luke strolled up to me and said, "Go for it." With a wink, he added, "She's moved over to the left a bit."

I threw the gold roses over my left shoulder, knowing they would fly straight to Sandy. I turned around in time to see Marcello stretch out his long arm and snatch them from the air right above Sandy's head.

What the hell is he doing? I thought. I looked over at Luke, who grunted and started to laugh. How could he?

All the women moved back to the seats as I stormed over to Marcello.

"What was *that*?" I said, hands on my hips.

"I caught them for you?" he countered, a look of the devil in his eyes. He said it almost like a question.

"They were meant for Sandy! What is your prob—" I started to say, pointing at Marcello, but then Luke grabbed my wrist and whirled me about to face him.

"Jane, we just spoke about this," he whispered harshly in my ear, pinning my arm at my side. "You will not disrespect my friends. Know you owe me for ...."

I wrenched my wrist free and ran toward the beach without looking back.

❦

Bolt, Christine. *American Indian Policy and American Reform*. London: Allen and Unwin, 1987.

Bremer, Richard G. *Indian Agent and Wilderness Scholar: The Life of Henry Rowe Schoolcraft*. Mount Pleasant, MI: Clarke Historical Library, Central Michigan University, 1987.

Burstein, Andrew. *Sentimental Democracy: The Evolution of America's Romantic Self-Image*. New York: Hill and Wang, 1999.

Burton, Clarence Monroe, William Stocking, and Gordon K. Miller, eds. *The City of Detroit*. Detroit: S.J. Clarke Pub. Co., 1922.

Burton, Irving F. "The Cholera Epidemic in Detroit 1832 and 1834." *Michigan Medicine* 68 (Oct. 1969): 1017–22.

Bushman, Richard L. *From Puritan to Yankee: Character and the Social Order in Connecticut, 1690–1765*. Cambridge: Harvard University Press, 1967.

Carnes, Mark C., and Clyde Griffen, eds. *Meanings for Manhood: Constructions of Masculinity in Victorian America*. Chicago: University of Chicago Press, 1990.

Castiglia, Christopher. *Bound and Determined: Captivity, Culture-Crossing, and White Womanhood from Mary Rowlandson to Patty Hearst*. Chicago: University of Chicago Press, 1996.

Catlin, George B. *The Story of Detroit*. Detroit: Detroit News, 1926.

Cayton, Andrew R. L., and Susan E. Gray, eds. *The American Midwest: Essays on Regional History*. Bloomington: Indiana University Press, 2001.

Cleland, Charles E. *Rites of Conquest: The History and Culture of Michigan's Native Americans*. Ann Arbor: University of Michigan Press, 1992.

Cole, Maurice F., ed. *Voices from the Wilderness*. Ann Arbor, MI: Edwards Brothers, 1961.

Cronon, William. *Changes in the Land: Indians, Colonists and the Ecology of New England*. New York: Hill and Wang, 1983.

Cronon, William, George Miles, and Jay Gitlin. "Becoming West: Toward a New Meaning for Western History." In *Under an Open Sky: Rethinking America's Western Past*. Edited by William Cronon, George Miles, and Jay Gitlin. New York: W. W. Norton, 1992.

———. eds. *Under an Open Sky: Rethinking America's Western Past*. New York: W. W. Norton, 1992.

Crowley, John. *This Sheba-Self: The Conceptualization of Economic Life in Eighteenth-Century America*. Baltimore: Johns Hopkins University Press, 1974.

Dain, Floyd Russell. *Every House a Frontier: Detroit's Economic Progress, 1815–1825*. Detroit, MI: Wayne State University Press, 1956.

Demos, John. *The Unredeemed Captive: A Family Story from Early America*. New York: Vintage Books, 1994.

Dunbar, Willis F., and George S. May. *Michigan: A History of the Wolverine State*. 3rd rev. ed. Grand Rapids, MI: Eerdmans, 1995.

Farmer, Silas. *The History of Detroit and Michigan; or, The Metropolis Illustrated*. 2nd ed. Detroit: Silas Farmer, 1889.

———. *History of Detroit and Wayne County and Early Michigan: A Chronological Cy-*

clopedia of the Past. Detroit: Silas Farmer, 1890. Reprint, Detroit, MI: Gale Research Company, 1969.

Feller, Daniel. *The Jacksonian Promise: America, 1815–1840*. Baltimore: Johns Hopkins University Press, 1995.

Finkelman, Paul, and Martin J. Hershock, eds. *The History of Michigan Law*. Athens: Ohio University Press, 2006.

Foner, Eric, ed. *The New American History*. Rev. and expanded ed. Philadelphia: Temple University Press, 1997.

Formisano, Ronald P. *The Birth of Mass Political Parties: Michigan, 1827–1861*. Princeton: Princeton University Press, 1971.

———. "The Edge of Caste: Colored Suffrage in Michigan, 1827–1861." *Michigan History* 56 (Spring 1972): 19–41.

Fuller, George N. *Economic and Social Beginnings of Michigan: A Study of the Settlement of the Lower Peninsula during the Territorial Period, 1805–1837*. Lansing: Wynkoop Hallenbeck Crawford, 1916.

———., ed. *Messages of the Governors of Michigan*. Lansing: Michigan Historical Commission, 1925.

Genser, Wallace. "'Habitants', 'Half-Breeds,' and Homeless Children: Transformations in Métis and Yankee-Yorker Relations in Early Michigan." *Michigan Historical Review* 24 (Spring 1998): 23–47.

Gilpin, Alec R. *The Territory of Michigan, 1805–1837*. Lansing: Michigan State University Press, 1970.

Haberly, David T. "Women and the Indians: 'The Last of the Mohicans' and the Captivity Tradition." *American Quarterly* 28 (1976): 431–43.

Halttunen, Karen. *Confidence Men and Painted Women: A Study of Middle-class Culture in America, 1830–1870*. New Haven: Yale University Press, 1982.

Hemans, Lawton T. *Life and Times of Stevens Thompson Mason: The Boy Governor of Michigan*. Lansing: Michigan Historical Commission, 1920.

Hershock, Martin J. *The Paradox of Progress: Economic Change, Individual Enterprise, and Political Culture in Michigan, 1837–1878*. Athens: University of Ohio Press, 2003.

Holli, Melvin G., and Peter Jones, eds. *The Ethnic Frontier: Essays in the History of Group Survival in Chicago and the Midwest*. Grand Rapids, MI: Eerdmans, 1977.

Howe, Daniel Walker. *What Hath God Wrought: The Transformation of America, 1815–1848*. New York; Oxford University Press, 2007.

Hurt, R. Douglas. *The Ohio Frontier: Crucible of the Old Northwest, 1720–1830*. Bloomington: Indiana University Press, 1996.

Johnson, Paul E. *A Shopkeeper's Millennium: Society and Revivals in Rochester, New York, 1815–1837*. New York: Hill and Wang, 1978.

Jordan, Tracey Sue. Braving New Worlds: Breed Fictions, Mixedblood Identities. PhD diss., Columbia University, 1999.

Kimmel, Michael. *Manhood in America: A Cultural History*. New York: Free Press, 1996.

Kudlick, Catherine J. *Cholera in Post-Revolutionary Paris: A Cultural History*. Berkley: University of California Press, 1996.

Blakely Bennett grew up in Southeast Florida and has been residing in the great Northwest for over seven years. She graduated from Nova Southeastern University with a degree in psychology, which accounts for her particular interest in crafting the personalities, struggles, and motivations of her characters. She is an avid reader of many genres of fiction, but especially erotica and romance. Writing has always been her bliss. She is attracted to stories of self-struggle and ultimate recovery.

Blakely is married to a wonderful, loving, and supportive husband, also a writer, who helps to keep her grounded. She is a mother, a communitarian, a lover of music (always on while she is writing—thank you, Pandora), and a good friend. An advocate of love and female empowerment, she is a facilitator for a women's group. She loves to walk and hike for exercise and finds that, since moving to Seattle, WA, she is now one of those "crazy" people who walk in the rain.

You can find Blakely on the Web at:

BlakelyBennett.fannypress.com.

Limerick, Patricia Nelson. *The Legacy of Conquest: The Unbroken Past of the American West.* New York: W. W. Norton, 1987.

Limerick, Patricia Nelson, Clyde A. Milner II, and Charles E. Rankin, eds. *Trails: Toward a New Western History.* Lawrence: University Press of Kansas, 1991.

Mancall, Peter C. *Deadly Medicine: Indians and Alcohol in Early America.* Ithaca: Cornell University Press, 1995.

Markel, Howard. "Medicine at Michigan." *Journal of the American Medical Association* 283 (Feb. 16, 2000): 915.

Marsh, Margaret. "Suburban Men and Masculine Domesticity, 1870–1915." In *Meanings for Manhood: Constructions of Masculinity in Victorian America.* Edited by Mark C. Carnes and Clyde Griffen. Chicago: University of Chicago Press, 1990.

McCoy, Alexandra. "Political Affiliations of American Economic Elites: Wayne County, Michigan, 1844, 1860, as a Test Case." PhD diss., Wayne State University, 1965.

McGrane, Reginald Charles. *The Panic of 1837: Some Financial Problems of the Jacksonian Era.* Chicago: University of Chicago Press, 1924.

Mousty, John A. "The Trammels of Territory: The Toledo Border War and Michigan's Admission Struggle." Master's thesis, Wayne State University, 1994.

Nobles, Gregory H. *American Frontier: Cultural Encounters and Continental Conquest.* New York: Hill and Wang, 1997.

Onuf, Peter S. *Statehood and Union: A History of the Northwest Ordinance.* 1st Midland Book ed. Bloomington: Indiana University Press, 1987.

———. *The Origins of the Federal Republic: Jurisdictional Controversies in the United States, 1775–1787.* Philadelphia: University of Pennsylvania Press, 1983.

Otis, Laura. *Membranes: Metaphors of Invasion in Nineteenth-Century Literature, Science, and Politics.* Baltimore: Johns Hopkins University Press, 1999.

Pearce, Roy Harvey. "The Significance of the Captivity Narrative." *American Literature* 19 (March 1947): 1–20.

Pocock, J.G.A. *The Machiavellian Moment: Florentine Political Thought and the Atlantic Republican Tradition.* Princeton: Princeton University Press, 1975.

Pomeroy, Earl. *The Territories and the United States, 1861–1890: Studies in Colonial Administration.* Seattle: University of Washington Press, reprt. 1969.

Prucha, Francis Paul. *The Indians in American Society.* Berkeley: University of California Press, 1985.

Quist, John W. "An Occasionally Dry State Surrounded by Water." In *The History of Michigan Law.* Edited by Paul Finkelman and Martin J. Hershock. Athens: Ohio University Press, 2006.

———. *Restless Visionaries: The Social Roots of Antebellum Reform in Alabama and Michigan.* Baton Rouge: Louisiana State University Press, 1998.

Ranger, Terence, and Paul Slack, eds. *Epidemics and Ideas.* Cambridge: Cambridge University Press, 1992.

Rosaldo, Renato. *Culture & Truth: The Remaking of Social Analysis.* Boston: Beacon Press, 1989.

Roscoe, Will. *Changing Ones: Third and Fourth Genders in Native North America.* New York: St. Martin's Press, 1998.

Rosenberg, Charles. *The Cholera Years: The United States in 1832, 1849, and 1866.* Chicago: University of Chicago Press, 1962.

Rosentreter, Roger L. "Michigan's Quest for State." In *Michigan: Visions of Our Past.* Edited by Richard J. Hathaway. East Lansing: Michigan State University Press, 1989.

Rotundo, E. Anthony. *American Manhood: Transformations in Masculinity from the Revolution to the Modern Era.* New York: Basic Books, 1993.

Rusk, Jerrold G. *A Statistical History of the American Electorate.* Washington DC: CQ Press, 2001.

Ryan, Mary P. *Cradle of the Middle Class: The Family in Oneida County, 1790–1865.* New York: Cambridge University Press, 1981.

Saler, Bethel. "Negotiating the Treaty Polity: Gender, Race and the Transformation of Wisconsin from Indian Country into an American State, 1776–1854." PhD diss., University of Wisconsin, 1999.

Schneider, John. *Detroit and the Problem of Order, 1830–1880.* Lincoln: University of Nebraska Press, 1980.

Sellers, Charles. *The Market Revolution: Jacksonian America, 1815–1846.* New York: Oxford University Press, 1991.

Shade, William Gerald. "The Background of the Michigan Free Banking Law." *Michigan History* 52, no. 3 (1968): 229–44.

———. "Banks and Politics in Michigan, 1835–1845: A Reconsideration." *Michigan History* 57, no. 1 (1973): 28–52.

Shields, David. "The Emergence of Civic Culture in the Colonies to about 1770." In *A Companion to the American Revolution.* Edited by Jack P. Greene and J. R. Pole. Malden, MA: Blackwell, 2000.

Silbey, Joel H. *The American Political Nation, 1838–1893.* Stanford, CA: Stanford University Press, 1991.

Slavcheff, Peter Donald. "The Temperate Republic: Liquor Control in Michigan, 1800–1860." PhD diss., Wayne State University, 1987.

Slotkin, Richard. *The Fatal Environment: The Myth of the Frontier in the Age of Industrialization, 1800–1890.* Norman: University of Oklahoma Press, 1985.

———. *Regeneration through Violence: The Mythology of the American Frontier, 1600–1860.* Middletown, CT: Wesleyan University Press, 1973.

Takaki, Ronald. *A Different Mirror: A History of Multicultural America.* Boston: Little, Brown, 1993.

Taylor, Alan. The Divided Ground: Indians, Settlers and the Northern Borderland of the American Revolution. New York: Vintage Books, 2006.

Taylor, George Rogers. *The Transportation Revolution, 1815–1860.* New York: Rinehart, 1951; rept., Armonk, NY: M. E. Sharpe, 1989.

Temin, Peter. *The Jacksonian Economy.* New York: W. W. Norton, 1969.

Thernstrom, Stephan, ed., *Harvard Encyclopedia of American Ethnic Groups.* Cambridge: Harvard University Press, 1980.

Thompson, E. P. *The Making of the English Working Class*. New York: Vintage, 1963.

Tomlins, Christopher L. "The Many Legalities of Colonization: A Manifesto of Destiny for Early American Legal History." In *The Many Legalities of Early America*. Edited by Christopher L. Tomlins and Bruce H. Mann. Chapel Hill, NC: University of North Carolina Press, 2001.

Trowbridge, M.E.D. *History of Baptists in Michigan*. Michigan State Baptist Convention, 1909.

Turner, Frederick Jackson. *The Frontier in American History*. New York: H. Holt, 1920; rept. New York: Holt, Rinehart and Winston, 1962w.

U.S. Bureau of the Census. *Historical Statistics of the United States from Colonial Times to 1970*, vol. 1. Washington, DC: Government Printing Office, 1975.

Utley, Henry M., and Byron M. Cutcheon. *Michigan as a Province, Territory and State, the Twenty-Sixth Member of the Federal Union*. Vols. 2 and 3. New York: Publishing Society of Michigan, 1906.

VanBurkleo, Sandra F. *Belonging to the World: Women's Rights and American Constitutional Culture*. New York: Oxford University Press, 2001.

VanDerBeets, Richard. "The Indian Captivity Narrative as Ritual." *American Literature* 43 (1972): 548–62.

Wallace, Anthony F. C. *Rockdale: The Growth of an American Village in the Early Industrial Revolution*. New York: Alfred A. Knopf, 1978.

Watson, Harry L. *Liberty and Power: The Politics of Jacksonian America*. New York: Hill and Wang, 1990.

Weber, David J. "Turner, the Boltonians, and the Borderlands." *American Historical Review* 91 (Feb. 1986): 66–81.

White, Richard. *The Middle Ground: Indians, Empires and Republics in the Great Lakes Region, 1650–1815*. New York: Cambridge University Press, 1991.

Wilentz, Sean. *The Rise of American Democracy: Jefferson to Lincoln*. New York: Norton, 2005.

———. "Society, Politics and the Market Revolution, 1815–1848." In Eric Foner, ed., *The New American History*. Rev. and expanded ed. Philadelphia: Temple University Press, 1997.

Wood, Gordon S. *The Creation of the American Republic, 1776–1787*. New York: W. W. Norton, 1972.

———. *The Radicalism of the American Revolution*. New York: Vintage Books, 1993.

Woodford, Frank B. *Mr. Jefferson's Disciple: A Life of Justice Woodward*. East Lansing: Michigan State College Press, 1953.

Index